Storytelling in Organizations

Storytelling in Organizations

Facts, Fictions, and Fantasies

YIANNIS GABRIEL

OXFORD
UNIVERSITY PRESS

OXFORD
UNIVERSITY PRESS

Great Clarendon Street, Oxford OX2 6DP

Oxford University Press is a department of the University of Oxford.
It furthers the University's objective of excellence in research, scholarship,
and education by publishing worldwide in

Oxford New York

Auckland   Cape Town   Dar es Salaam   Hong Kong   Karachi
Kuala Lumpur   Madrid   Melbourne   Mexico City   Nairobi
New Delhi   Shanghai   Taipei   Toronto
With offices in
Argentina   Austria   Brazil   Chile   Czech Republic   France   Greece
Guatemala   Hungary   Italy   Japan   South Korea   Poland   Portugal
Singapore   Switzerland   Thailand   Turkey   Ukraine   Vietnam

Published in the United States
by Oxford University Press Inc., New York

ISBN 978-0-19-829706-2

Printed in the United Kingdom by
Lightning Source UK Ltd., Milton Keynes

ACKNOWLEDGEMENTS

This book is the product of a ten-year study of organizational story-telling. Many people have helped me along the way during this period, friends, colleagues, students, storytellers, and story-lovers. I am indebted to all of them. Special thanks to my colleagues Steve Fineman, David Sims, and Andrew Sturdy, whose feedback has helped me greatly. I am also greatly indebted to David Musson, who offered me constant encouragement throughout the gestation and writing of the book.

CONTENTS

Introduction

'Once upon a time, a cat drank a bottle of green ink. At once, the cat turned green . . .' Thus is a story announced. Thus does it command attention, no less firmly than the opening bars of a Beethoven piano sonata or the first sight of a new mountain peak. Thus does each story hold a promise, a promise that, as every storyteller knows, will be tested. An audience that has swallowed the possibility of cats turning green does not easily forgive a poor story.

'Story' shares a common etymology with 'history'—they both derive from a Greek group of words that include *histos* meaning 'web', *histanai* meaning 'to stand', and *eidenai* meaning 'to know well'. Storytelling is an art of weaving, of constructing, the product of intimate knowledge. It is a delicate process, a process that can easily break down, failing to live up to its promise, disintegrating into mere text. This is why good storytellers and raconteurs have commanded power and esteem. Good stories are valuable; they can hardly be mass produced. Teachers, orators, and demagogues have long recognized their value—good stories entertain, explain, inspire, educate, and convince. Bad stories do not merely disappoint; they insult the intelligence of the audience, they undermine communication, and they can challenge the very possibility of sensical discourse.

This book is the product of a lifelong love of stories and story-telling. Some of my earliest childhood memories are those of stories, drawn from the Grimm brothers and Hans Christian Andersen, Aesop's fables, Greek myths, legends, and folklore. The characters of these stories are as vivid to me today as when I first encountered them, their plots endlessly fascinating. Much later, I discovered the pleasure of telling some of those same stories to my children and re-experienced the strong bond that unites storyteller and audience. Storytelling might not have become part of my academic work, however, had it not been for three experiences of stories in institutional settings. At 15, I travelled to Brazil as an apprentice aboard a

1

cargo ship. I heard numerous lively stories about life at sea and escapades at port, as valuable for passing long stretches of time as cigarettes and coffee. Later, as a conscript in the Greek Navy, I was exposed to constant stories about the sadistic pranks played by different officers on new recruits. I also witnessed the birth of stories, where different more or less infantile schemes were put into practice for the main purpose of spawning new stories. Most importantly, however, it was my research into the catering industry in the 1980s that triggered my fascination with organizational stories. What I found remarkable were two things. First, on several occasions, different workers and managers related to me the same story, as though they had agreed to do so before talking to me. These stories acted as symbolic landmarks in the cultural life of organizations. Secondly, several years after the end of my research, when the names and faces of the people I had interviewed had faded from my memory, what remained were the stories, their plots, and the faces of their characters.

This book is a study of storytelling in organizations. It argues that stories open valuable windows into the emotional, political, and symbolic lives of organizations, offering researchers a powerful instrument for carrying out research. By collecting stories in different organizations, by listening and comparing different accounts, by investigating how narratives are constructed around specific events, by examining which events in an organization's history generate stories and which ones fail to do so, we gain access to deeper organizational realities, closely linked to their members' experiences. In this way, stories enable us to study organizational politics, culture, and change in uniquely illuminating ways, revealing how wider organizational issues are viewed, commented upon, and worked upon by their members. The main questions addressed by the book are:

1. How can we study organizations through the stories that are told in them and about them?
2. What do stories tell us about the nature of organizations as distinct forms of human collectivity?
3. What do stories encountered in organizations tell us about the nature and functions of storytelling?

As a lover of stories and storytelling, I have some misgivings about the increasing popularity of stories in academic research. While I am pleased with the recognition of the value of stories, I am concerned about the increasing tendency to view every sign, every snippet of conversation, every image, and every cliché as either being a story or telling a story. At times, the concept of story is stretched to encompass virtually everything that is not a fact. The book is, therefore, also an attempt to vindicate stories as valuable but precarious artefacts and storytelling as an important narrative craft.

STORIES AND ACADEMIC RESEARCH

The relationship between academic research and storytelling has been ambiguous. In many ways, science has stood as the opposite of storytelling, seeking to replace the lore of 'old wives tales' with provable generalizations. History itself, from the time of Thucidides, sought to distinguish its own domain, the domain of ascertainable facts, of causes and effects, from the mere hearsay, fiction, and story that had fascinated his predecessor, Herodotus. Gradually history and storytelling moved into distinct and antagonistic terrains. As de Certeau (1986: 200) has argued:

Western historiography struggles against fiction. The internecine strife between history and storytelling is very old. Like an old family quarrel, positions and opinions are often fixed. In the struggle against genealogical storytelling, the myths and legends of the collective memory, and the meanderings of the oral tradition, historiography establishes a certain distance between itself and common assertion and belief; it locates itself in this difference and gives it the accreditation of erudition because it is separated from ordinary discourse.

For a period in the nineteenth century, storytelling, as the object of enquiry, was of interest only to folklorists, themselves a marginal group of the scientific community, the majority of whom preferred to focus on facts rather than stories. In the twentieth century, however, an ever-increasing range of scientific disciplines started to take an interest in stories. Cultural anthropology turned to the stories of pre-literate societies as a vital feature of their cultures and meaning systems. Psychoanalysis found in the stories told by its patients a route into the world of the unconscious almost as valuable as that offered by dreams. Even history, the declared adversary of fiction, came to acknowledge oral history, composed of personal narratives, reminiscences, and stories, as part of its remit.

By the end of the twentieth century, stories had made a spectacular comeback; far from being marginalized by their declared enemies, theories, information, and facts, stories suffused most popular culture and art, mass media, advertising, and journalism. Curiously enough, science itself has become popularized by being turned into stories—stories of intrigue, triumph, betrayal, deception, success against the odds, and so on. Gradually academic research in every field of the human sciences would turn its attention to stories. In one

3

of his last appearances, 'man' emerged as a storytelling animal, an animal whose main preoccupation is not truth or power or love or even pleasure, but meaning. 'The human being alone among creatures on the earth is a storytelling animal: sees the present rising out of a past, heading into a future; perceives reality in narrative form' (Novak 1975: 175–6). Stories emerged as the great factories of meaning, creating it, transforming it, testing it, sustaining it, fashioning it, and refashioning it. And storytelling, far from being the preserve of old grandmothers during those long Nordic winter nights, became ubiquitous—the craft and trade of artists and advertisers, the stuff of television talk shows, the preoccupation of lawyers and managers, the unending project of all people trying to make sense of their daily lives and experiences.

The interest of organizational studies in stories is as belated as it is enthusiastic. Although this interest is undoubtedly connected with the more general interest in narrative processes in organizations, it cannot be reduced to that. Organizational stories are currently studied in different ways—for example, as elements of organizational symbolism and culture, as expressions of unconscious wishes and fantasies, as vehicles for organizational communication and learning, as expressions of political domination and opposition, as dramatic performances, as occasions for emotional discharge, as narrative structures, and so forth.

The mileage that scholars of organizations are currently getting from the concept of stories (and other currently fashionable concepts) ought to alert us to certain risks. Are we being seduced by the idea of 'stories', just like that famous sultan who found himself addicted to the yarns spun by Sheherezade? And if stories are proving such a serviceable concept, could it be that they offer a smokescreen against awkward questions that we prefer to avoid? Postmodernism has invited us to mistrust many of the revered categories of the human sciences, including 'self', 'body', 'society', 'family', 'organization', and, above all, 'fact', revealing them to be linguistic mirages or constructs of convenience, indeed 'stories'. Is it not time that we sought to deconstruct the concept of a 'story' itself?

It is now widely agreed that stories are part of a sensemaking process that can be researched *in situ*, without that burdensome requirement of social science research—the need to establish the validity of claims, the facts behind allegations, the truth behind the tales. For, as it has been widely argued, the truth of a story lies not in *the facts*, but in *the meaning*. If people believe a story, if the story grips them, whether events actually happened or not is irrelevant. It is for the pedant or the unreconstructed positivist to question poetic licence, seeking to convert storytelling into testimony.

INTRODUCTION

Any analysis of the concept of story must be constantly aware of its juxtaposition to fact. If traditional positivist research privileged facts over narratives, steering stories in the direction of facts, the current tendency is increasingly that of privileging narrative over fact. Some research under postmodernism is happy to go about as though facts do not exist, or as if they do not matter, even if they do exist. What matters are narratives. Even when 'facts' do crop up in the text ('I saw him with my own eyes . . .'), they are sometimes seen as narrative constructions, amplifying or elaborating a story. Once narratives were freed from their enslavement to facts, an immense new landscape for organizational research opened—a landscape dominated by linguistic structures and rhetorical tropes, in which a wide variety of entities previously thought of as solid facts, such as 'organization', 'culture', 'commodities', 'the body', meekly surrendered to being treated as texts.

The arguments presented in this book will offer a different way of theorizing stories. In contrast to current trends of seeing stories everywhere, this book will argue that stories are not the only things that generate and sustain meaning, nor indeed do all stories generate and sustain meaning—some stories may actually undermine and destroy meaning. I shall argue that not all narratives are stories; in particular, factual or descriptive accounts of events that aspire at objectivity rather than emotional effect must not be treated as stories.[1] Stories in organizations are relatively special narrative phenomena competing with other types of discourse, including theories, clichés, statistics, and reports. The importance, quantity, quality, and character of folklore differ across organizations. Not all stories are good stories, nor are all individuals effective storytellers. Stories, it will be argued, should not be seen as automatically dissolving 'facts'. Instead, narratives and experience must be treated as having a

---

[1] In this I depart from Polkinghorne (1988: 14), who equates story and narrative, by adopting an excessively broad conceptualization of the former. Polkinghorne's lead has been followed by most organizational theorists, who, as we shall see, stretch the concept of story to encompass any meaning-giving text. I am happier with Barthes's view of narratives as ever present and of almost infinite variety; stories, according to this view, are but one type of narrative. 'The narratives of the world are without number. In the first place the word "narrative" covers an enormous variety of genres which are themselves divided up between different subjects, as if any material was suitable for the composition of the narrative; the narrative may incorporate articulate language, spoken or written; pictures, still and moving; gestures and the ordered arrangements of all the ingredients: it is present in myth, legend, fable, short story, epic, history, tragedy, comedy, pantomime, painting . . . stained glass windows, cinema, comic strips, journalism, conversation. In addition, under the almost infinite number of forms, the narrative is present at all times, in all places, in all societies; the history of narrative begins with the history of mankind; there does not exist, and never has existed, a people without narratives' (Barthes 1966/1977: 79; translation from Polkinghorne 1988: 14).

material basis, even if this material basis is opaque or inaccessible. The relationship between facts and story is plastic—stories interpret events, infusing them with meaning through distortions, omissions, embellishments, and other devices, without, however, obliterating the facts. Finally, the book will seek to draw a line between stories and myths. Organizational stories rarely achieve the depth and complexity of myths and should not be treated as part of a *mythology*. Instead, they may be profitably treated as folkloric elements that become part of organizational culture.

It will be noted that several of these points may be seen as matters of definition. Why should we not treat every text as a story? Why indeed not treat every object, including a gleaming motor car, a tattoo, or a building, as a story? I shall argue that, by obliterating distinctions between stories and other types of texts and narratives, stories lose precisely the power that they are meant to possess— namely, the power to generate and sustain meanings. They then disintegrate into chic clichés into which meaning disappears. Restricting the concept of stories to those narrative phenomena that can rightly claim to be stories is not an act of semantic policing but an attempt to preserve that which makes stories unique both as social phenomena and as instruments of social research.

I

TOWARDS A THEORY OF ORGANIZATIONAL STORYTELLING

1

Same Old Story or Changing Stories? Folkloric, Modern, and Postmodern Mutations

Storytelling has always been an art of the people, of 'ordinary folk'. In the early nineteenth century, a folkloric revival was signalled by the publication of the Grimm brothers' stories (in 1812 and 1835), collected by the two brothers with the assiduous zeal of archaeologists. As with other archaeological finds, the admiration and interest that the stories aroused at the time coincided with their transformation into museum pieces. For all the Grimm brothers' good intentions of recording the stories intact and preserving the dialect and nuance of their delivery, their work marked an ossification of storytelling from a folk art into written texts. Certainly, this ossification did not kill the stories' symbolic resonances, but it drastically altered their meanings. It also obscured what folklorists insist is the most important function of stories—namely, *entertainment*, which can be grasped only when stories are experienced *in situ*, as performances (Dorson 1969; Georges 1969, 1980, 1981; Newall 1980). Of course, stories have carried other functions, besides entertainment. They stimulate the imagination and offer reassurance (Bettelheim 1976), they provide moral education (MacIntyre 1981), they justify and explain (Kemper 1984; Lévi-Strauss 1958/1976, 1978), they inform, advise, and warn (Van Dijk 1975), but folklorists are adamant that, when seen in the practice of storytelling, stories were above all else recreational. As no less an authority than Campbell has argued (1975: 862):

The folk tale, in contrast to the myth, is a form of entertainment. The story teller fails or succeeds in proportion to the amusement he affords. His motifs may be plucked from the tree of the mythological order. His productions have to be judged, at last, not as science, sociology, psychology, or metaphysics, but as art.

Entertainment distinguishes stories from other narratives. In moral tales or fables, for example, the didactic function eclipses the recreational. Legends, on the other hand, are often said to have a historical grounding, though this is enhanced by supernatural accretions from myths or fairy tales. Myths, for their part, carry grand sacral meanings that are alien to stories; they seek to explain, justify, and console. They may exist in many variants, but they are not liable to the embellishments and elaborations that are part of the storyteller's craft. The folklorists' insistence on the entertainment value of stories accords with the storyteller's willingness to do virtually anything that will please his or her audience, unencumbered by considerations of morality, factual accuracy, or even decorum.[1] Aristotle was keenly aware that storytelling was a *poetic activity* involving the symbolic elaboration of narrative material.[2] *Poetic licence* is the sacrifice of everything for effect:

The fantastic quality is a source of pleasure, as appears from the fact that we all tend to embellish a story, in the belief that we are pleasing our listener. Homer more than anyone else has taught us how to tell lies in the right way. . . . [In stories] a likely impossibility is preferable to an unconvincing possibility. (*Poetics* 1460*a*)

And this relates to the second much-noted quality of folk stories, their plasticity. Vladimir Propp, the Russian folklorist known for his morphological analysis of wonder tales, has argued:

[Folk] performers do not repeat their texts word for word but introduce changes into them. Even if these changes are insignificant (but they can be

---

[1] This is one of the two reasons why Plato disapproved of storytelling, which subordinates truth and moral edification to pleasure. Plato was fully aware that the coarser, more fantastic stories are likely to generate much more entertainment that those of a higher and finer quality. See Plato (*Republic* 397*d*): ' "The mixed style does at least give pleasure, Adeimantus; and the one which gives by far the most pleasure to children and their attendants, and the general run of people, is the one which is the opposite of your choice." "Yes, that's because it is very enjoyable." "But perhaps you'd say that it isn't compatible with our community's political system," I went on.' In Book 10 of the *Republic*, Plato launches his well-known attack on poetry (even great poetry, like Homer's) for dealing with appearances and indulging the emotions, which, in turn, prompted Aristotle's defence of poetry.

[2] 'Poetics' derives from the Greek *poiesis*, which signifies the creation of something distinctly new from existing materials. Plato and Aristotle juxtapose *poiesis* (making) to *praxis* (doing), a motivated deed that aims not at transforming matter but at producing a result. *Poiesis* may apply equally to a carpenter making a table or to a poet fashioning an epic rhapsody; artefacts are products of *poiesis*. *Praxis*, on the other hand, may apply to a general leading an army or a tragic hero confronting a predicament. Among literary critics, 'poetics' has come to signify generally a theory of literature (Morson and Emerson 1990); I shall be using the term in its original sense of purposeful, creative transformation of material to form something distinct and new, something that may not be reduced to the original constituents. This includes the type of transformation that is entailed in turning opaque or inchoate facts into stories brimming with meanings.

very great), even if the changes that take place in folklore texts are some-times as slow as geological processes, what is important is the fact of *change-ability of folklore compared with stability of literature.* (Propp 1984: 8)

Folklorists have noted that the plasticity of stories is compounded by the nature of their dissemination. Unlike film or theatrical audi-ences, the audiences of stories are potential storytellers or dissemi-nators of the story; thus do stories travel from mouth to ear and from ear to mouth, undergoing embellishments and elaborations along the way, mutating, disappearing for long periods of time, and then resurfacing in new variants. Indeed, the quality of the story lies in its delivery as much as in its plot. The storyteller is understood by the audience to be inventing as a true 'poet' rather than merely recount-ing. Mark Twain has expressed this admirably by saying that 'If you wish to lower yourself in a person's favor, one good way is to tell his story over again, the way you heard it' (Flesch 1959: 124).

The fact that storytelling aims to entertain does not preclude unpleasant, sad, or terrifying twists in the plot. Such twists can be quite important in establishing a happy end, following a crisis or a cathartic conclusion. They also accentuate the oppositions between good and evil, young and old, success and failure, which lie at their heart.

The plots of folk tales are relatively uniform, in spite of an enorm-ous invention in matters of detail and embellishment. They can delight by coming up with new variants on old themes, and new twists to old plots, in short, through a creative blend of the totally familiar and the totally unexpected. Their characters are also quite one-dimensional. They may go through tremendous adventures, face moments of crisis or decision, and display great virtues and vices. But their action is essentially non-psychological—they experi-ence little inner conflict—and non-sociological—they are not the products of social conflicts and contradictions.[3] They are driven by the plot, instead of driving the plot. A villain behaves in villain-like ways, just as a princess behaves in princess-like ways. Consider the following story retold by MacIntyre (1981: 123):

In the saga account of the battle of Clontarf in 1014, where Brian Boru defeated a Viking army, one of the norsemen, Thorstein, did not flee when the rest of his army broke and ran, but remained where he was, tying his shoestring. An Irish leader, Kerthialfad, asked him why he was not running. 'I couldn't get home tonight,' said Thorstein. 'I live in Iceland.' Because of the joke, Kerthialfad spared his life.

---

[3] 'In [authentic folklore] a character is great in his own right, not on some other account; he himself is tall and strong, he alone is able to triumphantly repel enemy troops . . . Folkloric man is the great folk, great in his own right' (Bakhtin 1981: 150).

In this story, a classic plot is presented, that of a person extricating him or herself from an awkward situation through wit. The effect is compounded by the hero's apparent absence of fear (courage) and dry sense of humour, qualities attributed to Nordic people to this day. In this way, characters in stories manage to find new and strange ways of behaving true to form.

Characters of stories grow and mature, they experience powerful emotions, they learn or fail to learn from their adventures and mistakes. Yet, the changes they undergo are themselves specific to the plots and to the characters themselves (immature characters will mature, arrogant characters will be humbled, cunning characters will disentangle themselves against the odds) rather than psychological development. One may ponder at length on the motivation of a Hamlet or a Raskolnikov, though not of an Iron Hans or a Snowhite (see Propp (1968: 27) and Benjamin (1968*a*: 91)). Unlike the heroes of novels or plays, the characters of tales do not pose many psychological puzzles. The puzzle that they pose is whether they can find unpredictable ways of behaving predictably, a puzzle that mirrors the *challenge* facing the storyteller, that of telling an old story in a novel way, so as to entertain his or her audience. The storyteller buys his or her audience's suspension of disbelief at the cost of delivering a good story—the unbelievable must be made believable. The story is a dare, which he or she must pull off.

The more outrageous or unusual the beginning of the story, the greater the narrative feats that must be performed to redeem it. Failed stories may actually feed a good story, that of a pretentious person failing to deliver his promise. Alternatively, however, aborted stories and stories that are not understood may lead to a collapse of meaning, just like a text or a joke in a foreign language that leaves us suspecting that there is meant to be meaning somewhere though the meaning eludes us.

While the characters of stories remain entirely fixed by the plot (it is inconceivable, for instance, that a villain will display compassion even on a single occasion or that the pronouncement of a wise woman will fail to come true), unexpected elements are introduced by supernatural occurrences and especially magic. Magic not only introduces legitimate though temporary aberrations in the behaviour of the characters, but also allows for sudden shifts in the balance of power among the characters. A few magic words can budge the mighty rock that no amount of physical effort could move. Other features that enable the plot to move forward are coincidences, accidents, and misunderstandings.

To summarize then, within the folkloric universe storytelling is a process whose primary aim is to entertain audiences. This is achieved through a creative blend of the unfamiliar with the familiar, the natural with the supernatural, the reassuring oppositions between primary forces and the storyteller's performing craft. Stories travel easily, mutating along the way, resurfacing in unexpected places in unexpected shapes. Good stories represent a successfully met challenge, whereas poor stories may be seen either as personal failures on the part of the storytellers or as instances where meaning is drained out of discourse.

MODERNISM AND STORIES: STORIES AS NON-FACTS, STORIES AS SYMPTOMS

It is hard to imagine reading the folkloric discourse without the prism of modernist discourses—even committed folklorists doubt that it is possible to capture the storyteller's craft, as applied to audiences unacquainted with electric light, mass entertainment, and scientific theories (Colum 1975). The very word 'folklore', coined by W. J. Thoms in 1846, is itself an invention of the age of reason, denoting, at least initially, the customs, superstitions, and stories of the folk, a euphemism for the rural poor, the 'uncultured or backward classes in civilized nations'. Over the nineteenth century, the cultured classes of Europe appropriated elements of folklorism in their civilized discourses (as did Gustav Mahler in his song collection *Des Knaben Wunderhorn*), though folklore retained its connotation of rustic unsophistication. Stories, as part of their folkloric discourse, were redefined by modernism, primarily through their *opposition to fact*, losing much of their connection with entertainment or communication. Myths were more amenable to modernism than stories, whether as supports for massive projects of social transformation or as buffers against older pre-modernist myths. In fact, socialism, fascism, as well as liberal democracy all emerged with their own myths whose larger sacral meanings are part and parcel of the grand narratives of modernism. In contrast to these grand narratives, the small and parochial narratives of stories and storytelling occupied a very secondary position in the modernist pantheon—far inferior to scientific theories, vast novels, and painstakingly detailed historical texts. In their ongoing opposition to fact, stories have remained firmly subordinate, being part of the realm of fantasy and uncontrol rather than the world of science and control. While casting occasional nostalgic glances at this realm, modernism moved forward confidently with its large visions and projects.

In this way, modernism invented what the eminent American folklorist Alan Dundes has called 'folklore without folk'. Folklore scholarship, for its part, has come to be characterized by progressive dehumanization, a collection, comparison, and analysis of texts without regard for the fact that they were once used to entertain people or that they might have acted as media of communication in a universe without mass media. Modernist scholarship, especially as embodied in Propp's morphological studies, Lévi-Strauss's structuralism, as well as the more conventional historical and comparative approaches, is summed up by Dundes (1980: 33 ff.) as the 'folkless study of folklore'.

By the 1930s it was not rare to regard storytelling as virtually moribund, folk tales themselves being a part of the folkloric past and to be studied as such. Writing an entry on folklore for the *Encyclopaedia of the Social Sciences* in 1931, cultural anthropologist Ruth Benedict (1931: 288) wrote that 'folklore has not survived as a living trait in modern civilization' and 'thus in a strict sense folklore is a dead trait in the modern world'. Writing about the work of the Russian novelist Nicolai Leskov in 1936, Walter Benjamin (1968*b*: 83) laments the passing of the storyteller's art:

Familiar though his name may be to us, the storyteller in his living immediacy is by no means a present force. He has already become something remote from us and something that is getting even more distant. . . . The art of storytelling is coming to an end. Less and less frequently do we encounter people with the ability to tell a tale properly. More and more often there is embarrassment all around when the wish to hear a story is expressed. It is as if something that seemed inalienable to us, the securest among our possessions, were taken from us: the ability to exchange experiences.

In Benjamin's argument two factors have conspired to bring about the demise of storytelling. The first factor, widely recognized by diverse scholars, relates to technical and social changes that have caused the audiences of storytellers to disappear or turn elsewhere for entertainment—electricity has eliminated the long periods of winter darkness opening up huge opportunities of mass entertainment, urban living with its cultural abundance and privatized living has marginalized storytelling, and the mass media have delivered the finishing blow. The second factor is one that Benjamin terms intriguingly the 'decline of the value of experience' in modern times. Interestingly, the point he makes here is not that traditional know-how and lore accumulated through experience are supplanted by scientific knowledge. Instead, he remarks that 'with the [First] World War a process began to become apparent which has not halted since then. Was it not noticeable at the end of the war that men returned from the battlefield grown silent—not richer, but poorer in communicable experience?' (Benjamin 1968*b*: 84).

In Benjamin's imagery, the unanswerable brutality of modernity makes people silent—their experience eclipsed by information, storytelling silenced by facts, hard facts in every sense. In sharp contrast to the glib expression 'stories for the trenches', Benjamin argues with some justification that the trenches spawned few stories among those who experienced them first hand. (They did, of course, generate a new genre of poetry far removed from the heroic poetry of earlier wars.) In one way, Benjamin furthers the argument that modernity marginalizes stories as non-facts; interestingly, however, he shifts the meaning of stories away from *narratives about characters* towards *narratives about the self*. This is why he views the travelling artisan as the storyteller *par excellence*, the person who collects stories in his or her travels, but whose travels are stories in themselves. If the folklorist views the story as the product of invention and elaboration on traditional materials, Benjamin views the story as the product of personal experience—it is this personal experience that modernity devalues, debases, and ultimately obliterates.

Benjamin's argument contains in embryo the modernist treatment of stories: that stories grow out of subjective experience, that the social and technical conditions of modernity undermine the art of the storyteller, that modernity devalues subjective experience in favour of information (an argument further developed by Lévi-Strauss, who casts science in the crucial part of supplanting experience (1978: 6)). In all this, modernity does away with the art and craft of storytelling just as it deskills and destroys other old crafts. This is what I shall call 'narrative deskilling'. Mass entertainment is then to storytelling what Fordism is to artisan craft. Narrative silence is the equivalent of the lost skills of traditional artisans.

Interpretivism

Yet modernism spawned another discursive line on stories. This line, like Benjamin's, views them as products of experience shaped by conflict, domination and resistance, control and uncontrol. Instead of lamenting the passing of stories, however, this line has seen them as marginalized but present in various nooks and crannies of modernity, from the psychoanalyst's couch to the impersonal spaces of organizations, from the private spaces of parents reading to their children at bedtime to the public areas of shopping malls. This approach is broadly interpretivist, seeking to unmask the hidden symbolism of stories, reading them as depositories of meaning and expressions of deeper psychic, interpersonal, and social realities. Exponents of this approach include Geertz, Douglas, and Devereux among cultural anthropologists, Dundes among folklorists, Bettelheim, Ferenczi, and Freud among psychoanalysts, Studs Terkel among urban ethnographers. This approach draws from Marxism and phenomenology, literary criticism, ethnography, and psychoanalysis, but its ideological root lies undoubtedly in romanticism. It seeks to restore a kind of modern folk, a set of ways that people discover for behaving outside the large modernist structures and institutions, evading controls, laughing at the absurdities of impersonal systems, and rediscovering their humanity in their ability to mould reality to their wishes and fantasies through storytelling.

In contrast to the rationalist tradition within modernism, interpretivist approaches have tended to emphasize emotion and desire as well as their repression. Freud's *The Interpretation of Dreams* stands as an almost paradigmatic work in this tradition: dreams, far from being anomalies, are seen as compromise formations resulting from conflicting mental forces, whose interpretation opens up the royal road to the unconscious. The approach pioneered by this work, which treats texts as distorted expressions of unconscious wishes and desires, has found a bewildering array of applications in neurotic symptoms, works of art and literature, slips of the tongue or the pen, political ideas, material artefacts, jokes, and, of course, stories and folkloric creations. Dream interpretations come closest to interpretations of folkloric materials in respect of symbolism: 'This symbolism is not peculiar to dreams, but is characteristic of unconscious ideation, in particular among the people, and it is to be found in folklore, and in popular myths, legends, linguistic idioms, proverbial wisdom and current jokes, to a more complete extent than in dreams' (S. Freud 1900: 468).

Interpretivism found an awkward place in modernism, generating much hostility, and often being defended by its advocates erroneously as scientific. Yet, in truth what interpretivism achieved was to offer a model of explanation different from that of positive causality, which enjoyed a modicum of respectability, at least in the human sciences. When applied to stories, interpretivism, unlike the rationalist tradition, did not concern itself much with their opposition to facts but rather with their attachment to meanings. Unlike rationalism, interpretivism located stories at the symbolic margin of reality, one that gives clues *about* social and psychological reality, but not a pre-eminent component of reality. If folklorists (with some notable exceptions, like Dundes) have generally shied away from interpreting the symbolism of stories, believing that interpretation usually kills a story, interpretivists have been keen to unlock the symbolic riddles of stories, seeking to uncover different meanings. In his work *The Uses of Enchantment: The Meaning and Importance of Fairy Tales*, Bruno Bettelheim argued that stories are vital in children's development. They help children make sense of a threatening and seemingly cruel reality, reassuring them, stimulating them, and entertaining them. This work did to fairy tales what Freud's *Interpretation* did to dreams: it opened up their symbolism, while honouring the multiple meanings that fairy tales have for different audiences.[4]

POSTMODERNISM AND STORIES: SENSE AS STORIES

Interpretivism, while offering a different type of explanation from rationalism, remains firmly within the modernist tradition. It preserves distinctions between fact and story, story and other narratives, plot and embellishment, story and interpretation, strong and weak interpretations. Postmodernism has tended to blur such distinctions, along with many others. If modernism questioned the survival of stories, postmodernism sees stories everywhere.[5] Postmodernism has reinvented stories beyond the dreams of the most ardent folklorists. If narratives are favoured objects of postmodern discourses, stories are favoured among narratives. Virtually any piece of text, any sign, any object that has drawn a gaze unto itself, tells a story; indeed, the failure to tell a story is a story in its own right. Advertisements, material objects (including all commodities, branded and unbranded), images of all sorts, human bodies (especially when pierced, tattooed, or surgically modified), consultants' reports and performance appraisals, official documents and works of art, legal arguments and scientific 'theories', do not merely furnish the material for stories, but, in as much as they make sense, *are* stories.

Organization and management studies, no less than consumer studies, cultural studies, media and communication studies, oral history, as well as substantial segments of legal studies, accounting, and studies of the professions and science, have enthusiastically adopted the idea that, in creating a meaningful universe, people resort to

---

[4] In a similar way, Robert Bly's Iron John (1990) unlocks the multiplicity of meanings present in the Grimm story *Iron Hans*.

[5] I shall not enter the debate on defining postmodernism in its relation to modernism. I accept that many features of postmodernism are rooted in modernism. One obvious instance of this is the equation of story and interpretation, whose origin is to be found clearly in Lévi-Strauss's discussion of myth. According to Lévi-Strauss (1958/1976), a myth consists of all versions and all interpretations; no single version is privileged as the right one.

stories. The proliferation of information in late capitalism leads not to a 'decline of the value of experience' as Benjamin and the modernists imagined, but rather to a massive process of turning information into experience, of signifiers into signifieds, through the medium of stories. The more 'people are buried in a mind-numbing avalanche of information' (Boje and Dennehy 1993: 155), the greater the importance of stories: 'stories make experience meaningful, stories connect us with one another; stories make the characters come alive; stories provide an opportunity for a renewed sense of organizational community' (Boje and Dennehy 1993: 156).[6]

Stories and experience are linked in postmodern discourses like Siamese twins—not only do stories transform into experience, but experience turns into stories: 'If we listen carefully to the talk around, it is not difficult to think that storytelling goes on almost non-stop. People transform their lives and their experiences into stories with practised ease' (Mangham and Overington 1987: 193). Narrative emerges as the privileged form of sensemaking, as 'the primary form by which human experience is made meaningful' (Polkinghorne 1988: 1). If organizations are *par excellence* jungles of information, stories come to the rescue of meaning. Stories re-enchant the disenchanted, introducing wit and invention, laughter and tears, into the information iron cage.

'In organizations, storytelling is the preferred sensemaking currency of human relationships among internal and external stakeholders,' claims Boje (1991: 106) with characteristic aplomb, a point that can be found in endless variants. Stories appear to sweep all other sensemaking, explanatory, or indeed narrative devices aside. A few examples will illustrate the extent to which sensemaking in different contexts has become dominated by stories:

Members of organizations: 'Telling and listening to stories . . . is fundamental to human processes of making sense of the world. But storytelling, which might take the form in the broader management context of biographies of famous managers like Lee Iacocca, Michael Edwardes or John Harvey Jones, or be manifested in the corporate tales and legends retold by Peters and Waterman, does not just give us moral anchors and pragmatic guidelines to help us through life. The stories we engage with also provide the languages or "discourses" which . . . influence the very way we talk about the world and hence, the way we interpret and act towards it' (Watson 1994: 113).

---

[6] Giddens (1991: 54) has argued that the very idea of personal identity 'is not to be found in behaviour, nor—important though it is—in the reactions of others, but in the capacity to keep a particular narrative going. The individual's biography, if she is to maintain regular interaction with others in the day-to-day world, cannot be wholly fictive. It must continually integrate events which occur in the external world, and sort them into the ongoing "story" about the self.'

SAME OLD STORY OR CHANGING STORIES?

Management consultants: '[Management] consultants successfully satisfy and retain their customers by telling stories' (Clark and Salaman 1996: 167).

Material objects: 'Ours is a world in which it is our products that tell our stories for us' (Davidson 1992: 15).

Social workers: 'The theoretical vacuum existing in the "social" professions has been largely filled by a model of explanation we term "narrative"' (Harris and Timms 1993: 53).

To generalize, postmodernist discourses have privileged stories and storytelling as sensemaking devices; in so doing, many have lost sight of the qualities of storytelling as entertainment and challenge, and have blurred the boundaries between stories and other types of narratives, including interpretations, theories, and arguments. From a postmodern angle, this current text is itself a form of storytelling, a story about stories, at once reflexive and self-referential.

ORGANIZATIONAL STORYTELLING: TERSE NARRATIONS OR NARRATIVE DESKILLING?

This storytelling perspective now permeates a large part of organizational studies, generating quite a formidable bibliography.[7] Yet one searches in vain for massive volumes of organizational stories to match the painstaking labours of folklorists. A few collections of organizational stories have been published, mostly for their pedagogic rather than their research value (Boje and Dennehy 1993; Fineman and Gabriel 1996; Sims *et al.* 1993). A few research texts report several stories (Kunda 1992; Watson 1994), many include the odd 'story' or two, but several papers explicitly devoted to organizational storytelling fail to quote a single story.

A few research pieces have studied organizational storytelling *in situ* (e.g. Boyce 1995). This is the great virtue of a justly acclaimed piece of research by David Boje, who collected or rather extricated stories from some 100 hours of taped material in an office supply firm. Boje (1991: 106) views organizational storytelling as the 'institutional memory system of the organization'. It is reflexive, in the sense of continuously recreating the past according to the present, interpretations becoming stories in their own right. It is interactive in the sense that most stories are multi-authored, with organizational members alternating in the roles of teller and listener, adding 'factual' cues or interpretive twists as a story unravels. It is dialogical, in

---

[7] See Boyce (1996), who has diligently assembled five pages of references.

that the truth of the story lies not in any one variant as in the process through which the text emerges.[8] Thus stories hardly ever feature as integrated pieces of narrative with a full plot and a complete cast of characters; instead, they exist in a state of continuous flux, fragments, allusions, as people contribute bits, often talking together. Boje's (1991: 112–13) key finding is that 'people told their stories in bits and pieces, with excessive interruptions of story parts, with people talking over each other to share story fragments, and many aborted storytelling attempts'.

Boje describes the stories he collected as 'terse' and acknowledges that in all his transcripts hardly a single story bears repetition outside its home territory as a 'good story'. He offers only one story with a plot:

Doug [the recently appointed CEO], in almost his first meeting with the executives, uprooted a 'reserved for the CEO' (one was also reserved for each of the VPs) parking sign and threw it on the executive meeting table, demanding to know 'who put up this sign? This is not the kind of leadership I will have around here.' The offending executive, for this and other good reasons, was fired by the week's end.   (Boje 1991: 119)

Boje collected this in several variants, apparently without substantive differences; in his view 'a year from now this might be tersely referred to as the parking-sign story' (ibid.). Thus organizational stories have the tendency to shrink into coded signifiers devoid of narrative. Observers who are not familiar with such taken-for-granted information may miss the point or the catch or may not be aware that a story is actually being alluded to or performed at all. Boje (1991: 115) asks the logical question of 'just how abbreviated can a story be and still be classified as a story?' and gives the extreme answer that the mere exclamation 'You know the story!' constitutes a story. A single word may thus be seen as encompassing an entire story.

One suspects that Boje is driven to this conclusion because his commitment to viewing organizations as storytelling systems does not square with the anaemic quality of the stories he collected. Yet, in taking this extreme position (and the strength of Boje's argument lies in its extremism), Boje loses the very qualities that he cherishes in stories, perfomativity, memorableness, ingenuity, and symbolism. His terse stories amount to little more than delicate fragments of

---

[8] The concept of dialogical truth originates in Bakhtin's analysis of Dostoevsky's novel, the *non plus ultra* of dialogical consciousness. A dialogic or polyphonic genre is characterized by the absence of a unifying narrative consciousness that embodies all the consciousnesses of all the characters. There is no higher level of narrative that incorporates the partial narratives offered by characters. 'For the author the hero is not "he" and not "I", but a fully valued "thou", that is, another fully fledged "I" ("Thou art")' (Bakhtin 1929/1973: 51).

sense, communicating metonymically, as if they were product brands. Why do such stories shrivel over time? One suspects precisely because meaning drains out of them, so that the effort is hardly worth making to narrate them. Again, this is a quality shared with product brands, which, in spite of advertisers' attempts to turn them into signifiers of difference, are lost in a meaningless cacophony of freely floating signifiers (Baudrillard 1983*a*, *b*; Gabriel and Lang 1995). Doug's parking-sign heroic may end up reduced to something barely meaningful—yet another CEO pulling off another tantrum in order to appear different from his predecessor. In a similar way, many 'official' organizational stories reported by researchers may amount to little more than slogans, virtually drained of meaning and unable to generate emotion. This view would lead to the conclusion that organizational storytelling is a victim of the narrative deskilling noted by the modernists, which itself results from the increasingly fragile nature of experience when choked by information. Members of organizations, overwhelmed by data, are neither storytellers nor story-listeners, but information-handlers. All that remains are relics of stories, coded leftovers from impoverished narratives, uncrafted and unappreciated. Storytelling would then be silenced (as per Benjamin) by the semiotic cacophony of flying signifiers (as per Baudrillard).

It is, however, possible to retain the concept of a story for proper narratives, with beginnings and ends, held together by action, entertaining for audiences and challenging for tellers, while acknowledging that other narrative devices are used to sustain or negotiate meaning. These include three devices noted by Czarniawska-Joerges and Joerges (1990)—namely, clichés, platitudes (including traditional proverbs), and labels (and Boje's terse stories can aptly be described as labels of stories rather than stories). They also included many other sense-seeking and sense-saving devices, often used in combination, though not amounting to stories—arguments and explanations, theories and rules of thumb, slogans and soundbites, lists (especially acronymic ones or featuring in overhead transparencies) and numbers (occasionally acting as labels—e.g. the '£67 million fiasco'), logos and images, opinions and stereotypes, metaphors and metonymies (especially in the form of slogans, such as 'quality', 'service', etc.), symbols and signs of all types, fragments of information, puns and *jeux de mots*, fantasies and daydreams, gestures, body language, and other displays of emotion.[9]

---

[9] For an eloquent discussion of the place of stories among sensemaking frames, which include ideology, third-order controls, paradigms, theories of action, and traditions, see Weick (1995).

ORGANIZATIONAL STORIES

This book will not study any of these (or other) types of sensemaking devices; instead, drawing from the folklorists, it will focus on stories and storytelling in the narrow sense of narratives with simple but resonant plots and characters, involving narrative skill, entailing risk, and aiming to entertain, persuade, and win over. The arguments presented here try to vindicate the insights of folklorists, while also accepting some vital lessons from modernism and postmodernism. Organizational stories develop their characters and plots not from the folkloric universe of enchanted forests and crystal mountains, but, as the modernists argued, from the personal experiences of individuals in organizations. And, as the postmodernists have recognized, storytelling comes to the rescue of meaning in an epoch saturated by information in which meaning is constantly displaced and crowded by noise. The argument that will emerge through the pages of this book is that storytelling is not dead in most organizations. Organizations do possess a living folklore, though this is not equally dense or equally vibrant in all of them. This folklore, its vitality, breadth, and character, can give us valuable insights into the nature of organizations, the power relations within them, and the experiences of their members. My argument is based on a large database of stories that I have accumulated over the years. One source of stories was a piece of fieldwork in five organizations—a privatized utility, a hospital, a large manufacturing company, a research and publishing company, and a consultancy unit. A second source of stories has been my students who report on their placement experiences, analysing and interpreting stories that they had heard as members of organizations. I have also collected numerous *ad hoc* stories from friends and acquaintances, some of which I shall present in this book. In nearly all of these instances, I represented an audience interested in hearing good stories. This contrasts with that of other research on stories, whose 'fly-on-the-wall' approaches undermine the storyteller's challenge and pleasure.[10]

It was clear to me that the majority of people I interviewed had a very clear sense of what I meant by 'story'. A few individuals instantly responded with some story, others suggested I talked to a specific person known for his or her storytelling ability, some held back from answering until they had a clearer sense of what types of stories I was interested in, and some indicated that they knew what I meant but commented that 'Nothing interesting ever happens here' or 'People

---

[10] Details of my methodology will be presented in Chapter 6.

only ever talk about work in this place'. This is in itself a significant finding—respondents made sense of the category 'story' and clearly differentiated it from other types of talk or narrative. Some of them regarded their organizations as story-free spaces but the majority did not. Their willingness and ability to relate stories varied widely. Many failed to relate a single story, while a few related numerous stories. Some individuals were able to convert the flimsiest material into interesting narratives, whereas others seemed unable to convert into meaningful stories what seemed like rich symbolic, emotional, and narrative raw material.[11] Like Boje, I found few stories that would be highly rated by folklorists. Yet there were several stories that were good enough to bear repetition. Here is one as narrated by a clerk of a utility:

There was a chap driving a lorry and he hit a cat so he got out of the lorry and saw this cat on the side of the road and thought I'd better finish it off . . . smashed it over the head, got back in, and drove off. A lady or a chap phoned the police and said I've just seen a Board lorry driver get out and kill my cat. So they chased after the van and found it and asked the driver whether he had killed the cat so he said he had run over it and couldn't leave it like that . . . it's cruel so I finished it off. So they said can we examine your van and he said yes by all means so they examined the van and found a dead cat under the wheel arch. So it was the wrong cat [he had killed] sleeping at the side of the road.

A narrative like this meets most folkloric criteria of storytelling; it is entertaining, it is well timed, its plot is a road story involving a protagonist and other characters, its storyline contains typical elements such as accident, coincidence, mistaken identity (of the cat), and misdirected motives. It certainly invites repetition and further embellishment. It does *not* invite factual verification. (Did he *really* kill the cat? Did the police record the incident? etc.) Looking at such a narrative as a myth would be wrong.[12] A myth about the deaths of

---

[11] This point is analysed clearly by Wallemacq and Sims (1998: 122).

[12] There are numerous reasons why I am disinclined to see organizational stories as being part of a 'mythology'. The stories lack the sweeping grandeur, narrative complexity, or overwhelming emotional charge of ancient Greek, native American, and other myths. Their characters can be interesting, unusual, or even brilliant, but they lack the towering presence of true heroes. Bettelheim (1976: 37) makes a very similar point in contrasting myth and fairy tale. 'Put simply, the dominant feeling in myth is: that is absolutely unique; it could not have happened to any other person, or in any other setting; such events are grandiose, awe-inspiring, and could not possibly happen to an ordinary mortal like you or me . . . By contrast, although the events which occur in fairy tales are often unusual and most improbable, they are always presented as ordinary, something that could happen to you or me or the person next door when out on a walk in the woods.' The comic or humorous qualities that feature in numerous stories undermine any mythical pretences; as Campbell (1949/1988) has noted, comedy and myth do not inhabit the same narrative or psychological space. The stories we encounter in organizations lack the sacral qualities of myths: they rarely address the great universals of myths, good and evil, human and divine, wild and

two cats does not bear comparison with the great myths of humanity; it would lead to the conclusion that organizational mythology is trite. Looking at it as folklore, on the other hand, highlights its vitality and invention. Slang, jokes, and idiosyncrasies, which are so alien to myth, all lie at the very heart of folklore (Dundes 1965, 1980, 1989). It is perfectly possible and meaningful to talk of Xerox or Internet lore or the folklore of computers or, indeed, the folklore of lorry-drivers and net-surfers without debasing the concept of folklore. The story of the driver who killed two cats is a fine example of lorry-driver folklore, capable of yielding telling and fruitful interpretations. It illustrates that, contrary to modernist ideas, storytelling is still alive and story-tellers can be found in organizations. It also illustrates that, contrary to postmodernist tendencies, some organizational narratives *are* proper stories and can be seen as part of an organizational folklore. This is an idea that briefly appeared to be gaining currency in the 1980s, during the excitement generated by the rediscovery of culture by organizational theorists. Yet, in spite of notable contributions (Jones 1984, 1985, 1990, 1991; Turner 1983, 1986), the concept of organizational folklore has not found great currency among scholars. We shall refer to organizational folklore as a range of cultural practices and texts that fulfil three conditions: first, they are richly symbolic; secondly, they are not manufactured or legislated, but emerge spontaneously through informal interactions among participants; and, thirdly, they are not one-offs, but become part of traditions, emulated, reproduced, and re-enacted (Jones 1991: 201). Stories, proverbs, generalizations, nicknames, puns, jokes, rituals, slang, graffiti, cartoons, material objects of use or display, codes, gestures, uses of physical space, body language are among the many ingredients of organizational folklore.

Here is a piece of car-park folklore, resulting from the visit of one of the company's own engineers to fix a problem at regional headquarters. It is a 'proper' story and is reported exactly as told by a senior clerk.

Lakeside is [our regional] head office; our engineer went out there, he thought it was an emergency call. The area is murder to park, he couldn't park any-

tame, agency and fate, heroism and victimhood. Expressing a widely held view, Barthes (1973: 142) argues that 'myth is constituted by the loss of the historical quality of things: in it, things lose the memory that they once were made'. By contrast, organizational stories remain bound to the mundane realities of everyday experience, the provincial, parochial concerns of life in most organizations; they are tied to the concrete, the fact, the historical rather than the mythological past. Even a cursory reading of serious mythological texts (Calasso 1983; Campbell 1949/1988, 1976; Douglas, 1967; Lévi-Strauss 1963a, 1958/1976), enables one to understand the impatience of anthropologists or ethnographers when management and organizational theorists use the idea of myth to denote any symbolically charged organizational narrative (Helmers 1993).

where and as far as he knew, it's an emergency job, he's got to get there; he goes round the back of the building and there is the company's own car park, so he sees a vacant place and puts his van there. Goes into the main building, it wasn't an emergency job, just that they wanted priority treatment if you like, run of the mill job, he comes back out again and one of the senior managers had blocked him in with his car. And he wouldn't let him out . . . and that was one of the top cats in personnel department and he said to the car park attendant and he told him his name and he virtually refused to come down and shift his car. That's senior management and he just lost his rag because it is costing him money . . . and he threatened to smash his car with a hammer or get the police to tow it away for causing an obstruction, the engineer this was, he was raving and that's what they think of senior management. But by the same token that's what they think of them . . . You, you peasant, you dare park there and blocks him in. There was a lot of sympathy for him here.

This story, like the previous one, can rightly be seen as a piece of workplace folklore, whose analysis can yield substantial insights into the nature of the organization, its power relations, and its culture. Like the previous story, it describes events second-hand, the narrator being neither a character in the story, nor a direct eyewitness. His narration is replete with passionate commitment, anger interfering with the narrative's grammar, yet amplifying its poetic effect. Most of the good stories I collected refer to events in which the teller is the central hero or which were witnessed first-hand.

OPINIONS, PROTO-STORIES, AND REPORTS

In later chapters I will describe different ways of classifying, interpreting, and analysing such stories. What I wish to do here is to introduce three particular types of narratives that must be distinguished from proper stories, even if they are not unrelated to them. The first are *opinions*, often strongly held, often containing some factual or symbolic material, but lacking plot, characters, and action. In the following example the opinion expressed by a clerk is that repetitive work causes mistakes:

Certain tasks are repetitive and tedious, we've got a particular task on the computer screen, it is called work reading . . . It is very repetitive, the screen is not pleasant to look at . . . it is not an easy thing to do and you need a lot of knowledge to do that . . . some people do it for 8 hours a day and that is a boring job, being stuck in front of the computer for that time. Mistakes happen not because they don't know what they are doing but because of the tedium of it.

Opinions like this seem to announce a story, that never materializes. They receive support from generalized assertions, without singling out a particular incident around which to construct a story. The listener may then encourage a story by prompting 'Can you think of any such cases?', though, in my experience, such prompting rarely generated high-quality stories. Opinions may not be stories, though they are part of an organization's sensemaking apparatus.

The second type of narrative I wish to distinguish from stories are *proto-stories*. These are fragments of stories, similar to Boje's terse stories, sometimes highly charged emotionally and symbolically. Yet their plot is very rudimentary. Under certain conditions of repetition, embellishment, and cross-fertilization, such narratives may yield fully-fledged stories. Here are two examples, the first from a chemical company, the second from a hospital:

There is the gentleman across the corridor, I notice him because he's always working, he's such a nice gentleman, such a nice character, and I always say 'I just met him on the first floor, I think he's madly in love with me', silly things like that. We just laugh about them.

We have got a chap that lives on the streets, it is quite sad, he was a prisoner of war and he hates to be confined, and he comes in lots, he sort of lives in the centre. Occasionally he suffers from hypothermia and someone will call an ambulance and he will come in; he is quite a character and can be quite aggressive sometimes.

Both of these narratives focus on a potentially interesting character who acts as a spur for fantasy, but their plot is rudimentary; they have a beginning, but, unlike true stories, they lack a proper end. Distinctions between stories and proto-stories are not as clear-cut as those between opinions and stories. A narrative may have different symbolic resonances with different listeners; one listener may hear a story where another hears merely a proto-story, just as one listener may hear a weak story where another hears a strong one. However, the essential quality of poetic incompleteness sets proto-stories apart.

Unlike opinions and proto-stories, the third type of narrative I wish to distinguish from stories, *reports*, does have a plot and characters. Yet its attitude towards them is stubbornly 'factual', refusing to read any meaning in the events described. A merger, a sacking, an accident are described just as facts devoid of overt symbolism or emotion. Consider the following example:

Over the weekend one of our showrooms was broken into and it was burgled . . . they actually broke in. The police went out and they got a firm to come out and replace the glass panel in the bottom of the door. One of our keyholders went down late to check . . . the burglars had been back, broken the glass again—twice in one night. . . . He rang the glass guy to see why he hadn't repaired the door and he said I did it about an hour ago . . . no you haven't there is a big hole in the door. On the Monday, the general manager went down to get some details for the police report—while he was there someone broke into his car and stole his stereo.

Such factual accounts were common in the research organization I studied, where members prized the factual accuracy of their work and appeared generally reluctant to deviate from 'facts'. They can be seen as historical accounts in which accuracy is valued above effect, narratives in which no poetic licence is accorded to the narrator. This maintains the vital distinction, first noted by Aristotle, between history and poetry. Aristotle viewed stories as emotional-symbolic texts and used the term 'poetics' to describe the type of work that is involved in transforming facts into stories. By contrast, he viewed history as analytico-descriptive. While poetry is a discourse of meanings, history is a discourse of facts, causes, and effects. In contrast to stories, I shall refer to these as *descriptions* or *reports*; they may lack the compelling narrative power of stories but are not outside the sensemaking apparatus of organizations. A reporter, like the one above, acts like a historian or a forensic scientist, inviting a causative rather than a symbolic explanation of events, concerned about damage and cost limitations and preventative measures rather than about keeping listeners entertained.[13]

FACTS AND STORIES

This distinction between report and story seems problematic. Many would deny that it is possible to give a purely factual report of any event. The choice of facts to report, the choice of words used, the omissions made, the framing of the narrative suggest that all narratives involve the narrator's active engagement with his or her subject. Yet I believe that it is necessary to distinguish between description, which deals with facts-as-information, and stories, which represent facts-as-experience for both tellers and listeners (Benjamin 1968b). The former is the craft of the journalist, the recorder, the chronicler,

---

[13] The distinction between story and report is one that has been extensively documented by narrative theorists, such as Labov and Waletzky (1967), Van Dijk (1975), and Robinson (1981). Van Dijk, for example, compares two accounts which we may give of a bank robbery that we happen to witness, one to the police and one to our friends. The former is likely to stick to the facts as a report, the latter is likely to present a story. Labov and Waletzky build a strong argument that stories entail both description and evaluation, whereas reports are limited to description.

the latter is the task of the raconteur, the entertainer, the yarn-spinner.

Now, as Habermas (1977: 349), following Danto, has argued, the chronicler who simply describes events is an ideal fiction: 'Completely to describe an event is to locate it in all the right stories, and this we cannot do. We cannot because we are temporarily provincial with regard to the future . . . The imposition of a narrative involves us with an inexpungeable subjective factor.' Yet this ideal fiction is indispensable in distinguishing between two types of discourses, one whose loyalty ultimately rests with the facts and another whose loyalty rests with the story. The chronicler is committed to accuracy, the storyteller is committed to effect (Frye 1969). Chroniclers treat their material with the respect of archaeologists, wishing to discover, preserve, and display valuable objects, their own pride lying in their claim not to have tampered with the material. Storytellers treat their material in a far more cavalier manner; their skill lies precisely in turning plain material into something valuable and meaningful.[14] Of course, many archaeologists end up framing their findings, they (including celebrities such as Schliemann and Evans) tamper with their findings for effect, they display their discoveries in front of television cameras. They, like many chroniclers and their contemporary counterparts, journalists, can end up as storytellers. In a similar way, experimental scientists may falsify the results of their experiments in order to use them in support of a theory. Such 'distortions' differ fundamentally from the storyteller's distortions. No one would accuse a storyteller of distortion, although a storyteller may be accused of spoiling a good story. In fact, the narrative test for a story is relatively straightforward: would a listener respond by challenging the factual accuracy of the text.[15] By contrast, journalistic, experimental, and archaeological practices are factually challengeable and distortions constitute serious offences. It is essential, therefore, to preserve the distinction between narratives that purport to represent facts (even if they fail to do so) and narratives

---

[14] It is possible to map the two discourses against the two forms of human cognition, identified by Bruner, the logico-scientific and the narrative. These are 'two modes of cognitive functioning, two modes of thought, each providing distinctive ways of "ordering experience", of constructing reality. The two (though complementary) are irreducible to one another . . . Each of these ways of knowing, moreover, has operating principles of its own and its own criteria of well-formedness. they differ radically in their procedures for verification' (Bruner 1986: 21).

[15] Storytelling, like a child's play, involves a collusion on the part of the audience. Just as the adult colludes with the child's illusion of a old box turned into a shop or a palace, so too the storyteller's audience collude with the fantastic or unrealistic elements in the story. See Winnicott (1980). Thus suspension of disbelief and poetic licence are acknowledged privileges of the storyteller but not of the chronicler.

that make no secret of their purpose to use facts as poetic material, moulding them, twisting them, and embellishing them for effect.[16]

Only by treating stories as distinctive types of narrative, claiming special privileges and subject to special constraints, can we use them as windows into organizational life. Only then can we study the challenge that they represent for teller and listener alike, the meanings they carry or fail to carry, the pleasure or pain they afford, and the power they accord or deny. If we insist on treating every consultant's report, every cliché, every overhead transparency, and every statistical table as 'telling a story', we inevitably assist in making storytelling, as a meaning-bestowing activity, in its very ubiquity, moribund. Even worse, we allow our fascination with discourse and narrative to act as a smokescreen, obscuring the political, psychological, and social issues in organizations.

---

[16] De Certeau (1986: 199 ff.) has argued that the distinction between fact and fiction is the touchstone of a process that privileges the univocality of science at the expense of the plurivocal, polysemic quality of storytelling. Through this process, 'fiction is deported to the land of the unreal, but the discourse that is armed with the technical "know-how" to discern errors is given the supplementary privilege of representing something "real" ' (201).

2

Storytelling and Sensemaking

Poetic licence is every storyteller's prerogative—the acknowledged right to twist the facts for effect. This is the basis of the bond that unites storyteller and audience. The audience suspends disbelief, allowing the storyteller to apply his or her craft on the material. Many of the stories that I collected in different organizations are highly charged narratives, not merely recounting 'events', but inter-preting them, enriching them, enhancing them, and infusing them with meaning. Omissions, exaggerations, subtle shifts in emphasis, timing, innuendo, metaphors are some of the mechanisms used. Far from being an obstacle to further study, such 'distortions' can be approached as attempts to re-create reality *poetically*. As Walter Benjamin (1968*b*) argued in his article on Leskov, the storyteller is concerned not with 'facts-as-information' but with 'facts-as-experience'. The response invited by a story is, then, not to challenge 'the facts', but to engage with its meaning (Reason and Hawkins 1988). This neither denies the factual basis of stories, nor reduces the stories to elaborations of facts. Instead, it disengages the narrative from the fact, in a similar way that a psychoanalytic approach to dreams disengages the text of a dream from the 'day's residues' or the bodily stimuli that provide its raw materials.

In this chapter we shall examine the process whereby events within an organization turn into stories. We shall look at an instance where a single incident fed three different stories, each based on a distinct interpretation of the event. We shall then look at three instances where particular stories had become part of organizational folklore, in each case crystallized around a single interpretation. Each of these stories was related to me by several members in each organization. Faced with such narratives, researchers have certain choices. They may dismiss them as trifles of organizational life, which do not affect the basic organizational realities of management, control, resistance, and so on. Alternatively, they may treat stories as clues leading to the 'truth' about the organization. They may then seek to elucidate 'the facts' of each case by asking questions such as 'Did the incident "really" take place? When? Where? How?', reasserting the dominance of the rational discourse of causes and effects. Alternatively, the researcher may adopt the role of audience in a storytelling event, becoming a *fellow-traveller* on a narrative, sharing its emotional tone, seeking to expand it, and enrich it, and ultimately sustaining its disengaged, pleasure-seeking qualities. This is the approach of one eager to appreciate a good story and explore its meaning for an individual or a group. The chapter will test whether the folklorists' tenet that the primary function of storytelling is entertainment is valid in organizations. It will be shown that even sad and anxiety-provoking stories can afford pleasure, albeit in oblique and unexpected ways. Yet it will be argued that, in contrast to the telling of fairy tales or folk tales, the telling of organizational stories frequently moves beyond entertainment, seeking to educate, persuade, warn, reassure, justify, explain, and console.

DIFFERENT ACCOUNTS OF THE SAME INCIDENT: THE HALON EXPLOSION

Consider, for instance, an incident involving the explosion of a pressurized fire extinguisher (Halon) at a research and publishing organization. The brass nozzle of the extinguisher flew through a glass partition, scattering glass everywhere; it narrowly missed a computer operator, and caused substantial damage but no injuries. The incident was recounted without prompting to me by four different witnesses, for whom the incident had been an important event of their working lives. Their accounts varied factually; more significantly, as I shall try to show presently, they varied poetically.

The first account of the incident, offered by Raymond, a manager, was a detached report that made no attempt to entertain, evaluate, or interpret. It emphasized the material damage (the fact that the room was flooded by the sprinklers and that the e-mail was out of commission for some time) without investing the events with any emotion or symbolic significance. For him, the incident was 'just an accident', an event without intentionality or agency, whose implications were essentially 'bureaucratic': ensuring that such an accident could not happen again in the future.

The most memorable thing I can think of was when the emergency fire control system in the computer room blew up. The pressurized system blew a cap off and punched a hole through the glass separating the computer room and

32

went through just over our heads; it nearly took our heads off. A couple of months ago. [How much damage did it cause?] It looked worse than it was; but it was pretty spectacular. The safety officer had just moved the compressed whatever it was, so the cap on the compressed system was facing across rather than up and when it blew off, a fairly substantial piece of brass came off like a bullet and went through the glass, so there was glass everywhere. Of course, the computer went down, the place was then flooded. It was out of operation for a couple of days. It didn't affect the working of my department very much other than the e-mail going down.

Organizations seek to eliminate or reduce the number of ruptures and minimize their impact. This is part of a discourse incorporating planning, precautions, insurance claims, and so on. There is little doubt that all organizational members are routinely engaged in this discourse. Accidents lead to factual reports, written and verbal, like the one above. This, however, is not the *only* discourse generated by accidents. Accidents often invite symbolic constructions; as Aristotle argued in *Poetics* (1452*a*), even the accidental collapse of a statue is seen as an incident 'not devoid of meaning'. In fact, numerous stories, including fairy tales, incorporate an accident as an omen or as a sign, which the heroes may or may not be able to 'read' correctly. In a similar way, accidents in organizations invite diverse interpretations.

This is precisely what the remaining three accounts did. Maureen, the computer operator who had the narrow escape, presented the incident in a half-serious, half-amusing tone, not only as a sign of management's neglect of the organization, its employees, and the fire system, but also as a personal attack on her:

I suppose they tried to kill me; I was sitting at my desk and the gas cylinder exploded which meant that the cylinder was directed at my desk and the nozzle hadn't been properly fixed . . . and it exploded and the projectile hit the window above my desk and caused an almighty explosion and shattered glass everywhere. They failed on that attempt to kill me! [Who?] The management.

In this account, the incident is presented not as a chance event, but as a *personal attack* on the subject, which directly enters the narrative. Not only is Maureen casting management in the role of the villain, but she also casts herself in the roles of target and survivor seeking to apportion blame and responsibility. Her account illustrates some of the choices facing the researcher. By saying 'They didn't *really* try to kill you, did they?', one can direct the discourse back to the domain of facts-as-information. Alternatively, by saying 'Have there been any other such attempts?', one can join in the story, stimulating the storyteller to build on or fantasize around the earlier narrative. It can be seen from this account that the story entails both an interpretation of the incident (an attribution of meaning) and also the beginnings of a fantasy of persecution and victimization.

Maureen's was not the only account of the accident that sought to bring the subject directly into the narrative. Chris, another eyewitness, recounted the incident in a light-hearted manner:

I heard this huge bang and this rattling sound because the windows were double-glazed and one window was banging against the other. And then Jim was crawling around on all fours trying to get out. Then I realized that everyone was trying to get out of the room, so I thought 'I better go then'.

Chris's account both denied the real danger presented by the explosion and cast himself in the role of a person who is not easily rattled or panic-stricken, in contrast to the others. Unlike Maureen, Chris did not seek to apportion blame, but rather interpreted the event as a *test of character*, meant to distinguish between those who get easily rattled and those who do not. Maureen's and Chris's narratives happily coexisted within the organization's folklore, as did the third account of the incident. Peter's account was, like Chris's, light-hearted, but very differently constructed. Peter explained how the service engineer had not fixed the nozzle properly on the fire extinguisher, placing the blame squarely on him, in a way that an independent inspector might have done; in fact, his account would, like Raymond's, have been a report rather than a story had he not concluded it in a most unexpected manner:

This is the sort of thing that people have been referring to jokingly, like 'Next time Maureen will aim better'. [What should she aim for?] Upstairs, of course!

This account illustrates how a report becomes a story almost as an afterthought, but acting as the trigger of a fantasy in which the near victim is transformed into an active agent, indeed an agent of retribution. It is not Maureen being threatened, but rather Maureen who threatens to cause damage; only Maureen should do the job properly next time and aim at management. This fantasy reverses the relations between prosecutor and prosecuted in a manner common, for example, among children's fantasies of ritually killing a hated teacher.

STORY-WORK AND THE POETICS OF STORYTELLING

This symbolic reversal of persecuted into persecutor and the turning of passivity into activity can be ascribed to a type of psychological work. This work is similar to what Freud (1900) called 'dreamwork', whereby a set of raw materials, which include memory residues from the previous day and unconscious desires, are converted into the content of a dream. By analogy, we shall view story-work as the process whereby a symbolically charged narrative is constructed out of an engagement of deep desires with organizational life. Story-work is the psychological counterpart of poetical work that seeks to transcend the literal truth of events by drawing out a different type of truth, one that may claim to be deeper, more powerful, or even transcendental.

Each of the four narratives above constructs the event differently, but only the last three entail story-work. If Raymond's account, with its emphasis on precision and unambiguity, is one of 'facts-as-information', the other three, with their emphasis on meaning, represent 'facts-as-experience'. And, in each case, story-work leads to a different 'reading' of the incident: Maureen's as dereliction of duty and personal attack, Chris's as test of character, and Peter's as opportunity for retribution. Story-work then involves the discovery of an underlying meaning to the events—a meaning that results from a core interpretation of the events (Labov and Waletzky 1967). We shall refer to these interpretations as *poetic interpretations* to distinguish them from the very different type of interpretation undertaken not by the storyteller, but by the student of stories. This latter type will be referred to as *analytic interpretations.*[1]

Poetic interpretation and the tropes of story-work

Interpretation is the core part of story-work in organizations, through which events are 'infused' with meaning or meaning is 'discovered' in the facts. How exactly does this 'infusion' take place? The importance of rhetorical tropes, metaphors, metonymies ('upstairs, of course'), synecdoches ('The management'), and ironies ('they failed . . . I suppose') have been well rehearsed as devices in the storyteller's armour and more generally as sensemaking mechanisms (Burke 1945/1969, 1962; Manning 1979; Weick 1995; White 1978). In addition, storytellers rely on various narrative and stylistic devices,

[1] This distinction between the two types of interpretation is related to Eco's (1990) distinction between the semantic or naïve reader and the semiotic or critical one. The former 'buys' the narrator's poetic interpretation, while the latter seeks to subsume it in an interpretation of his or her own. Czarniawska (Czarniawska 1997; Czarniawska-Joerges 1995) has developed Eco's idea in respect of the relation between the narratives of organizational researchers and those of organizational participants. In her work, the narratives of the field are not qualitatively distinct from those of academia or, for that matter, of literature, all of which represent genres of narrative knowledge.

such as deliberate ambiguities[2] ('directed'), omissions ('And then, Jim . . .'), distortions, exaggerations ('crawling on all fours'), rearrangement of materials, timing, and so on, to enliven their stories. What has been less well analysed are the mechanisms through which an underlying set of meanings is generated. Our example enables us to draw out some of these mechanisms through which meaning is generated, turning information into experience. We shall refer to them as 'poetic tropes', in contrast to the rhetorical tropes that have already been noted.[3] Without these poetic tropes, it seems to me, no amount of symbolic, rhetorical, or narrative elaboration can be effective, and it is for this reason that I regard them as the storyteller's central interpretive devices. Each one of these tropes represents a way of either making sense of specific parts in the narrative or making connections between different parts. Eight such poetic tropes can be noted:

- attribution of motive
- attribution of causal connections
- attribution of responsibility, namely, blame and credit
- attribution of unity
- attribution of fixed qualities, especially in opposition
- attribution of emotion

---

[2] For an interesting discussion of ambiguity as a narrative resource, see Burke (1945/1969: pp. xviii–xix): 'Insofar as men cannot themselves create the universe, there must remain something essentially enigmatic about the problem of motives, and that this underlying enigma will manifest itself in inevitable ambiguities and inconsistencies among the terms for motives. Accordingly, what we want is not terms that avoid ambiguity, but terms that clearly reveal the strategic spots at which ambiguities necessarily arise . . . Hence, instead of considering it our task to "dispose of" any ambiguity by merely disclosing the fact that it is an ambiguity, we rather consider it our task to study and clarify the resources of ambiguity.'

[3] The relation between poetics and rhetoric is a complex and ambiguous one. Todorov (1981: 11) viewed them as mutually supportive disciplines. 'Poetics might find a certain assistance in each of these sciences [anthropology, psychoanalysis, philosophy of language], to the degree that language constitutes part of their object. Its closest relatives will be other disciplines that deal with discourse—the group forming the field of rhetoric, understood in the broadest sense as a general science of discourses.' His view of poetics, however, is close to a general theory of literary discourse. The argument put forward here takes a broader view of the poetic (see Ch. 1 n. 2]. It is distinct from those of both Czarniawska, who de-emphasizes distinctions between poetry and rhetoric (Czarniawska 1997; Czarniawska-Joerges 1995) and Höpfl, who, following de Certeau, views rhetoric and poetry as opposed to narrative and experiential principles, associated with masculine and feminine respectively (de Certeau 1986; Höpfl 1995). De Certeau (1986: 208), for his part, views storytelling as engendering both rhetorical and poetic accretions, in contrast to history, which systematically seeks to extirpate such influences from the 'surrounding culture'. Following Burke (1966: 302), we view poetics and rhetoric as distinct but overlapping and potentially reinforcing narrative principles. Thus, a rhetorical trope, such as irony or metaphor, may strengthen a character's position in the plot, or alternatively a story may be used to amplify the rhetorical effect of a particular position. After all, tragedians were master ironists and orators master storytellers.

- attribution of agency
- attribution of providential significance

Maureen's interpretation of the incident reveals one of the primary tropes, the *attribution of motive* to a seemingly motiveless event: the explosion was not an accident, but a motivated event, aimed at killing her. Attribution of motive is central to any interpretation. Was a particular event aimed at achieving an outcome or was the outcome not intended? Was a comment aimed at insulting or at deceiving, or not? Attribution of motive is vital in criminal cases, where it decides the nature and magnitude of an offence, whether, for instance, a death was murder, manslaughter, the product of negligence or misadventure. It is also characteristic of numerous organizational stories that feature in this book. One special type of this attribution is the attribution of the motive to harm, to injure, or, more generally, to oppose and frustrate. In general, attribution of motive is vital in determining whether the predicament facing the protagonist is one that he or she deserves or not; this, in turn, affects the construction of the protagonist as hero, victim, villain, survivor, fool, and so forth. Attribution of *unconscious* motive is the fundamental psychoanalytic contribution to sensemaking in the twentieth century. The agent, under this conceptualization, may not be aware of his or her own motive, may vehemently deny it, or may seek to rationalize and neutralize it—yet, since Freud, we have learnt not only to reject such claims, but, if anything, to use them to reinforce our attributions. Attribution of motive is one of the most powerful sensemaking devices and features prominently in storytelling. It would be virtually impossible to construct a story with unmotivated characters.

Related to attribution of motive, is the *attribution of causal connections*, whereby two or more incidents in the narrative are linked as cause and effect. Goffman (1974: 503 ff.) has noted how storytelling overestimates the 'causal fabric of experience', representing actions and events as necessary rather than accidental or conditional; establishing orderly sequences of causes and effects is a means of organizing and rationalizing remembered experience. This is especially so when two events can be presented as simultaneous or as being in close temporal proximity (Polkinghorne 1988; Weick 1995). In attributing causal connections, poetry eschews multi-causality, covariation, probabilistic causation, as well as distinctions between sufficient and necessary conditions. Instead, it invariably opts for a simple chain of causes and effects, which are automatically linked together.[4]

---

[4] An extreme form of attribution of causal connections is superstition.

Associated with attribution of causal connections is *attribution of blame and credit*, which has deep psychological consequences, since it determines whether an individual will be cast in the role of a villain (he or she caused the disaster), a victim (he or she suffered from it), or even a hero (he or she managed heroically in the aftermath). In organizational stories, attribution of credit and blame is frequently associated with lack of recognition (someone else claimed the credit), scapegoating (finding someone suitable to blame), and heroic achievement (she single-handedly saved the day). Attribution of credit and blame is in essence an attribution of moral responsibility, allowing the storyteller a means of determining right and wrong and assigning them to appropriate agents.[5]

Maureen's narrative also reveals two further poetic tropes: *attribution of unity*, whereby an entire class of people ('they') are treated as an undifferentiated entity, all of them equally responsible, and *attribution of fixed qualities*, most notably magical powers of bringing about explosions. These two tropes both hinge on the quality of sameness and come together in collective representations—labelling, generalization (Robinson 1981), and stereotyping. As a poetical mechanism, attribution of fixed qualities is extremely important: a person who lies once can be treated as a liar on every subsequent occasion, just as a person who once performed a heroic deed is treated as incapable of cowardice at any later stage. Thus the label 'liar' or 'hero' acts as a full signifier of the person and his or her qualities. These qualities may range from total malevolence to total perfection, from omnipotence to omniscience; they may be accorded equally to individuals, groups, organizations, or physical objects. The attribution of superhuman powers to particular individuals, groups, or machines in organizations echoes directly the attribution of similar powers to witches, magicians, magic wands, and magic droughts in folkloric tales. Later we shall identify some of the fixed qualities associated with particular characters in different plots. One especially important means of attributing fixed qualities involves the juxtaposition of two objects, people, groups, or situations whose qualities are meant to be exact opposites of each other. Through opposition, qualities become both fixed and exaggerated. Thus, for instance, the bravery of the hero is juxtaposed to the cowardice of the villain, the ease of one task to the difficulty of another, the peace and tranquillity of one moment to the death and devastation of another.[6] One important poetic use of

---

[5] Martin *et al.* (1983: 450) have noted the fundamental difference between attribution of causality and attribution of responsibility. Yet they unaccountably go on to focus exclusively on attribution of responsibility.

[6] Poetic opposition or contrast is a technique especially useful to film- and documentary-makers as well as other narrative-makers who rely on visual images.

opposition is the opposition of important and unimportant—an event or a situation is devalued and diminished in opposition to ones that are constructed as self-evidently important.

Chris's narrative offers an example of a different type of attribution, *attribution of emotion*. Of course, the emotional tone of stories can be quite complex and ambiguous. In evaluating the emotional tone of a story, it becomes essential to distinguish between the emotions with which the characters are invested and the emotions aroused by the story itself. The emotions with which the central characters are endowed crucially influence our understanding of their actions and bring into relief the behaviour of other characters. Thus, Chris's friend Jim is clearly presented as being terrified, to draw the nonchalant character of the hero's response ('I better go then'). Whether a person is seen as enjoying an act or doing it while being in terror or shock crucially affects the interpretation of an incident and its conversion into story. An evil deed committed in ignorance is very different from an identical deed committed with gleeful satisfaction or one perpetrated with scientific precision and apparent lack of emotion.

Peter's account offers an example of another poetic trope that we note here—*attribution of agency*. This turns something passive or even inanimate into something active, purposeful, and conscious, something capable of being an agent. In one account of the Halon explosion, Maureen becomes an agent, indeed an agent of retribution, rather than someone who just happened to be sitting near the place of the explosion; in another account, management is an agent, knowingly and consciously causing explosions to eliminate particular employees. While attribution of agency is related to attribution of motive, it goes well beyond it. A motive may drive one action whereas agency turns an object into subject, governing its entire range of cognitions and actions. Thus, in folkloric tales, animals, forests, stellar objects, and objects of daily use turn into characters in the plot, able to act in a meaningful and purposeful way. In organizational stories, one of the commonest attributions of agency is to the organization itself which is treated anthropomorphically as an independent and sovereign agent.[7]

A special type of attribution of agency is the attribution of a divine purpose an event, which we shall refer to as *attribution of*

[7] This use of agency is distinct from Burke's. Burke views agency as one of the five key terms of dramatism, the others being act, scene, agent, and purpose. Agency represents the means or instrument that enables the actor to pursue his or her purpose (Burke 1945/1969). While Burke defends this use of 'agency' strongly, it seems odd, given the current practice of using 'agency' as the quality or potential of being or acting as an agent. This is the meaning adopted here. The terms 'instrument' and 'resource' have been used as equivalent to Burke's agency.

providential significance. This presents an incident as having been engineered by a superior intelligence in order to achieve a particular end, such as a radical conversion in the hero (a Road-to-Damascus type of incident), a test of character (Chris's story, above), or an *ex machina* intervention that restores justice and brings about the punishment of the villains and a happy end for all the rest. Providential significance may be benevolent or it may assume the form of a malignant or persecuting fate from which the protagonist cannot escape, no matter what he or she does. This is an important trope in tragedy.

If the eight poetic tropes identified here act to infuse events with meanings, the same can be said of their opposites, the negative tropes. For example, instead of attributing agency to an individual, the storyteller may deny agency and in so doing cast a possible villain in the role of a victim. Was Judas an instrument of divine will or a psychological agent? Denying agency sometimes assumes the form of presenting the protagonist as lacking a certain knowledge or information that would enable him or her to act as a conscious agent. A storyteller may deny all emotion ('precise, scientific killers') or specific emotions ('sadistic, entirely without conscience) of some characters. Important qualities can be denied ('non-human, animals'). Alternatively, motive may be denied ('It was an accident—he never intended to endanger her life'), as can unity ('She was not one of them – she could see that . . .').

Poetic tropes may be combined through story-work to generate complex narrative constructions out of simple events. A manager fails to inform one of his colleagues that she has left the headlights of her car on in the company car park. His car was parked next to hers, but he claims not to have noticed. The dead battery in the woman's car causes her to spend several hours in the frozen car park waiting for it to be repaired. The next day she accuses him of deliberately not telling her, while he protests his innocence. In her story, he is attributed with *motive*—he meant to cause her harm. This extends into attribution of *emotion*—he meant to hurt her because he is envious of her. This, in turn, may be supported by an attribution of *causal connection*—he was envious of her because she was promoted over him—and an attribution of *fixed qualities*—he is a petty and vindictive man. Besides, he is just a man, like all the others (attribution of *unity*), wanting to have a laugh at her expense with his mates (further attribution of *motive* and *emotion*). He, of course, is entirely to blame for her misfortune (attribution of *blame*). And the whole incident only serves to show what a rotten individual he is (attribution of *agency/providential significance*). In this way, a poetic interpretation of the incident emerges which makes sense to the woman and possibly to her audience and turns a simple incident into a minor drama of organizational life.

Poetic tropes are used to support particular interpretations; these may be reinforced through additional rhetorical, narrative, and symbolic devices. Thus a particular interpretation may be announced through a metaphor, an oxymoron, or a paradox. The interpretation may be offered directly in the course of the story or may be delayed in order to build up a sense of mystery and suspense. Thus, an expert storyteller may build up a narrative out of material that does not appear to add up to a story, only to offer, almost as an afterthought, the key that unlocks the narrative, revealing its meaning. This symbolic construction of events is not arbitrary—it is carried out in accordance with desires and wishes, with emotions and feelings, rather than with great concern for accuracy and consistency. Poetic interpretations may set off fantasies (for instance, a fantasy of retaliation in the example above) or may actually merge with fantasies (for instance, a fantasy of persecution in the example above, where all male managers are envisaged as seeking to harm her). In the earlier example of the Halon explosion, each one of the three interpretations (whether the accident is interpreted as a trial of character, a dereliction of duty or an opportunity for retribution) sets off a different fantasy. Some fantasies are more developed than others, though they each have a distinct emotional tone, unleashing a different set of feelings, such as self-pity, pride, defiance, or mirth.[8]

Story-work involves the transformation of everyday experience into meaningful stories. In doing so, the storytellers neither accept nor reject 'reality'. Instead, they seek to mould it, shape it, and infuse it with meaning, each in a distinct and individual way through the use of poetic tropes. Through this activity they shape their personal and organizational identities—for instance, as heroes, as heroic survivors, as victims, or as bystanders. They also cast other individuals into a relatively narrow range of roles, some of which will become clearer as we examine the central plots of organizational stories. Story-work permits the narrator to rearrange his or her cast of characters, to turn allies into enemies, defeats into victories, traumas into triumphs. Story-work is not always a purely personal process. Some

---

[8] These fantasies maintain a firm link with reality. As Bakhtin (1981: 150–1) argued, 'the fantastic in folklore is a realistic fantastic: in no way does it exceed the limits of the real, here-and-now material world . . . Such a fantastic relies on the real-life possibilities of human development—possibilities not in the sense of a program for immediate practical action, but in the sense of the needs and possibilities of men, those eternal demands of human nature that will not be denied. These demands will remain forever, as long as there are men; they will not be suppressed, they are real, as real as human nature itself, and therefore sooner or later they will force their way to a full realization.'

stories are virtually multi-authored, being co-narrated simultaneously by two or more individuals (Robinson 1981: 72). Others emerge
accidentally during conversations out of small narrative fragments,
referred to earlier as 'proto-stories', which entail the seed of a story.
Several people may respond by offering significant clues or relating
the material to another story. Different participants to the conversation may then offer further elements, trading interpretations (Boje
1991). Some of these elements are discarded, others are incorporated
or elaborated. The story emerges as a collage from a complex inter-
subjective process. Even then different participants may retain different versions. Each version may then travel, undergoing further
elaborations with each recital. In one incident that I witnessed, a
number of managers were deriding their department for its extrava-
gant brochures and stationery, at a time when many other departments were carrying out cuts in expenditure. Such gripes must have
been daily occurrences at the department in question; but what
turned them into a story and a 'good story' at that time was when
someone revealed that the head of the department was having an
illicit liaison with the graphic artist responsible for the material.
Whether true or not, this was the missing piece necessary to turn the
earlier gripes (proto-stories) into a proper story. The story was subsequently embellished, fusing with other narratives regarding the head
of department's sexual behaviour and his financial mismanagement.

Organizational stories do not stand as obelisks or pyramids in a
barren landscape. Instead, their texts constantly evolve, they compete, they merge, they often disappear, at times to reappear out of
nowhere. Many stories, like the one described above, often coexist in
different versions, rarely coming into direct conflict or competition,
pursuing errant careers within organizations, like furtive thoughts or
fantasies. As long as a story remains 'live', new meanings may be
uncovered and different symbolic elements may be highlighted. In
this way, stories evolve, some of them becoming gradually embellished and augmented eventually becoming part of the folklore.
Others may atrophy and disappear altogether, or may be rediscov-
ered later and start new careers.

CRYSTALLIZATION OF STORIES

There are times, however, when stories crystallize around particular
interpretations. Different versions may diverge in numerous details
but seem to agree on the story's core symbolism. This symbolism
seems very powerful, the stories being treated as part of the heritage

of an organization or of a group. When researchers encounter such stories, they may sense that what is being related is no mere trifle of organizational life but something deeply significant. It is offered to them on the basis of trust and respect, the way that a valuable artefact might have been. Questioning or doubting such stories is not easy and may lead to the exclusion or ostracism of the researcher and the breakdown of the research relationship.

In such situations, the researcher may try to delve deeper into the story, seeking to analyse the reasons why it has such a powerful grip over a group or an organization, whether indeed it has a deeper meaning. As Paul Ricœur (1970: 8) has argued 'to interpret is to understand a double meaning'. Storytellers propose such interpretations, which the audience may test, trying them out in their own imagination and seeing whether they work or not. If a particular interpretation 'resonates' with them, they may accept it; alternatively, they may reject or modify it. As fellow-travellers on a story, researchers will engage in their own interpretations. However, analytic interpretations are rather different from the storytellers' poetic interpretations. Instead of adding new layers of story-work after the manner of collages, further embellishing and elaborating the narrative, analytic interpretations aim at unlocking the inner meaning of a story, a meaning that may be present and yet not acknowledged by storyteller and audience. If poetic interpretation allows the storyteller to align events with desires and construct them in a meaningful way, analytic interpretation asks why such constructions resonate with meaning; whether they possess a deeper layer of significance.

It is, after all, for this reason that researchers turn their attention to stories—because they wish to use the stories as ways of gaining insights into the deeper organizational, political, and psychological realities that they contain. While the storyteller interprets in order to make events meaningful to his or her audience, the researcher interprets in order to get to the truth behind the changes undergone by meaning. Consider the case of the collapse of the statue of a ruler. A poet or a storyteller may endow such an event with diverse meanings, interpreting it as retribution, omen, sign of neglect, and so forth. A political scientist, on the other hand, would want to know why such interpretations make sense: why, for instance the downfall of the empire is seen as imminent or why the leader is seen as deserving assassination. A psychologist may be interested to find out what the leader symbolizes for the followers. This type of interpretation is according to Ricœur (1970: 32), a 'systematic exercise of suspicion', forever mistrusting the obvious and forever looking for the hidden. Stories are undoubted repositories of meaning—yet, these meanings can be contorted, ambiguous, and contradictory.

The three interpretations that follow are offered as examples of analytic interpretations. They suggest that the meanings read into events by the storyteller may differ from the deeper meanings revealed by the story itself. The stories have no special claims to uniqueness; they do, however, represent three distinct modes of story-making, the epic, the tragic, and the comic, each displaying a different range of vicissitudes of meanings and each generating a distinct amalgam of emotions. Each story poses a bigger hermeneutic challenge than its predecessor; yet the interpretation of each suggests that many stories conceal as much as they reveal—pride may conceal hurt, defiance may conceal weakness, mirth may conceal anxiety. Suspicion is an appropriate stance for the analytic interpreter, even if it is not one appropriate for a storytelling audience. The first two stories are drawn from a series of field interviews in two different catering establishments (Gabriel 1988), while the third is drawn from my personal experience during a period of military service in a naval camp.

The epic story: Gill gives a piece of her mind

You ought to be here when Miss McDermott is expected on a visit. The bosses run around like mad all day making sure that the place is spotless, last time they even threw the mops away in their panic, they didn't have time to put them away . . . They never dare open their mouth [in the presence of Miss McDermott], it's Gill from school-meals who does all the talking.

This is how a dinner lady described, in the course of an interview (Gabriel 1988), the visits of the council's catering officer to inspect a kitchen in a large school and community centre. The meaning of the story appears self-evident and I might have brushed it aside had several subsequent interviewees not brought it up, unprompted. Individual accounts of the story varied. They varied factually, in elaboration and in quality of delivery. Each telling of the story constituted a unique performance or 'recital'. Each omitted certain details (for instance, I only heard about the throwing-away of the mops once) or included different ones. In some accounts, the story was a one-off, in others, it was a regular event. Some accounts have Gill talking to one bureaucrat from headquarters, others have her talking to many. What Gill said differs in different accounts, and in some it does not feature at all. What was constant, however, was that Gill apparently spoke her mind without fear. Unlike the earlier story of the accident involving the fire extinguisher, which led to different poetic interpretations, the meaning read into this story was consistent, even if the means of conveying it varied. The question then is why the story was seen by several workers as something worth relating to an acade-

44

mic researcher. What made it a telling story? The answer seems to lie in the core of the story, the text that underpinned all individual recitals. The core poetical interpretation around which Gill's outburst had crystallized is not hard to identify. 'Gill lashes out at HQ chief' would read the headline, followed by 'Gill gives a piece of her mind to visiting administrators, while the local managers sit in awe'. In all accounts of the incident, the core characters are the defiant Gill, the out-of-touch administrator(s), and the sycophantic local managers. The story attributes various positive qualities (outspokenness, courage, concern for quality) and emotions (fearlessness, defiance, pride) to Gill and correspondingly negative ones (obsequiousness, timidity, cowardice) to the local managers.

Stripped of its secondary features, Gill's outburst expresses an important reality about relations between staff and management at this organization. The managers were seen as weak and ineffectual, unwilling to make any decision that could have brought them into conflict with headquarters and generally unable to run the department. Contempt rather than hostility seemed to be the prevailing feeling of the workers towards their managers, summed up in what became a ritual refrain of my interviews: 'The bosses are not running this department, the girls are' (Gabriel 1988: 78). The incident could, therefore, be seen as typifying the kind of relations that the workers perceived as existing between themselves and their managers. The workers saw themselves as outspoken, courageous, and sincere, and they saw their managers as indecisive, weak, and deferential (attribution of unity, attribution of fixed qualities by juxtaposition of opposites). Gill's outburst epitomizes such an attitude. Yet, if Gill's outburst is typical, why did her fellow-workers choose to relate it to me in preference to other typical incidents? And, if it is typical, could Gill's act be attributed to any one of the other workers? Finally, if it is typical, why did the story generate such pleasure among those who recounted it?

It seems to me that we shall be closer to answering these questions if the incident is not regarded as typical of a relationship (between managers and workers) or even of the workers' perception of this relation. Instead, the story's value lies in its fulfilment of what was undoubtedly a potent wish for her fellow-workers. Far from being typical, Gill's outburst is untypical, in the sense that it was not common, it could not have been undertaken by any other worker, and it represents in deed what for the remaining workers remained a desire or a fantasy.[9]

---

[9] The tendency to view something untypical as typical is quite common in organizational storytelling. It involves an attribution of unity, whereby many different incidents are meant to amount to the same or carry the same symbolism. The issue of whether stories focus on typical or untypical events will be discussed in Chapter 4.

Catering workers come from some of the most vulnerable and stigmatized sections of the population. Two of Gill's colleagues commented eloquently on what they experienced as low status and demeaning work:

Because they see you in an overall, they think that you've got no brains at all.

Working in catering you feel sometimes that the job lacks dignity. Kitchen ladies and catering staff in general are treated as inferior people by everyone.

Certainly, gossiping and joking (especially at the expense of the managers) were two of the women's major survival mechanisms. But interviews with forty-nine women in this organization indicated that their outspokenness had its limits. Far from being fearless, they tolerated grievances and injuries to their pride with quiet resignation, something that the managers of the organization alluded to through the popular 1980s euphemism of 'new realism'.

As the individual who speaks her mind freely, without being intimidated by status or by the big brass, Gill is a true heroine for the many who suffer in silence. It is the fact that she speaks her mind rather than what she says exactly that makes her a heroine. Speaking one's mind, after all, is not something to be scoffed at in large impersonal organizations where people must often stay silent if they wish to keep their jobs. For the individual entangled in organizational politics, whose freedom and power are constrained internally and externally, Gill offers an object of admiration. What she does is what her colleagues would like to do, but for much of the time are not able to do.

Gill's outspokenness does not only articulate feelings and views that are shared by many; more importantly, her outspokenness is the proof that she has overcome fear, and this is indeed the mark of a hero. Gill's act, far from being an organizational trifle, may be seen as the basis of an epic story of heroic defiance. By identifying with Gill's deed, her colleagues can temporarily overcome fear, they are no longer silent. But by the same token, recounting Gill's exploit projects fear onto the managers—that is, onto those who are the objects of fear. Symbolically, the story enables the workers to swap sides. 'It is not we who are afraid of the bosses, but the bosses who are afraid of their bosses.' By this process of identification, a simple episode of organizational life becomes a narrative of emancipation from fear. First, it expresses in words what cannot ordinarily be expressed because of fear, and, secondly, it projects the fear onto the person who is feared. As a story, it represents a wish as already fulfilled, and hence it generates both pleasure and pride. Each narrator feels free to present a number of significant (in his or her opinion) details and with every retelling the story is dramatically re-created, in the epic manner, without departing from the core interpretation. The details, significant in themselves, add spice, credibility, and substance to the main message. Such elaborations and embellishments emphasize its heroic quality.

The tragic story: The cook's suicide

The story of Gill's outburst suggests that in organizational story-telling the wish to entertain the listener is frequently subordinated to the wish to fashion a story that fulfils deeper desires, such as a desire for pride and self-esteem. Unlike the story of Gill's outburst, the second story generated no pride. The story offered no pleasure in any evident sense. The telling of this story could not, in any sensible way, be said to be entertaining. On the contrary, one of the interviewees was in tears while telling me how one of her fellow-workers had been driven by management to hang himself. The worker, an elderly Italian cook, had been found dead in the kitchen of Saint Theresa, a historic hospital in London.

This organization had a history of bitter confrontations, as management tightened discipline and cracked down on what they regarded as restrictive practices. The continuous skirmishes between managers and workers fed a rich lore, making the catering department a veritable treasure trove of anecdotes, rumours, and stories. Many of the staff related lengthy stories about past events. For example, a cook had been enticed to break a strike and had been smuggled into the hospital huddled in the back of a taxi; he had later been rewarded with a car-parking place 'right next to the places reserved for consultants'. A young woman cook had fallen 'for the Spanish lover stereotype' represented by foreign cooks, to find that compromising pictures of her were freely changing hands in the department.

One of the most persistent stories, however, was the cook's suicide, reported without prompting by five interviewees, including the following account:

[The managers] are not really fair. They show too much favouritism. That's why they get so much sickness. Their own people they treat like a syndicate, for the rest they don't care. Their bad manners and the war of nerves they set up make life very hard and at times unbearable. A few years ago, an Italian cook . . . he killed himself in the kitchen, he couldn't take any more.

The way the incident is referred to in one brief sentence, as if to crown a heartfelt litany of grievances, is characteristic. All accounts of the incident were equally laconic. In none of them was the name of the cook mentioned. Unlike the myth of Gill's outburst, this one seemed to speak for itself without need of ornamentation.

In contrast to the heroic quality of Gill's outburst, the cook's suicide possesses a tragic character; while Gill's story is the story of a great deed, the cook's story is a story of great suffering. Deaths (including suicides) can, like heroic deeds, be favourite topics of epic myths. The cook's suicide, however, possesses none of the qualities of noble sacrifice with which epic deaths are endowed; nor does it have the sacrificial qualities of some organizational myths, in which success is seen as the product of the hardships and sacrifices endured by the organization's early pioneers. In none of the accounts did his suicide serve a redemptive purpose, nor was the cook an object of pride or admiration. Instead, his suffering generated the classic mixture of pity and fear, noted by Aristotle: 'Pity is reserved for undeserved misfortune and fear for the misfortune of people just like ourselves' (*Poetics* 1453*a*).

If the first myth centres on agency (Gill did *X*), the second centres on victimhood (*Y* happened to the cook). Like heroes, victims carry a potent cultural symbolism. Victims of natural and man-made disasters, never far from the news broadcasts' opening headlines or the front pages of the press, epitomize one aspect of the experience of the modern individual who finds him or herself faced with forces over which he or she has no control—government, powerful bureaucracy, mystifying technology, escalating crime, and arbitrary nature (Lasch 1984: 59). For the catering staff at this establishment, victimization was at the core of their experience. Many described themselves as 'trapped' in their jobs, trapped by their age and lack of qualifications, trapped by their inability to find alternative employment and their poor command of the language. Such a claustrophobic environment bred bitterness and an anxiety bordering on the paranoid. Many workers reported deep insecurity, not knowing who would be next to incur the arbitrary wrath of those in authority. Management arbitrariness was perceived as a force of nature, threatening their very existence. One of the dead cook's workmates described his experience in these terms:

We just hang on and hang on. What else is there to do? I will end my days as a worker here, either for retirement or for the dole. Every day I come here and I feel depressed: after fifteen years of working here and I still don't know if there will be a job for me next week or not . . . You work like a machine here. You do what they tell you. You work for eight hours, you go home, and that's that. Respect for each other is the most important thing and is lacking here. People are demoralized, especially the older people. Many times I feel depressed, I do my eight hours work here, go home, and try to forget about it.

It is hardly surprising that the cook's suicide was a seminal event for his colleagues and became part of Saint Theresa's unwritten history.

I asked one of the managers about the event. He casually brushed it aside and, in doing so, offered an alternative interpretation of the incident. The cook had been depressed, he explained, he had had serious problems at home, besides, the kitchen at the time had been divided up into cliques and some of the others had been picking on him.

I went back with this interpretation of the incident to the five workers who had mentioned it—three of them passionately denied that there was any truth in this version, while two granted that the atmosphere in the kitchen at the time had been bitter, but insisted that responsibility for the suicide lay with management (attribution of blame). This seemed extremely important, as if the story's central text was 'management drive cook to suicide'; I felt that questioning this construction of events made me highly unpopular with the interviewees. The cook's suicide, then, gave rise to competing interpretations, or competing accounts. By accepting an interpretation, one inevitably had to take sides. The contestation of the story became itself a political act.

In both versions, the cook's suicide can be seen as one of those stories that Boje, Fedor, and Rowland (1982: 19) classify as 'help[ing] explain and create cause and effect relationships under conditions of incomplete knowledge'. For the manager, the cook's suicide was due to personal and other factors beyond his power—a sad incident, to be sure, but of no outstanding moral significance. For the workers, on the other hand, the cook's unbearable suffering and its tragic conclusion are ineluctably linked to the callousness of the managers (attribution of causal connection). Any notion that others may have a share of the guilt is strictly taboo. The attribution of guilt to a malevolent agent or to a suitable scapegoat is a central theme of tragic stories—it is what turns purposeless human suffering and pain into tragedy. This is what turned the cook's suicide into a symbolic watershed for the workers, while remaining merely a 'sad incident' for management.

Like the previous story, the cook's suicide suggests that many organizational stories cannot be seen as 'entertaining' after the folkloric model. And, like the story of Gill's outburst, it possesses a strong wish-fulfilling quality, by crowning an elaborate demonology of suffering and injustice. The suicide is no longer a suicide; symbolically it stands for murder. The story becomes the final and conclusive evidence of management malevolence: 'They stop at nothing, not even murder. What more proof is needed?' (attribution of motive). In both stories the narrators identified with their subject. The workers identified with Gill, who said and did what they would like to have done. They identified with the cook, who suffered just like they suffered. In this way, while the suicide story may not have been 'entertaining', it offered pleasure in the form of the moral satisfaction of those who have suffered injustice and whose suffering is finally displayed for all to see. The very anonymity of the cook (another nameless victim, like those that haunt the history of the twentieth century) strengthened his emblematic victimhood. Thus, in its own way, the story represented the fulfilment of the wish to have the injustice brought to light.

Both stories reconstruct events according to a primal opposition between the forces of decency, courage, and integrity and the forces of duplicity, malice, and oppression (attribution of unity); this is a characteristic of many fairy tales (Bettelheim 1976: 8), whose regressive character offers an occasion for catharsis and consolation for the discontents of life. Tired with the endless complexities of the real world, where the face of the oppressor is rarely seen, the individual seeks solace in the Manichean clarity of the story, where good is good and evil is evil. It is also a feature of most story-work. By regressing to the reassuring simplicities of such stories, the individual defends him or herself against anxiety 'when [his or her] self-esteem is seriously threatened' (Kets de Vries and Miller 1984: 138). The consolation offered by the story is substantially strengthened when the story is shared with others. This not only further accentuates the Manichean qualities of the story, but it guards it against most objective evidence. The story may not be 'entertaining' in an obvious way, but it represents a collective wish-fulfilment, and as such it becomes a group's prized possession, a genuine heritage. Anyone who challenges the verity of the story (as I tried to do by questioning the reasons for the cook' suicide) is frequently cast with the forces of darkness, thus reinforcing the hold of the story over the group.

Neither Gill's outburst nor the cook's suicide can be seen as myths, similar to humanity's great epic or tragic myths. They do, however, entail the wish-fulfilling and consoling functions of myths. Individuals seem quite unwilling to give them up, even in the face of strong 'factual' opposition (Zaleznik 1989) In the first place, as Bowles (1989: 412) has argued, there is a level on which a story, unlike an ideology, cannot be negated. Questioning a story is the task of a pedant and a spoilsport. Alternatively, combating a story (like rejecting a rumour) may be dismissed as bad faith, in which case it simply adds fuel to it. As wish-fulfilment, the story satisfies powerful psychological needs. In such situations, as was recognized long ago, reality offers a modest corrective. 'Men are nearly always willing to believe what they wish' (*Julius Caesar*, III. xviii). As Schwartz (1985: 35) has argued:

from the standpoint of psychological dynamics, the important thing to recognize is that [stories and myths] are self-deceptions: vital self-deceptions, to be sure, since self-confident action and coherent life could not take place without them, but self-deceptions nonetheless . . . Indeed, it is this very process of psychological avoidance [of reality] that constitutes the vitality of the myth.

To sum up. Both stories explored so far can be seen as expressing deep psychological truths about the members of the two organizations and fulfilling important needs for the members. The stories become detached from reality, although the belief that the events they described did happen is an important part of both narratives. By turning facts into stories and stories into facts, the stories offer an opportunity for emotional release in tune with the symbolic universe that they construct.

The comic story: Trial by fire

The story to which I now turn shares some of the features of the previous two but also reveals some crucial differences. I heard it during a period of military service, and it circulated widely among navy conscripts, along with many similar stories that flourish in such environments.

Sentry duty is one of the most tedious aspects of a conscript's life, whether aboard a ship or on land. Alone for four long hours in a sentry box, he rarely meets anyone and practically never an enemy. The only regular visitor is the sentry officer, who will come to check that the sentry has not nodded off, lit a cigarette, or surreptitiously smuggled a transistor radio into the sentry box. Above all, he will come to check that he has not abandoned his post, that he has not moved more than a dozen steps from his box. This is the cardinal rule of sentry duty—under no circumstance is one to leave one's post. Should anything untoward happen, one is to contact the sentry officer on the telephone or, failing that, to fire one's rifle.

During the briefing of new recruits by the officer responsible for sentries in a navy training camp, the following exchange took place.

OFFICER. *Do you understand? You are never to leave your post, under any circumstance.*
MEN *[nodding that they understand].*
OFFICER. *So, what would you do if you saw a fire?*
BRIGHT RECRUIT. *I'll phone the sentry officer on duty.*
OFFICER. *Good. And if there is no answer from the sentry officer?*
BRIGHT RECRUIT. *I'll phone the commander.*
OFFICER. *And if all the lines are dead?*

BRIGHT RECRUIT. *I'll fire my rifle.*

OFFICER. *And if the fire is spreading rapidly in the direction of the munitions depot?*

BRIGHT RECRUIT. *I'll run and try to put it out.*

OFFICER *[besides himself with rage]. Idiot, if you are lucky you'll end up court-martialled, and in prison for six months, if you are unlucky, you'll get a dagger in your back. This is what the enemy wants you to do—he distracts you with a diversion, you quit your post, he polishes you off. Now do you understand? You are never to leave your post, you should sooner see the whole camp go up in flames than quit your post. So, what do you do if you see something suspect and the phone lines are dead?*

RECRUITS *[convinced]. We fire our rifles.*

The broader message of this exchange seems straightforward enough—do not ask questions, do not take any initiative, just follow the rules. The officer's rhetoric, however, goes beyond direct exhortation. 'There are reasons for the rules being what they are', he seems to be saying, 'reasons, that you needn't bother your little heads with understanding, but that we, who know about matters of war and peace, life and death, have long understood and incorporated in the rules'.

Like all rhetoric, the rhetoric of the officer, rehearsed on generations of unsuspecting 'idiots', convinces through brutality and simple, if deceitful logic. It would take a recruit of surpassing sophistry and masochism to point out to the officer that (*a*) different rules may usefully apply in peacetime from wartime, (*b*) the cost of a catastrophic fire may justify the risk of temporarily quitting one's post, (*c*) a guard may be equally well overcome while in his post as away from his post, or that (*d*) the vast majority of sentries are wasting their time in watches of utter pointlessness.

These and numerous other objections to the officer's strictures are effectively obliterated by his virtuosic performance, which gives the new recruits a fine introduction to life in total institutions. Subsequently, I related this exchange to some of the older recruits. This immediately elicited a story, according to which a sentry officer had deliberately started a fire to test the sentries. He had also made sure to disconnect their telephone lines, and, when the sentries went to put out the fire, they were arrested and court-martialled for quitting their posts.

It is apparent that the story as told by the recruits directly reflects the performance of the sentry officer: what was a hypothetical situation in the officer's performance became a 'fact' in the recruits' story. At first, this may not seem especially significant. It could, for instance, be said that the recruits had 'livened the story up', dramatized it, by presenting as a fact what was at best a threat. Having witnessed the officer's routine themselves and internalized its message, they ornamented it by having the officer actually start a fire to test them. Alternatively, though perhaps less likely, it is possible that the officer used the routine described above to save himself the trouble of actually testing the recruits by starting a real fire.

This story shares the traumatic quality of the cook's suicide; but there is nothing tragic about it. In none of the recitals that I heard did it generate pity for the victims; nor was there ever any anger at the callousness of the officer. The strong emotion displayed in the telling of the story of the cook's suicide was absent. Instead, the story was related in a *half-jocular half-menacing* manner, in which many military stories are recounted. In most of these stories the good soldier is the victim of some more or less funny, more or less unpleasant prank staged by his officers or seniors. Some officers specialized in inflicting colourful punishments in arbitrary or whimsical ways on new recruits, such as shaving a statue in the barracks forecourt or (as we shall see in the next chapter) refusing them leave after inspecting their underwear and finding that it did not meet the regulations. Such pranks range from innocent teasing to vicious bullying and they feed a continuous lore of half-amusing half-menacing stories.

Recounting such stories rarely evokes horror (or the horror is rarely admitted) but generates anxiety lest one should share the fate of the victims. This is the reason I have chosen this genre of story rather than a more direct comic story—for example, a joke—for the story resists the familiar interpretation of being a safety valve for anxiety. On the contrary, alarmist stories like the one described above maintain a continuous and tangible level of anxiety, which permeates the culture of such organizations. It seems that this anxiety affects both the teller of the story and, to a much greater extent, the listener.

But why should such anxiety-creating stories remain popular with the recruits? Would it not be easier collectively to repress them, or at least to deny them and seek to neutralize them? Following the discussion of the first two stories, it would be tempting to argue that all organizational stories—epic, tragic, and comic—function as collective fantasies that exorcise anxieties and allay fears. This would accord with the views of those humour theorists who have argued that jokes act as safety valves (Benton 1988; Coser 1959; Fine 1983; Pollio 1980, 1983), as well as those theorists who have highlighted various mechanisms within organizations for coping with anxiety (Jaques 1955; Menzies 1960). My interest in 'Trial by Fire' and similar stories is that they appear to do quite the opposite—as if the hardships of military life were not enough, the stories generate additional degrees of discomfort. In this sense, this story is still further away from a simple 'entertainment' function than the suicide.

The psychic function of this story becomes a lot clearer if we view anxiety not as a dysfunctional by-product of mental processes, but, following the tradition established by McDougall (1908/1932), as a warning signal in situations of real danger that alerts, protects, and reduces the severity of potential trauma. There are few contexts calling for anxiety to fulfil such functions with the same urgency as the navy camp. Earlier, we saw how the arbitrariness of management rule was perceived as a force of nature, feeding the imagery of victimhood. If anything, the arbitrariness of life's fortunes is even greater in a navy camp, where misfortune and favour are dished out on an apparently random basis and where rules are applied in the most whimsical manner. It would not be too fanciful to liken the new conscripts' experience at the camp with that of crossing a minefield, with mines, some known, some suspected, and some totally unexpected, lurking at every step (Born 1979: 91).

Going through such a minefield, one may be fortunate to escape without injury numerous times—one's vigilance may loosen. Anxiety, produced and reproduced through alarmist gossip and horror stories (attribution of causal connections), ensures that the recruits are constantly prepared for the worst; and, when the worst happens, the shock is somewhat diluted, the magnitude of the injury reduced. As one becomes more familiar with such stories, through repeated recitals, the ability of each story to generate anxiety becomes reduced. The recruit himself becomes increasingly familiar with army life and comes to accept its misfortunes without rebelling. His need for anxiety-sustaining stories may be lessened. His identification with the victims of the story is weakened; he sees himself as a seasoned warrior rather than a wide-eyed new recruit. He may continue to recount the story, in an increasingly detached manner, getting more and more satisfaction in observing its effect on new recruits.

In my experience of listening to such stories, there were occasions when the teller became so detached from the fate of the stories' victims that he ended up identifying with the officers inflicting the ordeals on the recruits. As the pleasure of the teller in unsettling the listener attained an almost malicious level, the stories were ornamented for greater effect. The verbal embellishments seemed to match the officer's virtuosity in humiliating and bullying. As a prankster, the officer became an object of admiration and even identification for those who may well have been the victims of such pranks but managed to survive them. Some of the officers appeared as master pranksters (attribution of fixed qualities), surrounded by tissues of lore. We can now understand why so many of the stories of this type have a comic, humorous, or creative quality about them. An officer who is merely a bully is less likely to become an object of admiration and identification than one whose sadism is expressed in imaginative, mischievous ways, like the example of this story.

'Trial by Fire' reveals a greater ambiguity than either of the two earlier stories. If the teller of the story of Gill's outburst identifies with the hero and the teller of the story of the cook's suicide identifies with the victim, the teller of the military story stands precariously between two identifications, identification with the victim and identification with the aggressor (A. Freud 1936; Kets de Vries and Miller 1984). The officer is at once an object of fear and a person of extraordinary qualities, whose deeds defeat boredom and break the oppressive military routine. 'Trial by Fire' is one of those stories whose symbolism is 'polysemic' (Rosen 1985b), evoking different, at times conflicting, meanings. Different groups found it telling for different reasons (Davies 1984: 155). To the new recruit, the story's predominant meaning may be 'Army life is dangerous, harsh and unfair: you should be prepared for the worst'. The old recruit, approaching release, may already be surrounding the story in a shroud of nostalgia: 'Army life was never boring—where else could you meet such characters?' The philosophical recruit may read it as a sad reflection of the irrationality of the military, whereas the wit may turn it into an occasion for a blistering satire. It is possible that the same story was circulating in the officers' mess in an epic form, the officers competing against each other as to who would inflict the most colourful humiliations on the new recruits. Thus, the same story may feed alternative poetic interpretations, some of which may be competing and some not.

To sum up then, 'Trial by Fire' can be seen, in the first place, as a warning story, an attempt to generate anxiety among newer recruits that will enable them to cope psychologically with the ordeals in store for them. Gradually, this anxiety may be mastered through a process whereby the victim identifies with the aggressor, turning the perpetrator of sadistic deeds into an object of admiration and even imitation. This process restores the wish-fulfilling quality to the story, since it enables the victim to swap camps, albeit in fantasy; the story provides a symbolic mechanism for turning passivity into activity, helplessness into control. It is no longer the conscript who is afraid of the officer, it is he who frightens his audience.

Interpretation is part of the story-work carried out by the storyteller, who reads meaning into events, infusing them with symbolic significance, which resonates with his or her audience. These interpretations make use of eight poetic tropes and can be enhanced and supported by rhetorical, symbolic, and narrative devices; they are referred to as poetic interpretations—poetry being the art of moulding something meaningful out of relatively inert material. Interpretation is also part of researchers' work, as they seek to unravel each story's deeper meanings. This type of interpretation, referred to as analytic interpretation, seeks to explain how and why poetic interpretation works—why people believe a story to be true, why they espouse it with fervour, why they may be unconcerned about factual accuracy.

Not all stories in organizations can be said to entertain in a direct sense. However, the stories examined in this chapter were seen as serving functions broadly similar to those they serve in mythologies and folklore. In other words, they support a universe of meanings and values that integrates individuals into their groups, helps them make sense of everyday experiences, and allows them to endure or make light of the hardships and injustices of life. All the stories interpreted in this chapter were shown to have pronounced elements of wish-fulfilment. The fire-extinguisher accident was shown to generate three very different stories, each of which expressed the personal fantasies of their narrators. The subsequent three stories seemed to express emotional experiences shared by numerous organizational participants, having become *crystallized in the folklore* of their organizations. The first was a story of heroic defiance, in which individuals can identify with a hero, whose acts echo their desires. Pride and pleasure are the dominant emotions it aroused. The second was a story of great suffering, through which individuals can identify with the victim of oppression, expiate their guilt, and attribute responsibility to an evil agency. It generated the classic tragic mixture of pity and fear. It was argued that both stories offered, in their different ways, solace for the hardships of organizational life, and that they displayed two important qualities—a regression into a Manichean universe of pure good and pure evil, and an opportunity for cathartic discharge.

The third story shared the traumatic quality of the second, but displayed a pronounced comic quality. Instead of an overtly cathartic effect, this story generated mirth mixed with anxiety, especially among those listening. It was argued that anxiety-generating stories act as protective devices in preparing the individual for random misfortune and offer a vehicle whereby the victim identifies with the aggressor. In this way, this story can also be seen as fulfilling a deep desire, which accords with the rigid authoritarian ethos of the organization that spawned it.

All three stories express collective fantasies, with different degrees of distortion. All three, in their different ways, imparted meaning and value on organizational life. Stories, along with gossip and jokes, represent attempts to humanize the impersonal spaces of bureaucratic organizations, to mark them as human territory, as does the vase of flowers or the family picture on the executive desk. When much of the information traded in organizations is symbolically and emotionally impoverished, as impersonal paperwork and, increasingly, data on computer monitors (Weick 1985), stories, jokes, and gossip reintroduce a symbolically charged narrative to everyday life in organizations. Many organizations are not generally pleasant places in which to live or work. They place severe restrictions on the individual's rights and freedoms and allow little room for those aspects of the human soul that are not directly relevant to the organizational objectives. Emotions, spontaneity, and play are largely disenfranchised, as is, in any meaningful sense, the pursuit of pleasure and happiness (Biggart 1988). If vast areas of the human soul are systematically excluded from organization, is it not possible to argue that stories represent attempts to gain readmission in surreptitious ways and diverse guises?

If stories are attempts to humanize organizations, the stories discussed in this chapter reveal an equally significant function: they all represent symbolic means of coping with pain. In the last resort, these stories represent efforts to deal with life's harshness, unpredictability, and arbitrariness and to make bearable something that is even harder to endure than the unequal distribution of wealth and power, the unequal distribution of suffering. The first two may invite social and political solutions, but not the last. Here, only symbols can offer consolations.

3

Poetic Modes: Characters, Plots, and Emotions

Classifications and taxonomies are not glamorous pursuits. Only pedants and obsessives are meant to enjoy them. Yet, as Gould (1996: 39) has argued, classifications 'are not passive ordering devices in a world objectively divided into obvious categories'. Dividing the members of the human species into females and males is no more natural than dividing them by class, weight, or zodiac sign. Classification involves identifications of similarities and differences; it requires decisions as to what is meaningful and important and what is insignificant, decisions that result from theories on the very subject to be classified. Classification and theory stand in mutual definition, continuously redefining each other. As one of them evolves, it necessitates adjustments in the other. We do not, therefore, need to apologize for devoting this chapter to developing the classification of stories that we started in the previous chapter through the examples of an epic, a tragic, and a comic story. The classification of narratives is a topic that, since Aristotle, has been examined by many, including philologists, folklorists, mythologists, as well as organizational theorists. We shall propose a typology of organizational stories that is helpful for the analysis of such stories, accepting that folklorists or literary critics may opt for different typologies. Like all typologies, it is imperfect; its object is to advance theory in our area of interest, storytelling in organizations. Besides advancing theory, the classification of organizational stories has some practical implications. Once the major types have been identified, comparisons can be made across organizations, examining the prevalence of particular types and its significance. Comparisons can also be made between variants of the same story, establishing important similarities and differences in a systematic way.

The classification that follows is the product of an iterative process, whereby 404 narratives were gradually classified into ever more precise categories. Early on in the analysis it became clear that some of the narratives were either proto-stories—that is, they contained the seed of a story without actually achieving the poetic imagination and narrative complexity that would make them proper stories—or reports—that is, descriptive accounts of events, emphasizing factual accuracy rather than narrative effect. Subsequently, stories started to find their places in a fairly narrow range of types, primarily through their emotional tone. Soon it was clear that some stories generated pride in the narrator and were meant to generate admiration in the listener; these were classified as epic stories. They usually dealt with achievements, contests, and trials and almost always had a happy end. Comic stories were instantly identifiable by generating laughter, amusement, and levity. Their themes were mishaps, breakdowns of communication, or cock-ups and were frequently aimed at a target or butt. Tragic stories, on the other hand, generated pity and sorrow—the audience was invited to treat them with respect and compassion. Their themes were frequently traumas and insults that left lasting scars on their victims. Eventually, a fourth type was identified, the romantic story, which has a lighter sentimental quality and deals with love, gratitude, appreciation, and affection. Combinations of the different types led to a number of hybrids, like the tragi-comic or the epic–tragic.

In addition to its distinct emotional tone, each story type employs a characteristic set of poetic tropes through which meaning is infused into events, some types treating the protagonist as active agent, others as passive victim, some treating the protagonist's predicament as deserved and some as fortuitous. The cast of each type of story and the relations between them are distinct; although the same character—for example, a villain, may feature in both epic and tragic stories, his or her relation to the protagonist is different in each case. While most types of story address human misfortune trying to make sense of it, they do so in highly differentiated ways. Finally, each type of story builds a rather different type of relationship between narrator and audience. The narrator of an epic story invites the audience to marvel at the hero's achievements, the narrator of the comic story invites the audience to laugh, the narrator of the tragic story invites the audience to feel compassion and awe at the protagonist's sufferings, and the narrator of the romantic story invites the audience to cherish a precious moment and partake of a love fantasy. Thus each story type represents a distinct *poetic mode* or way of infusing meaning into events.

THE COMIC STORY: THE PROTAGONIST AS DESERVING VICTIM OR FOOL

Misfortune is a favourite theme of many stories. Misfortune can be at the centre equally of tragic or comic stories. Banana skins and pies in the face have long been part of the stock in trade of comics. Similar comic stories abound in organizations. Computer experts swap stories celebrating the foibles of naïve users and doctors relish in swapping stories about curious items swallowed by their patients or objects that they recover from their patients' intimate cavities. Comic stories unleash mirth and amusement, often laughter. In many cases mirth can be mixed with other emotions, including bitterness, sadness, anger, hate, nostalgia, envy, and love. However, a story can hardly be comic unless it generates some amusement and merriment.

What are the basic narrative elements of comic stories? Using ideas from Stein and Policastro, Robinson and Hawke (1986) propose that a prototypical story contains five features:

1. a protagonist;
2. a predicament;
3. attempts to resolve the predicament;
4. the outcome of these attempts;
5. the reactions of the protagonist.

In their simplest form, comic stories entail a protagonist who is a victim and a predicament that is a misfortune. The protagonist can be an individual, a group, or even an organization. Elements 3, 4, and 5 may be absent, though, if present, they usually reinforce the victim's misfortune and the audience's amusement. The notion that the misfortunes and infirmities of others can be a source of amusement for the rest dates back to Plato and Aristotle, but more especially to Hobbes, who saw such calamities as conferring a superiority upon the storyteller and the audience. Hobbes argued that our own imperfections are forgotten as we relish in the misfortunes of others (Hobbes 1651/1962). Psychologists and sociologists have developed this view of malice residing in funny stories, arguing that misfortune is funnier when it befalls enemies rather than friends (Davies 1984, 1988; Powell 1988; Zillmann 1983; Zillmann and Cantor 1976).[1]

In his classic study of laughter, Henri Bergson (1980) saw humour as an essential human quality, one that distinguishes us from other animals, and viewed laughter as a release achieved by the

---

[1] For a different view, see Zijderveld (1983).

chastisement of 'the mechanical encrusted in the human'. We laugh at people behaving like machines (e.g. making compulsive/mechanical movements), at the mercy of machines (e.g. Charlie Chaplin being fed by the machine in *Modern Times*), or suffering as a result of their naïve assumption that the human spirit can be contained and controlled, for example, by bureaucratic or technological automatism. Anyone who enters into a pact with such automatisms is begging for a well-deserved comeuppance—and every such comeuppance is likely to be celebrated, embellished, and remembered. So Bergson accurately points out that the comic quality results from the dissociation of an action from its consequences—slipping on a banana skin instantly converts an agent into an inert physical body, at the mercy of the laws of mechanics. But Bergson also realizes that feelings of sympathy or kindness for the victim would undermine the comic quality of a story. 'Laughter is, above all, a corrective. Being intended to humiliate, it must make a painful impression on the person against whom it is directed. By laughter, society avenges itself for the liberties taken with it. It would fail in its object if it bore the stamp of sympathy or kindness' (Bergson 1980: 187).

The victim's predicament must, therefore, be seen as 'deserved' and the victim must be seen as a 'deserving fool' bringing misfortune to him or herself. In this sense, he or she is both agent, albeit unwitting, and victim. This is achieved by poetically constructing the misfortune as 'punishment'. The point is illustrated by a myriad organizational stories. One of my colleagues related to me the story of a businessman delivering a well-rehearsed lecture to an audience of academics. The lecture made heavy use of audio-visual aids and built a gradual crescendo to a final climax presented in the form of a slide; predictably, the projector jammed at the crucial moment, leaving the lecturer in acute embarrassment amidst the general mirth and merriment. A good story, undoubtedly, given the ambivalent relations between academia and business. The story suggests that the audience may have felt both envious and dismissive of the businessman's heavy use of sophisticated gadgetry. They relish his misfortune because, as professional lecturers, they have long known how to cope with unforeseen mishaps. At a deeper level they may be resenting the fact of being 'lectured' by a businessman. The comic story's elementary plot of deserved misfortune and deserving victim then may also involve an unacknowledged character represented by storyteller and audience who are protected from the misfortune by their savvy, skill, or general superiority.

Several poetical tropes are at work in generating such comic stories. In the first place, as noted by Bergson above, the conversion of the victim's misfortune into a deserved punishment for failure of character or past transgression is achieved through an attribution of providential significance to the event—a superior agency is at work, ensuring that justice is done. In ensuring that the victim is constructed as deserving the misfortune, fixed qualities may be also attributed to him or her. He or she is thus presented as pompous, vain, foolish, ill-tempered, arrogant, fat, miserly, greedy, cruel, immature, overconfident, rich, and so forth, qualities that trigger off the hubris inviting retribution. In many instances, these qualities combine with attribution of unity, as in the case above, where the lecturer is presented as a typical businessman. Stereotypes, products of this combined attribution, are frequent poetic devices of comic stories.

Perhaps the most delicate attribution in comic stories concerns agency: in order for the targets of misfortune to be cast as 'deserving', they must appear to be active even if unwitting agents in their own downfall. However, while they suffer misfortune, agency must be denied to them, as noted by Bergson, the misfortune reducing them to something physical and material at the mercy of mechanical laws beyond their control. To the extent that they may seek to extricate themselves from the misfortune they only manage to make themselves more ridiculous still—generating more unanticipated consequences through their actions. Thus, people who deliberately punish themselves by some means like self-mutilation are hardly amusing, if they are doing so, as conscious agents, in full knowledge of their actions. Such people may be constructed as martyrs, victims, or madmen. On the other hand, people doing exactly the same thing because they regard it as fashionable or 'cool' may instantly draw ridicule upon themselves, just like people who follow fashions out of keeping with their age, class or personality.

Cock-up stories: The protagonist as hero/fixer

If personal misfortunes are frequently turned into organizational stories or jokes, so too are organizational misfortunes. Military, business, and operatic disasters invariably find captive audiences. Within organizations, mechanical breakdowns and their close relatives, systems failures, are favourite topics. Accidents, breakdowns and their attendant misfortunes are the source of rich narrative material. Just as the arrival of a pompous, expensively dressed individual in slapstick comedy signals the imminent flight of a pie or a fatal encounter with a banana skin, the installation of fancy hardware in an organization, poetically at least, may cry out for a cock-up, a breakdown, or a failure. Cock-ups, breakdowns, and systems failures are chinks in the armour of the controlling organization, which when turned into stories promote an image of the organization as an absurd farce.

The poetical tropes at work in such cases are not unlike those aimed at individuals. The organization must be cast in the role of an arrogant, overconfident, and foolish entity that invites retribution, the more so the more advanced its reliance on sophisticated systems, technology, wealth, and power. However, such stories frequently add a poetic twist, whereby the cock-up is repaired through ingenuity, good luck, or further unexpected turns of event. The following is a story reported by the librarian of a large manufacturing firm; the library had been extensively computerized in the previous few years at great cost, rendering many traditional librarianship skills obsolete.

One of the directors asked for an article about the company in The Times. *No problem, I mean, it's the sort of thing we could get to his desk in five minutes. Fair enough. Then, what happens? We can't find it; the computer knows nothing about it. On this particular occasion, we [library staff] did actually remember the piece, we all remembered it, which is even more frustrating. In the end I rang* The Times *newspaper and said 'We know that it exists but the computer can't find it, explain!' and then they came back. That particular article had been written by a freelance writer and he had the copyright and wouldn't sanction it being put on the electronic database.*

This is an almost archetypal story in which the perceived failure of sophisticated machinery necessitates a fallback on traditional skills or common sense. Such stories add a new character to the basic elements of deserved misfortune plus deserving victim or fool—the hero/fixer who prevails over adversity through his or her individual qualities. Such stories, which are much loved by Hollywood, pitch the individual against the blind forces of bureaucracy and technology and can be found in many organizations. For instance, a student returning from a placement in a prestigious accounting firm that had invested in the last word in information technology reported how the staff had lost faith in the bug-ridden system and relied for the manual retrieval of files on 'a little fellow buried in the basement stacked to the ceiling with files'; he alone in the organization knew where every document was kept. Such stories (and the mere mention of mechanical breakdown is often enough to elicit them) seem to celebrate the failure of expensive, hyper-controlling, systems, and the re-emergence of human shrewdness, art, savvy, or plain common sense, fully substantiating Bergson's view. In this way, such stories reverse the classic scenario of the *deus ex machina*. Instead of the god from the machine coming to solve the problems of the erring humans, an ordinary person with wits comes to the rescue of expensive, arrogant, and disagreeable systems. The story-work generating this story deploys attribution of credit to the hero for fixing the problem. Thus, while the simple comic story presents the predicament as punishment, the cock-up story may shift the emphasis to the predicament as test or trial for the hero. In this way, it introduces epic or mock-epic qualities to the narrative.

HUMOROUS STORIES: THE PROTAGONIST AS SURVIVOR, HUMORIST, IRONIST, OR WIZARD

Organizational failures do not feature only as situations inviting fixing by a hero. Instead, in numerous stories, they are constructed as predicaments to be survived by the victims. 'You don't have to be mad to work here but it helps' is a favourite if hackneyed piece of xerox lore in many organizations. In contrast to the mock-epic quality of the 'little-man-in-the-basement' story, some of the stories spawned by organizational life display the characteristic defiance of gallows humour. Here, the legitimacy or rationality of the system is *not* undermined by its malfunction or breakdown, but its supposed irrationality is to be found deeper. In a baked-bean processing plant, women liked to recount the story of how management had, with the help of some psychologists, trained pigeons to do the extraordinarily tedious job of identifying the defective beans and picking them out of a continuously moving conveyor. However, the RSPCA was alerted to this fact and ruled that it amounted to cruelty to the animals, whereupon the job was assigned once again to the women. The bitter-sweet irony of this story refuses to seek solace in the system's mechanical failures, but, instead, invites any *bona fide* listener to witness and attest to the system's moral failure.

The teller of such stories rejects self-pity, escapism, or scapegoating, symbolically making light of the hardships, and turning victimhood into survival against the odds, if not outright victory. Freud rightly distinguished this type of humour from the wit of the straight comic stories. Humour, he argues, 'refuses to be hurt by the arrows of reality or to be compelled to suffer . . . Humour is not resigned; it is rebellious. It signifies the triumph not only of the ego, but also of the pleasure principle, which is strong enough to assert itself here in the face of adverse circumstances' (S. Freud 1927: 429). The self-mocking aspect of this type of story gives it a higher and finer quality. Stories of this genre reveal a proud and defiant protagonist, who, while stopping short of rebellion or confrontation, refuses to capitulate to the big mechanical forces of bureaucracy and technology. The audience of such stories experiences sympathy and pity for the character's predicament but also a degree of admiration for his or her proud and defiant attitude. This attitude is essential in order to stop the story lapsing into the tragic type.

Freud observed astutely that the essence of this type of humour lies in the replacement of emotions, such as anger, bitterness, or despair by a jest, a quality that characterizes the humorist: 'There is no doubt that the essence of humour is that one spares oneself the affects to which the situation would naturally give rise and dismisses the possibility of such expressions of emotion with a jest' (S. Freud 1927: 428). The characters of such stories are able to adopt a playful, ironic, witty, or graceful attitude in the face of adversity. These are the essential qualities attributed to them, along with an ability to detach themselves from the emotions called for by the situation. Not dissimilar story-work is at play with self-disparaging humour, famously attributed to Jewish jokes (Davies 1984; Zijderveld 1983), where subjects' willingness to mock themselves or their social grouping serves as an occasion for celebration of individual or collective survival against the odds.

There are instances when the humorist ceases to be cast as a survivor and becomes a hero in his or her own right. The funnier the jest and the greater the adversity, the greater our admiration becomes for the humorist. Some humorists are true virtuosos, wizards capable of producing a witticism in virtually any situation, however trying or embarrassing. Our admiration for the masters of the pun and the one-liner is akin to that for the trapeze artist or the juggler who takes outrageous risks and is able to pull them off. The humorist in the following story risks offending people's sensitivities but the witticism saves the day:

We were talking about a new logo for the hospital. We had been waiting some months for a logo to be drawn and somebody submitted this yesterday. It was just a bird flying off; it was the same bird, but they had drawn it from several angles. But the hospital weren't very keen and asked us whether we could come up with something better. Sue, a nurse, said she had been messing about on the computer and her husband had come up with a logo; he had drawn these wreaths and he had put at the bottom 'patients are dying to meet us'. That is awful but I really laughed!

Self-pity and scapegoating *are* features of a related type of story, which Coser (1959) termed the jocular gripe; the classic one is the hospital patients' complaint that the nurse woke them up to give them their sleeping pill. While highlighting the absurdity of the system and subverting the authority of those in power, such stories highlight victimhood rather than survival or agency, seeking to elicit sympathy. In many similar stories that I collected, the comic quality was virtually non-existent, the gripe quite unadulterated by humour.

Practical jokes: The protagonist as prankster or joker

A different type of virtuosity is at play in practical jokes, already familiar to us from our discussion of the navy camp story in Chapter 2. If the humorist's virtuosity lies in his or her use of words, pranksters are masters at stagecraft, planning and executing mischievous pranks at the expense of a target, a butt, or a dupe, often with the assistance of accomplices and in the presence of an audience (Tallman 1974). In carrying out a prank, the target must be constructed as deserving, either because of some fixed quality (pompous, arrogant, naïve, etc.) or because a situation calls for it (April Fool's Day, stag or hen party, wedding party, etc.). The social functions of practical jokes are not of interest to us here, what concerns us is their transformation into story material. When recounted as stories, pranks can be fashioned in different ways. For example, they can be presented as part of a joking relationship, reinforcing mutual trust. Alternatively, they may be presented as comic stories where well-deserved ridicule is heaped on a victim, in such cases, the misfortune befalling the target is not accidental or self-inflicted but carefully planned and orchestrated by a prankster. On occasion, the prank becomes a trial from which the subject emerges victorious through, for example, an ability to laugh at him or herself or to come up with an appropriate and amusing retaliation. Some practical jokes recounted long after an event are shrouded by nostalgia and presented as evidence of the trust that prevailed in the good old days or will be tinted by guilt at subjecting someone to something unpleasant. In general, the cruelty or sadism of many practical jokes is overlooked or underplayed as they turn into stories (Dundes 1989).

Many of these meanings can coexist within a single account of a practical joke, as in the example below. It is told by the chief librarian of the manufacturing company we encountered earlier as a narrator, fully fifteen years after the incident:

The best practical joke I did, it near enough backfired on me [Laughter]. During the three-day week, the archives were in the basement; we used to lose power all the time, you remember? This student chap, we'd just had him for 6 months just to do the humping of the boxes of archives. And we had an Irish chap who was very superstitious. And I felt that it was time to get one back on him. So I used to say to John, the Irish chap, 'There's probably a lot of ghosts down that basement' and that sort of thing. There was also a rumour that someone had died down there in the 1930s and that his ghost used to wander around. Anyway, I had enough of this teasing of John, so one day Philip, the student, came back from lunch and we didn't go down to the archives because it was all dark. We had a candle and a torch. By chance, we had a photographic studio in those days, and there was a dummy there with a hand that was detachable. One of the secretaries got her lipstick out and made it look all bloody and we had the hand and we put it in one of the boxes, so that when you opened the box the hand dropped out. We put the box away and gave it a number. The chap came back from lunch and we said to him 'Philip, one of the directors has requested a file from inside box such and such. I'm sorry, it's urgent and it can't wait till 3 o'clock when the lights come back.' Off he went. Normally it would have taken him 10 to 15 minutes to find the box; three-quarters of an hour went by and he hadn't reappeared and we thought 'Oh my God, he's had a heart attack', so we went down there and found him. 'Hi' he said, he sounded in a terrible shock, 'this hand came out', and that was it really [Laughter]. The funny thing is that we rehid this hand in a box and one day someone is going to find it. Nobody knows where it is because they've renumbered the boxes.

In this account, amusement merges with remorse, pride with nostalgia, and the aggression entailed is attenuated. The emphasis shifts from the predicament of the target to the mischievous and creative qualities of the perpetrator—he or she is the central character, the true hero of the story. The story then is more a story of a funny deed, rather than a story of a deserved chastisement, which accords it an epic quality to which we shall return later in this chapter.

A type of humour that is related both to this and to the 'grace in adversity humour' discussed earlier is what may be rightly called sadistic humour, since physical and symbolic violence is perpetrated at the expense of a powerless, naïve or defective character, who becomes the constant butt of all jokes. This humour beloved of certain British television series, such as *Fawlty Towers* and *Black Adder*, is not so common in organizational stories, although it is not uncommon in media portrayal of organizational politics. Its key feature is that it denies the quality of wit or imagination from both the hero and the victim. In the story above, there is a possible allusion to it in the sentence 'I had enough of this teasing of John', which suggests that John may have been the normal target of hardly amusing ribbing. In fact, the plots of sadistic humour stories are remarkably like those of tragic stories in which a bully terrifies a weak or disabled target, which we shall examine shortly. What stops characters such as Manuel in *Fawlty Towers* or Baldrick in *Black Adder* from becoming figures of pathos are two features: first, in spite of repeated affronts and in spite of their lack of humour, these characters 'survive'; in effect, their very inadequacies (linguistic inadequacies or low intelligence) inoculate them from being insulted and broken, since they fail to comprehend the abuse they sustain. Secondly, the perpetrators of the symbolic and physical violence are themselves ambiguous figures of mixed qualities rather than clear-cut bullies or villains. Often the abuse of the powerless target is presented as the venting of frustration against a non-sentient being (a punchbag), thus offering the audience a moral amnesty that enables them to laugh. Such stories, however, lie at the border between the comic and the tragic, something that becomes clear when a joke backfires or when the target suddenly displays his or her human ability to be hurt and broken.

THE TRAGIC STORY: THE PROTAGONIST AS UNDESERVING VICTIM

Tragic stories, like comic ones, generate a substantial degree of emotion, albeit of a different kind. Instead of the mirth and amusement generated by comic stories, tragic stories are accompanied by grief, pain, fear, anger, and, possibly, guilt and shame. Tragic stories share a number of features with comic stories: they too grow out of human misfortunes and they too often deal with the unintended consequences of human actions. Like comic stories, tragic stories cast the protagonist as a victim. At a first glance it may seem that the difference between a tragic and a comic story originates in the magnitude of the misfortune. A minor injury or blow to one's ego may generate jokes, death or severe mutilation may generate tragic stories. A predicament will, in other words, generate tragic rather than comic folklore if the feeling is that 'One does not joke about such matters'. All the same, there is evidence that even the deranged carnage of Auschwitz generated its own brands of humour, both among victims and among perpetrators (see, e.g., Bravo *et al.* (1990)). Many of us would not find such grotesquerie amusing, but the fact that some do suggests that no amount of suffering offers adequate protection against ridicule.

More important than the magnitude of the misfortune is the fact that tragic stories rarely have the quality of comeuppance, which characterizes comic ones, or of sacrifice, which characterizes epic ones. Instead, misfortune assumes the character of painful trauma, shock, or disillusionment. Punishment may be a feature of tragic stories (as it is of comic ones) but this punishment, far from restoring justice, seems to reinforce injustice by being entirely incommensurable with the magnitude of the offence. If, in comic stories, we convince ourselves that the misfortune was 'deserved' or that it was not really serious enough, or that it might have been much worse, or, at any rate it could not happen to us, tragic stories generate no moral amnesty. Even if victims bring about their own downfall through their own actions, such downfall is no cause for celebration. Instead, as Aristotle (*Poetics* 1453*a*) pointed out, tragedy generates feelings of compassion and anxiety, or pity and fear. They also generate much anger, if agency (even unwitting) can be attributed as the cause of the catastrophe. Pity and awe may be our emotional response if a hundred people die as a result of a 'freak' natural disaster; anger is more likely to be our response if a hundred people die as a result of criminal behaviour or wanton negligence. Anger is commonly our emotional response to injustice and unfairness (see Chapter 10).

Tragic stories are somewhat less common in most organizations than comic stories. One example, the cook's suicide, was discussed at length in Chapter 2, in which the suicide symbolically stood for murder. Other predicaments that functioned as sources of tragic stories were forced redundancies, disciplinary incidents, strikes, industrial disputes, and serious accidents. In all of these cases, the plot can be summarized as a trauma to an individual or group, of which the narrator is part. The trauma is usually experienced as being 'surplus to rational requirements', assuming the character of an insult superimposed on an injury. If the point of many comic stories is that suffering is the just reward for foolishness or stupidity, the point of most tragic stories is that the world in general and organizations in particular are unjust and unkind. The individual's happiness or pride counts for little, in spite of most organizations' clichéd affirmations of the opposite. Far from being an invaluable resource, the individual is a pawn to be manipulated, controlled, and finally discarded as dead wood when his or her usefulness is finished. Thus, suffering is meted out with arbitrariness and with impunity (Stein 1994).

The key poetic trope of such tragic stories is the attribution of blame to a supernatural principle such as fate, or, more commonly, a malevolent agent or a scapegoat. This could be 'all management' (a case of simultaneous attribution of unity), a supervisor, a strike-breaker, or some other individual or group. In the following example, a clerical worker with a teacher's qualification describes being snubbed by a supervisor who was both younger and less educated than her:

When I started working here, I immediately got into trouble. I think that being a teacher you are used to being in charge. When I came here I was told what to do and I had to do it. It was continuous ordering, there was no discussion. And this particular lady, who was in charge . . . after about four weeks I thought I would have to leave the company, because she was, as far as I was concerned, impossible. Things were missing and I was constantly blamed, you know, and I was getting to the point where I was going to go to personnel and she asked me, 'Are you all right?' and I said, 'No, I'm not, I'm sorry but you're going to have to treat me as an equal.' This lady is about 34–35, she's been with the company since she was 17, and she just turned around and said, 'Well, you're not I'm afraid.' And that summed it up for me. It's how many years you've been here that counts. The fact that you are a teacher is neither here nor there, the fact that you have a degree is neither here nor there.

The plot of this standard type of story is fairly rudimentary, consisting of a slur, a perpetrator, and a victim. It is the product of a very precise type of story-work. The narrator casts herself in the part of powerless victim of an unprovoked attack or insult and attributes to her assailant the motive of deliberately insulting or hurting. Thus the assailant is cast as a villain, intent on inflicting injustice. Can such a story be properly referred to as tragic? There can be little doubt that the story lacks several qualities of a tragedy such as *Othello* or *Oedipus Rex*. There is no question of witnessing the fall of a great tragic figure, nor does the tragedy stem from the hero's 'hamartia', Aristotle's notion of a tragic error, deriving from a flaw in character, heritage, or past actions. Instead, there is a slightly pathetic quality in the story, that of witnessing an already weak person being the victim of surplus injustice. Not all tragedies, however, entail these qualities. In his classic analysis of fictional modes, Frye (1957) identifies five distinct types of tragic mode, adopting as the key criterion one first proposed by Aristotle—namely, the importance of the victim in relation to the audience. The highest tragedy is one involving god, such as Christ dying on the cross or the destruction of the Valhalla in the last act of *Götterdämmerung*, referred to as Dionysiac tragedy. Less apocalyptic is the demise of the epic demi-god, such as Beowulf or Roland, in what Frye calls 'romance', a tragedy unspoilt by irony or hamartia. The downfall of the great leader, like Othello or Oedipus, is the third type of tragedy, blending heroic stature with a flaw in the hero. This is referred to as the high mimetic tragedy, in contrast to the low mimetic tragedy in which the protagonist is a person whom the audience regard 'like themselves', as in the case of Hardy's Tess or Verdi's La Traviata.

The best word for low mimetic or domestic tragedy is, perhaps, pathos, and pathos has a close relation to the sensational reflex of tears. Pathos presents its hero as isolated by a weakness which appeals to our sympathy because it is on our own level of experience. I speak of a hero, but the central figure is often a woman or a child . . . We notice that while tragedy may massacre a whole cast, pathos is usually concentrated on a single character, partly because low mimetic society is more strongly individualized.   (Frye 1957: 38)

The lowest tragic form is one that centres around a victim lower than ourselves, such as a person of defective intelligence, such as Benjy in Faulkner's *The Sound and the Fury* or Berg's *Wozzeck*, or one of vastly inferior social standing. This too is characterized by pathos, a 'queer ghoulish emotion' (Frye 1957: 39), quite common in contemporary media stories on helpless victims of natural or social disasters.

Trauma stories, like the one above, are accurately described by Frye's low mimetic tragedy, a misfortune visited on a person like ourselves and attributed to a villain, a thoroughly heartless person who is denied any redeeming qualities. Such stories drain agency from the undeserving victim and place it squarely on the villain or on a malign fate. Some authors (Lasch 1984; Schwartz 1993) have claimed that victimhood, rather than heroism, defines *the* dominant form of subjectivity in contemporary America. Groups and individuals, it is argued, construct their identities not on the basis of their achievements and triumphs but on the basis of the injustices done to them. Ethnic groups may vie to define themselves as oppressed by others, women by men, homosexuals by gay-bashers, and even white males by their mothers, their fathers, or the zealots of political correctness. In a similar way, organizational participants whose experience is profoundly shaped by powerlessness or, to use Schwartz's term, 'under-appreciation', may derive their sense of selfhood and fashion their identity, neither through conformity with the oppressing organization, nor through rejection and rebellion, but through the respect accorded to those who suffer—the victims.[2]

An attenuated version of the tragic story is the non-jocular or chagrined gripe, which also focuses on victimhood. Attribution of agency here takes the standard form of 'passing the buck'. Here humour does not come to make light of the hardships as in the jocular gripe. If the moral of the jocular gripe is 'You don't have to be mad to survive in this organization, but it helps', the moral of the chagrined gripe is 'grin and bear it'. Gripes are tragic stories without a villain, the victim usually attributing his or her misfortunes to error, negligence, or system failures. For example, clerks in the office of a privatised utility that had recently undergone massive computerization routinely griped about the system's inflexibility, which led to a proliferation of errors. Here are some simple examples; their plot lines are so indistinct, their characters so emaciated, that they hardly qualify as stories.

Bloody typical. We ask the boys upstairs what exactly they want, receive no reply, and then when we use our initiative what happens? They throw the report back in our faces and tell us to start again.

A secretary got me out of bed early one Saturday morning. She had to prepare a report for her boss and her machine had packed up—nothing showed on the

---

[2] A victim can easily be recast as martyr, if his or her suffering can be shown to have been willing and to serve an accepted superior goal. Martyrdom, unlike victimhood, is almost always linked to epic or heroic qualities.

*screen. I asked her to check that the machine was switched on and properly
booted. No use. I got there to discover that the brightness control was turned
all the way down. And she got me out of bed for this!*

Such routine gripes which are extremely common in some organizations, stand at the border line of what constitutes a story, and can
more accurately be seen as proto-stories—their plot is quite rudimentary, their characters sketchy, and they hardly seem to warrant
repetition or embellishment. They do, however, display the two features of the tragic story: they grow out of misfortune experienced as
trauma, rather than as chastisement, and they seek not always successfully to apportion blame and responsibility.

Tragic–comic stories

Zijderveld (1983: 23) has observed that 'with the lapse of time many
tragedies are slowly transformed into comedies'. The same can be
said of some tragic organizational stories. With time, we learn to see
the funny side of things, including unpleasant things. We have
already observed four types of stories that combine comic with tragic
qualities. First, humorous stories in which the protagonist refuses to
give into despair but improvises a witticism that makes light of his or
her predicament. Secondly, jocular gripes that lack humour's finer
and higher quality, but nevertheless seek to mock adversity and satirize the situation. Thirdly, pranks, bizarre tests, and punishments or
initiation rites, which are common in public schools, military organizations, the police, and other such institutions (Holdaway 1988).
These may initially be experienced as traumatic events, but with time
they become shrouded in blithe nostalgia, as the emphasis shifts
from the humiliation of the victims to the wit of the perpetrators.
Fourthly, sadistic humour stories, in which a small boundary has to
be crossed converting the survivor into undeserving victim and the
wit or prankster into an unalloyed villain.

EPIC STORIES: THE PROTAGONIST AS HERO

We now turn to the third main type of organizational story, the epic
or heroic story. The epic is an important element in folklore, assuming different forms such as heroic poetry, songs, legends. and
laments (Propp 1968: 149). Epic stories, like all epics, are distinguished by their heroic character, centring on battles or contests
won. If most tragic stories and a great many comic ones focus on

victimhood, epic stories focus on *agency* and in particular on noble or heroic achievements, such as missions accomplished, contests won, challenges met, or crises resolved. In organizations, these are the stories that are sometimes elevated from folklore to official 'mythology'. The employee who defies storms, earthquakes, and other adversities to discharge his or her mission, the executive who cuts the red tape of bureaucracy with aplomb, the little man rising to the top, the big man coming to the rescue of everyone else. Epic stories, like comic and tragic ones, may spring from dramas and crises, but, unlike the other two, highlight the resolution of the crisis through great acts of courage, force, or wit. The emotional content of epic stories is quite distinct from those of comic and tragic. They invariably generate pride and admiration. They also generate commitment and even a sense of duty to emulate the hero or maintain the tradition that he or she started; thus, epic stories are occasionally tinged with insecurity and envy. Will the audience and the narrator be the equal to the story's heroes?

Epic stories in organizations come at the micro-level, epitomized in the 'Bill and Dave' anecdotes that celebrate the founding fathers of Hewlett Packard (Peters and Waterman 1982), as well as the macro-level of the type 'Iacocca saves Chrysler'. The popularity of such stories coincides with the rediscovery by capitalism of its heroic heritage. In the last twenty years of the twentieth century, business became again an arena for heroes, whose exploits were narrated and celebrated, like those of King Arthur and his knights. It is not accidental that epic stories are the ones that have caught the attention of organizational theorists (Bowles 1989; Ingersoll and Adams 1986; Kanter 1983; Martin *et al.*, 1983; Martin and Powers, 1983; Mitroff 1984; Mitroff and Kilman 1976). Such authors have argued that organizations have their own corporate mythologies, full of heroes and villains, martyrs and traitors, great courage and noble sacrifices, missions, struggles and ordeals, reinforcing the organization's values and strengthening its culture. People crave for heroes, hence they mythologize them. Few things are as inspiring as full identification with a hero, few quite as painful as the cutting to size of a hero. The potential of heroes for enriching organizational culture has been emphasized by authors such as Deal and Kennedy; they argue (1982: 57):

It is time that American industry recognized the potential of heroes. If companies treated people like heroes even for a short time, they might end up being heroes . . . When companies make heroes out of bosses and workers—that is when we all accept the responsibility of playing to a world stage—will we banish the sterility of modern organization.

Such arguments have encouraged the view that organizations can virtually manufacture heroes; this is a foolhardy conclusion. Just as people may interpret everyday actions as heroic, if they wish to perceive someone as a hero, the self-same actions may be constructed as devious or plain stupid by people determined to cast someone as villain or fool. The need for villains and fools may be every bit as strong as the need for heroes.

Not all epic stories, then, automatically reinforce corporate values. Even strongly integrated organizations involve competing and opposing values, some of which cannot be assimilated in the official culture. Some epic stories are distinctly counter-cultural. The Honda employee who walks back home in the evenings straightening the windscreen wipers of every Honda car parked on the side of the road or the man who invents Sellotape in his spare time may be turned into part of the organization's official 'mythology'. By contrast, the following incident described by Hochschild (1983: 127) remained firmly part of the unofficial organizational lore: 'A young businessman said to a flight attendant, "Why aren't you smiling?" She put her tray back on the food cart, looked him in the eye, and said, "I'll tell you what. You smile first, then I smile." The businessman smiled at her. "Good," she replied. "Now freeze, and hold that for fifteen hours." Then she walked away.'

Some epic stories are narrated by the central character, who casts him or herself as hero dealing with a crisis or a challenge. Such unadulterated accounts of personal heroics were not very common in my research in organizations—they invite criticism and even ridicule, as being boastful or exaggerated. Here is an account offered by an engineer dealing with a potentially dangerous pipe leak. It is clear that the narrator tries to underplay the heroic quality:

I've had some near misses when I'm on stand-by; they are a bit nasty and I get landed with them because nobody else . . . because I've got the experience and have been around a long time and I find young engineers . . . avoid situations and all of a sudden I find it in my lap . . . we had one recently with chaps' lives at stake . . . basically what it was was a ten-inch medium pressure main and it was leaking and when I say medium pressure I mean 30 psi. It was leaking badly outside a house and it was ten feet down in moving ground, moving because it was unstable ground, so you had the problem, and this medium pressure main actually fed an entire town so I had the problem of actually, I had to repair the main with limited equipment on site, which meant digging a massive hole and then sending blokes down to repair it when gas was actually belting out and the ground was moving and water actually filled the hole up at one stage. I had to take the responsibility of someone going down and repairing it and getting that chap out again and hoping nothing would happen.

This account paints a tense picture of the potential disaster and casts the narrator as one who has the courage and the expertise to tackle it. It fits precisely Propp's (1968: 149) description of epic plot as 'struggle and victory'. The struggle, as Propp (ibid.) notes, 'is waged not for narrow, petty goals, nor for personal interests, not for the well-being of the individual hero but for the people's highest ideals. The struggle is difficult; it demands the concentration of all the hero's powers and the ability to sacrifice himself.'

The struggle undertaken by the hero is often waged against the blind forces of bureaucracy and petty officialdom. In the following example, a privatized utility clerk describes her struggles to meet the consumers' demands for an urgent repair visit:

When all the odds are against me, you know, I'm trying to help this consumer and everybody is saying no you can't have an engineer—I won't let anything go, because I get on to it and go on and on, and then I will start going up the line higher and eventually somebody will listen and then the job gets done; and someone rings up and she says I'm happy and then I put the phone down and I think 'hurrah we have done it!' but then why is it necessary to go through all this trouble . . . it is more of a challenge then and I get more excited.

The hero's perseverance in the face of adversity, courage and dedication to the task, and willingness to submit to various ordeals uncomplainingly, these are all features of epic stories. The epic hero can have flaws, make mistakes, and suffer reversals, but the overall integrity of his or her character can never be doubted, unless he or she is under the influence of magic or other external powers. The epic hero is loyal, impetuous, decisive, wise, controlled, dedicated, compassionate, approachable, loving, and caring. Such qualities virtually never enter into conflict with each other, nor is the epic hero riven by self-doubts or anxieties.

It is characteristic how the protagonist's burning ambition, which can easily lead to tragic or comic downfalls, in the case of the epic hero generates unadulterated admiration, as illustrated by the following story. It was narrated by an office supervisor at a chemical firm:

I had a friend whom I met while she was on secondment; in fact, she was the first American woman secondee, she was a personnel assistant from the US, and she came here and one day I went out to lunch with her, and I said, 'Damn me', I was in that sort of mood, I said, 'I want to be a director' and she looked at me, I wasn't being serious, and she looked at me and said, 'Well, I'm going to be one.' And I said 'Pardon?' and she said, 'No, I . . .' I said, 'I'm only joking, Roberta', and she said 'No, one day I'll get one of the top three positions in this country [Freudian slip] . . . in this company.' And now, years later, she has come back over here as the personnel director. So, she made it happen. It

*could not have happened here, very unlikely [for a woman to rise] to that posi-
tion in England.*

It is telling how in this story what was an idle fantasy for one woman
(being a director and having power) was a driving force for the other,
one that drew the unqualified admiration of her ex-colleague.

Epic stories lack the poetic complexity and ambiguity of tragic and
comic stories; their plot invariably revolves around one axis, success
and failure, which is decided by the qualities attributed to the hero
and the magnitude of the forces that oppose him or her. Defeats are
important parts of epic plots, though their main purpose is to allow
the hero to show his or her fortitude and sacrifice, helping to reinforce the poetic effect of the crowning triumph. This is not just any
victory or success. A victory against an inferior opponent, a victory
achieved through luck or treachery, a victory achieved through rational and careful husbanding of resources, a victory diplomatically
downplayed so as not to provoke retaliation—these are not epic victories. Victories in epic stories must be achieved in great style and
with maximum display, resulting in unalloyed glory and admiration
heaped on the hero. Emotionally, too, epic stories are less ambivalent, by offering the audience an even more one-dimensional view of
good and evil than the low mimetic tragedy. The story-work of epic
stories is very straightforward, relying on exaggeration of all positive
qualities in the hero and obliteration of even the smallest trace of
weakness and placing him or her squarely at the centre of the action.

Epic hybrids

Like tragic stories, epic stories can come in humorous or comic variants. One such type that is especially interesting is where a crisis is
resolved through cunning and wit rather than courage and force.
This is a favourite theme in mythology and folklore, whether in
Aesop's fables, in Hermes outsmarting his brother Apollo, or Jerry
outwitting Tom. In organizational stories, we have already discussed
the theme of the little man who outsmarts the bureaucratic obs-
tacles, often by using the bureaucracy's own provisions against
itself—that is, by 'playing the system'. Numerous examples spring to
mind: the worker who refuses to work until all health and safety provisions are fully observed, the official who gleefully applies every let-
ter of every regulation to harass superiors and customers alike. The
protagonist of this type of epic-comic story is the trickster, a character familiar to anthropologists (Apte 1983), sociologists (Fine 1983),
and increasingly organization theorists (Kets de Vries 1990; Turner
1986). Tricksters and jokers have inspired some of the world's great

myths, and it comes as no surprise that they also feature prominently in organizational stories.

A different combination of comic and epic features a crisis that is the product of human or organizational blunders, yet where no scapegoat is sought but a mixture of improvisatory qualities, wit, luck, humour, and providential help, enable the protagonist to overcome crises and difficulties. The hero here is not a trickster but an Odysseus- or Figaro-like figure, one who has an answer for every question and proves equal to every crisis. The story that follows is representative of this type. It is based on an incident that had been much discussed in the communications department of a large chemical firm and is based on the movement of a heavy mainframe computer from one building to another. It was related to me in a different variant, according to which the computer was seriously damaged during the move, and it concluded, 'Lucky that the data on it weren't lost, but a few heads could have rolled at the time.' By contrast, the version that follows combines a slapstick humour with a happy end. It was told by the Communications Director of the firm:

The funniest incident I have witnessed was when we moved from the old building to the building across the road while the refurbishment was going on. And we had a lot of fairly old mainframes and we found that one of them was too big to get in the lift the other end, so the lift had to be taken out of the lift-shaft and let the computer dangle down the shaft. The remaining IBMs we could get out in the lifts, so we had this crowd of six carpenters, who were marvellous guys, whose job was at such and such time, such and such day, to seal the room up. And I expected them to screw the doors up or whatever. We'd got two of the mainframes out one was still in there with four IBM engineers in there; and we suddenly heard this screaming. The six had come along with railway sleepers and about 24 inch nails and they'd nailed the railway sleepers over the door frame and trapped these guys [Laughter]. Got the IBM lot out, and this was one of the big guys, just fitted in the lift, and the idea was that we had the lifts strengthened before we got the computer in the lift, slowly lower it down to the basement, where the heavy haulage gang were waiting to carry it to the other building. We put the thing in the lift, and there is a guy sitting on top of it, so we say 'press the button', so he presses the button, the door shuts, the lift drops two feet and jams. Luckily we still had the lift engineers in, so they came along, and they found that all the springs that held the door and all the rest had fouled up. So they managed to get the guy out, sort of pumped him out, and it took three hours to winch the lift to the basement, with the computer in, by which time the haulage gang had disappeared for a fish and chips supper. This was 11 o'clock on a Friday night, and we didn't see them again until the following Tuesday. The fact that they are Irish and they'd just been paid had something to do with it. So the three of us moved this computer on our own on a trolley, right in the middle of the road. All in all, it was quite an interesting weekend.

If achievement can be part of a comic narrative like this one, it can also be part of a tragic one. In Frye's categorization of fictional modes, the romance combines the epic emphasis on great achievement and contests won with an unhappy end, whereby a hero, such as Roland or Beowulf, meets his tragic fate. The *Iliad* represents a classic combination of epic and tragic, as fate claims for her victims the greatest of heroes. I found very few organizational stories that combined tragic and epic elements. The nearest that stories came to this description are epic stories in which the injuries sustained by the hero leave permanent marks. In Part Two, we shall discuss the instance of retaliation against an insult, a predominantly epic theme with possible tragic resonances.

A few stories in my collection turned out to combine features of all three types, tragic, comic, and epic. All but one of these stories were poetically very weak; it seemed clear that a narrator trying to combine all three elements in a single narrative is likely to lose the plot. This, of course, does not mean that the same incident cannot lead to all three types of stories. As we have already seen, it is perfectly possible for the same accident or the same practical joke to lead to tragic, comic, and epic renderings. What seems almost impossible is to construct a single narrative that effectively combines all three poetic modes. The exception was a long narrative with several characters that is composed of several incidents. The narrative, once again told by the librarian of the multinational, started with the appearance of the company's CEO on national TV in which he pledged his support for local business. Subsequently, a small local bookshop in financial difficulties phoned up the CEO's office and asked why it did not receive any orders from the company. The Chairman then asked the company's librarian to put some orders through this local bookshop. The librarian stalled by asking for very rare and specialist books, which the small bookshop could not possibly provide; he already had well-established suppliers and was not prepared to place orders with a small non-specialist outfit. The bookshop went out of business within a few months. The story concludes thus:

I think it was the only time I felt that I was actually killing somebody off, really because this had been his last hope . . . Later the chairman asked for a report. Back I trotted to his office and I explained, so he said, 'OK, we've done our best, we've shown him why we can't use him. We can't take it any further than that.' Then he said, 'What kind of train were you hoping to get back home today?' 'Well,' I said, 'ten to three', so he shouted through the open door, 'Edna, get my car ready'. So I was driven home by his chauffeur in his pale blue Rolls Royce. I was chairman for the day [Laughter], people looking in and thinking 'Who's that?' [Laughter].

This narrative, which could form the basis of a television script, combines epic elements (the chairman trying to help the little fellow), tragic elements (the little fellow going out of business as a result of the librarian's unwillingness to help), and even some comic elements (the librarian being unexpectedly rewarded in style). The chairman emerges as an unconventional, well-intentioned individual but also one whose whims generate unreasonable demands on his subordinates. He is also a bit of a fool; outsmarted by the librarian but oblivious of it, he rewards him in an unorthodox way. The librarian, for his part, is potential victim, villain, and victor. All in all, the story, in spite of its narrative richness, lacks the clear emotional tone of most others.

ROMANTIC STORIES: THE SUBJECT AS LOVE OBJECT

The comic, tragic, and epic types and their combinations account for the large majority of organizational stories. Yet, in classifying the narratives at my disposal I found a residual class of stories that could not meaningfully be seen as belonging to any of the previous types. Alone among stories, these could make reasonably compelling narrative material without there being any conflict or any crisis. The protagonist appeared to confront no 'predicament', and no fate, benevolent or malign, was at play. The emotional tone of these stories too was quite distinct: a gentle, tender feeling, at times bordering on sentimentality, occasionally pity (or self-pity) but without its tragic companion, fear; some of these stories had a nostalgic quality. Poetically, such stories had some lyrical qualities. Like epic stories, they eschewed irony, though an unkind listener could easily twist them into nasty sarcasm. Following a suggestion from one of my students, I refer to these stories as romantic, a label that can unfortunately create false associations with romance (an epic–tragic genre). This is entirely alien to the romantic story type, which has more in common with the sentimentality of Valentine's Day, 'romantic fiction', and the like.

The plots of romantic stories revolve around romantic love and tokens of love, gratitude, and appreciation. Not surprisingly perhaps, most of the romantic narratives were collected in a hospital, where staff talked of grateful patients bringing them cards, chocolates, or other presents after successful treatment. These narratives tended to be somewhat sketchy, lacking those features of plot, character, and unexpectedness that characterize 'good' stories. The present situations combine affectionate feeling for a fellow human being with the reciprocation of this feeling. The following example was recounted by a hospital receptionist:

Recently a lady brought this great big box of chocolates to me. Actually she is a member of the catering staff and she had come to see me about her mother who was ill and to ask me if there was anything we could do to get her an early appointment. So I said 'Leave it to me', and I sorted something out. The lady's mother was seen without having to wait long for an appointment, and I had a box of chocolates bought for me. I said, 'I don't want this, it is my job,' but she insisted, 'Take it please.'

This text presents the 'good turn' done by the receptionist not as a heroic deed, but as a show of compassion for a colleague, as an act of love rather than an act of duty or courage. The gift then serves to construct both the protagonist and the giver of the present as objects of affection within the narrative. Another romantic story was told by a female secretary working for a privatized utility. It concerned the one day per year when office staff accompanied engineers on house calls, aimed at promoting greater understanding between the two groups of employees.

We had a day out with the lads (engineers) and we had a really good time. We saw how they did their job and, later, they came into the office to see how we did our job. Well, Roy and I went to check an appliance for this dear old couple, who had a beautiful house in Chipping Camden. It was lovely this house, and she said, 'my dear you could have a glass of sherry but I drank it all'. She then went down to the cellar and found some and I said to Roy, 'I've never been offered sherry in my life'. The old girl was lovely; she couldn't make coffee, she said, as they came from France. All these houses we went to were great.

It is characteristic of the romantic character of this story that the wealth of the lady does not create envy, nor does her being foreign generate any hostility—the tender feeling is allowed to rule unchallenged.

The 'day out with the lads' also fed a different type of romantic narrative in the office, not involving gifts but straight love fantasies. This was partly due to the fact that one of the secretaries eventually married 'her engineer', whom she had met on a joint visit. Love fantasies, like gift stories, also constitute the subject as an object of love, though not for 'what they have done' but for 'who they are' (Schwartz 1993), as in the following example, recounted by a secretary:

The Finance Director who was here before Mr Rogerson, Mr Harrison, he was brilliant with everybody. He used to come every Christmas to our [the secretaries'] party and eat awful sausage rolls that we'd made, drink cheap wine and still look pleased about it. Last year, at the party he made me do a waltz with him. He was a really nice guy.

In my experience, office romances featured in two main types of narratives; on the one hand, they fed comic and often malicious gossip, the central characters being constructed as 'fools'. Alternatively, however, office romances fed romantic narratives, in which individuals clearly identified with one or both of the lovers, treating them as objects of love and affection. The very vulnerability of the romantic couple, the fantasizing love object, and the appreciated gift-receiver (in all cases they could so easily turn into figures of sarcasm) is reflected in the vulnerability of the narrator, whose story can easily be challenged or even 'defiled'. Such narratives require a considerable degree of trust on the part of the narrator in his or her audience.

At a deeper level, romantic stories also represent a way of dealing with suffering and misfortune. Instead of turning misfortune into deserved chastisement, like comic stories, a test of character and an occasion for heroic deeds, like epic stories, or the product of a malignant fate that must be endured and may be survived, like tragic stories, romantic stories appear to proclaim that love conquers all. The hardships and injustices of work, the pains inflicted on us by culture, fortune, and nature, they can all be endured and even overcome with the assistance of love, both in its sensuous and its non-sensuous embodiments. In organizations, we cautiously celebrate instances where ordinary human emotions, such as compassion, gratitude, and love, become the instigators of altruistic action in lieu of rational–instrumental factors and institutional emotions such as greed, cowardice, and selfishness. A gift converts an impersonal organizational transaction into something personal, emotional, and unique—it stands for caring and for relations outside the organizational cash nexus. In a similar way, the romantic couple may be celebrated for its supposed self-contentment and self-containment, its independence from the slings and arrows of fortune, and its discovery of happiness in love and emotion. Of course, these connections are sensitive and easily undermined, as any cynic knows. Hence, romantic stories entail a vulnerability like no other, one that afflicts a narrator who has placed maybe all his or her faith in love and stands to be rudely corrected. The narrator, therefore, feels quite protective of the objects of love, seeking to shelter them from criticism and disparagement by loving them.

One interesting feature of romantic stories is the entirely novel treatment that they accord to any flaw in the central love object or indeed some of the other characters. Instead of it being an occasion for laughter or disparagement or the cause of the hero's downfall, this flaw generates protective and reparatory feelings. For example, in the first of the romantic stories above, the mother's sickness is treated as something calling for help on the part of the narrator.[3] This reinforces the tender protective qualities of romantic stories. Within the romantic story, then, love is not a sickness or an affliction but a redemptive power, a cure, which brings with it its own vulnerabilities.[4]

THE POETIC MODES

But then, all types of story require trust between the narrator and the audience. An unsympathetic audience can throw a narrator off course, by challenging the way that sense is infused into the events. A comic story can be undermined by pointing out the tragic consequences of what seemed like an amusing incident, the real pain and injury that it caused. A tragic story can be undermined by finding a way of presenting the victim as a fool, a villain, or a victim of his or her own actions. An epic story can be undermined by finding chinks in the hero's armour or by pointing out the unnecessary suffering that his or her heroics caused for others. These distinct spoiling techniques (in which contemporary journalists have become experts) reinforce our confidence in our classification of stories into the four major types. Each type represents a distinct poetic mode—in other words, a distinct way of turning facts into meaningful, emotionally charged stories. Each mode casts the protagonist in a different light, uses a distinct set of poetic tropes and triggers off a specific emotional response in the audience. At the cost of simplification, these can be presented as shown in Tables 3.1 and 3.2.

A relatively small change in emphasis can radically alter the poetic mode at work in a narrative. Thus, acknowledging that a 'villain' acted unknowingly or without intention to harm dramatically alters the narrative, as does evidence that the villain acted nobly on a particular occasion. Discovering that a hero has acted in a mean or

---

[3] This is very close to the reparatory feelings that have been explored by Kleinian analysts as part of what Klein calls the 'depressive position' (Klein and Riviere 1974).

[4] Does the romantic mode form its own hybrids with other modes? Undoubtedly, as a literary genre, it combines with the tragic in what is wrongly known as melodrama and with the humorous in romantic comedy. The character of the 'simpleton' or 'holy fool' can be seen as the product of the marriage of epic and romantic, combining vulnerability with unwitting achievement (see Bettelheim (1976: 75) and Kets De Vries (1990)). As a storytelling mode, however, the romantic rarely mixes with others; occasionally an epic or comic story may have romantic resonances, but it is rare for it to merge with one of the other modes.

Table 3.1. Generic poetic modes

Characteristic	Mode			
	Comic	Tragic	Epic	Romantic
Protagonist	Deserving victim, fool	Non-deserving victim	Hero	Love object
Other characters	Trickster	Villain, supportive helper	Rescue object, assistant, villain	Gift-giver, lover, injured or sick person
Plot focus	Misfortune as deserved chastisement	Undeserved misfortune, trauma	Achievement, noble victory, success	Love triumphant; misfortune conquered by love
Predicament	Accident, mistake, coincidence, repetition, the unexpected and unpredictable	Crime, accident, insult, injury, loss, mistake, repetition, misrecognition	Contest, challenge, trial, test, mission, quest, sacrifice	Gift, romantic fantasy, falling in love, reciprocation, recognition
Poetic tropes	1. Providential significance 2. Unity 3. Agency before misfortune 4. Denial of agency during misfortune 5. Fixed qualities (pomposity, arrogance, vanity etc.)	1. Malevolent fate 2. Blame 3. Unity 4. Motive (to the villain) 5. Fixed qualities by juxtaposition (victim: noble, decent, worthy, good; villain: evil, devious, mean etc.)	1. Agency 2. Motive 3. Credit 4. Fixed qualities (nobility, courage, loyalty, selflessness, honour, ambition)	1. Emotion (loving, caring) 2. Motive 3. Credit (worthy love object) 4. Fixed qualities (gratitude, caring, loving, vulnerable, pathetic)
Emotions	Mirth, aggression, (hate), scorn	Sorrow, pity, fear, anger, pathos	Pride, admiration, nostalgia, (envy)	Love, care, kindness, generosity, gratitude (nostalgia)

Table 3.2. Some secondary poetic modes

Characteristic	Mode			
	Humour	Cock-up	Tragi-comic	Epic-comic
Source modes	Comic	Comic, epic	Tragic, comic	Epic, comic
Protagonist	Survivor, humorist, wizard, ironist	Hero-fixer, wizard	Victim who turns out to be unheroic hero and vice versa	Unwitting hero, hero with humour, prankster, trickster
Other characters	(Villain, unjust system)			Villain, victim, accomplice
Plot focus	Misfortune as occasion for wit	Cock-up as test for non-heroic hero	Misfortune, both deserved and undeserved, leading to comic twists and tragic results	Unorthodox achievement, display of wit
Predicament	Accident, mishap, reversal of fortune, injustice, repetition, coincidence	Crisis, problem, mistake, breakdown, puzzle	Boon turns into misfortune or vice versa	Prank, puzzle, challenge, wager, the unexpected
Poetic tropes	1. Denial of emotion 2. Fixed qualities (grace, sense of humour, self-possession, fortitude)	1. Agency 2. Credit 3. Fixed qualities (wit, imagination, cunning, speed, common sense)	1. Providential significance 2. Fixed qualities (fortitude, moral courage, defiance, wit)	1. Agency 2. Motive 3. Credit 4. Fixed qualities (sense of humour, irony, imagination, bravado)
Emotions	Mirth, admiration, (pity)	Mirth, admiration	Amusement, pity, fear, guilt, pathos	Mirth, admiration, levity

cowardly way on a single occasion virtually undoes him or her as a hero. This is why an entire narrative can be undone by contesting a single piece of evidence or introducing a single new clue. The presence or absence of consent is necessary in establishing rape, whereas premeditation is necessary to establish a particular type of murder. These are contestable elements, more often subject to interpretation rather than factual verification. Stories are delicate narrative structures allowing relatively little scope for dissonant elements. Within each poetic mode, the scope for variation is limited. Complications are in order, so long as they reinforce the story's main point—the hero's brave deeds, the villain's capacity for villainy, the trickster's imaginative qualities, the humorist's wit, the injustice done to a victim, the comeuppance inflicted on a fool. In this respect, storytelling is quite different from many literary genres where psychological complexity is necessary to sustain the narrative. In the last resort, storytelling relies on a relatively narrow array of plots, characters, and motives to make sense of an endlessly complex, ambiguous, ambivalent, and perplexing reality. This is the source of its strength and also its weakness.

4

Stories, Symbolism, and Culture

'When I hear the word culture, I reach for my gun,' said Heinz Johst, the expressionist novelist and head of the Nazi Chamber of Literature, in a phrase later made famous by Hermann Goering. For the Nazis, culture had no solutions to offer to the sickness of Germany. Indeed, culture was part of the problem, whose solution required far more radical measures. Max Weber might have been amused (or might have reached for *his* gun; Weber reputedly was a fine shot), had he been alive to witness the 1980s' vogue for the concept of organizational culture. As a result of this popularity, meaning and emotion were written back into the theory of organizations. The days of studying organizations as grey Weberian bureaucracies, made up of rules and hierarchies, are now gone, as are the days of looking at people as anonymous functionaries or well-oiled cogs. Organizational culture has emerged as the concept mediating between changing forms of production and administration, on the one hand, and lived human experience, on the other. It enables individuals to make sense of their experience and to share it with others; it infuses their actions with meaning and value; and it supplies them with a sense of belonging. Instead of disregarding organizational culture as superfluous, effective management takes hold of shaping, guiding and invigorating the culture.

The initial enthusiasm generated by the concept of organizational culture and the management of meaning has now been tempered. Numerous authors have warned of the dangers of conceptualizing culture as a unitary force enhancing cohesion and integration, and have questioned whether culture is automatically internalized by individuals and whether it is invariably consonant with structural features of the organization (Gregory 1983; Meek 1988; Smircich 1983*a*, *b*; B. A. Turner 1986). Others have criticized the assumption that culture may be managed or controlled (Bate 1990, 1994; Gabriel 1995).

A THEORY OF ORGANIZATIONAL STORYTELLING

This chapter locates storytelling within the cultural fabric of different organizations and examines what stories can tell us about these organizations and their cultures. The chapter offers further illustrations of interpretation, elaborating the relationship between the fantasy life of individuals and groups and an organization's cultural artefacts, such as stories, jokes, and symbols. The chapter concludes with a detailed discussion of one particular story, encountered in a navy training camp. This story is shown to be the point of convergence for a number of fantasies held by organizational participants. We shall argue that certain fantasies, instead of integrating individual and group into the organization, enable participants to distance themselves from it by presenting the organization as an object of derision and disparagement. Extending the conclusion of Chapter 2, we shall argue that organizational culture and its artefacts equip the individual with a protective armour against the types of misfortune and suffering that characterize contemporary organizations. Organizational culture, like all culture, in addition to imparting meaning and value, has a consolatory function, compensating for the frustrations of life in organizations.

CULTURE AND STORYTELLING

The place of stories within culture has been widely discussed. Stories help communities to pass their spiritual, moral, and cultural heritage from generation to generation, they are vital for the instruction of young people, they generate behavioural expectations, and they offer models of emulation and avoidance. In some respects they resemble symbolically endowed material artefacts; like symbolic artefacts, stories are repositories of meaning, a meaning that both changes and is timeless. Like artefacts, they sustain a set of values and form part of wide networks through which meaning travels. They are also valued in their own right, as we have seen in earlier chapters, both as products of narrative craft and as objects with integrity that well-intentioned listeners treat with some respect. It is not accidental then that Schein (1985) groups them together as 'artifacts and creations', those phenomena lying at the surface of culture, being easily perceptible, but demanding deciphering and/or interpretation.

Since the study of culture became a major topic in organizational theory, numerous authors have sought to elucidate the functions of storytelling for organizational culture. While not the first to use organizational stories, Peters and Waterman (1982) can undoubtedly claim the credit for placing stories centre-stage in analysing organizational life. Their best-selling book expertly weaves numerous fine stories in a discourse of corporate excellence. Stories are approached as a sign of strong corporate culture, a culture that penetrates deeply into the lives of its members drastically, shaping their meaning systems. Such strong cultures were initially seen as the basic precondition of excellence. Perhaps an even more important contribution of Peters and Waterman is the demonstration of the extraordinary power of stories as didactic devices in the moral and practical education of managers—what sets their book apart from other contributions to the excellence thesis is the memorable qualities of their stories and the economy with which they make their point. The 'Bill and Dave' stories, for example, the folklore surrounding the founders of Hewlett Packard, their exploits, witticisms, and inspirational qualities, were brought to a far wider audience of eager businessmen and management students than they could ever have reached within the company. Such stories, occasionally, embark on separate careers in academic circles, like the foibles of Schmidt, Taylor's famous human ox. While the sentimentality of the romantic and the subversiveness of humour creep into some of Peters and Waterman's stories, the predominant type on which they focus is the epic, the tale of achievement, perseverance, hardship endured, loyalty, devotion, heroism, and crowning triumph.

Before Peters and Waterman brought organizational storytelling to a wider public, Wilkins with his collaborators at Stanford University had already started to explore organizational stories as cognitive repositories in which important ideas are mapped and stored (Wilkins 1978; Wilkins and Martin 1979). Wilkins and Martin proposed three major functions for stories and legends: sensemaking and the transmission of knowledge among organizational participants, generation of commitment, and social control (Boyce 1996; Wilkins 1983; Wilkins and Martin 1979). Wilkins's work has influenced numerous scholars who have expanded on the cognitive and sensemaking properties of stories within an organization's culture. Stories guide action and strategy, by providing precedents for times of crisis or change (Boje 1991); they act as maps, helping people make sense of unfamiliar situations by linking them to familiar ones (Weick 1995), making 'the unexpected expectable, hence manageable' (Robinson, 1981: 60).

What seems absent from this line of investigation is the emotional quality of stories, their ability to generate a far wider palette of emotions than mere commitment. After all, the symbolism of a map is a very precise mathematical one, quite different from the symbolism employed by an artist who sets out to paint a landscape or describe it in prose or rhyme. The study of stories as symbols capable of generating emotions has been pursued by a line of researchers, who have drawn from the ethnographic tradition, treating stories, along with myths, rituals, ceremonies, and material artefacts, as expressions of shared belief systems. Such researchers have sought to identify the meanings and symbolism of stories for organizational members and place this symbolism within a wider set of cultural meanings particular to organizations (Allaire and Firsirotu 1984; Boyce 1995, 1996; Hansen and Kahnweiler 1993; Mahler 1988; Meek 1988).

Yet another group of writers, inspired by the work of Goffman and folklore theorists like Georges, have examined storytelling in action. Using a dramaturgical perspective, these writers have sought to elucidate the relations between storyteller and listeners, the storyteller's authority, the nature of shared assumptions, meanings, and emotions, and the quality of the performance (Boje 1991; Mangham 1986, 1995; Mangham and Overington 1987; Rosen 1985*a*; Rosen and Astley 1988; Wallemacq and Sims 1998; Weick 1995). What this approach has highlighted is the delicate and ambiguous quality of symbolism in organizations. Stories are polysemic, resonating in different ways with different people but also entailing diverse and even contradictory meanings for a single person. While capable of generating cohesion and commitment, they can also function as the basis of resistance and opposition. This is especially but not exclusively true of stories describing injustice, oppression, and trauma.

This brings me to my particular interest in stories as part of organizational cultures. While the approach taken in this book grows from insights offered by many of the theorists above, it departs from their approaches in three important respects. First, within an organization's culture, we view stories as a highly problematic and difficult type of artefact. Important events in an organization's history do not automatically generate stories, nor are stories able to survive unless they are regularly reinforced. While stories may appear to be highly spontaneous and economical sensemaking devices, they compete against other sensemaking devices and do not automatically spring into action as soon as something unusual or remarkable happens. Moreover, as was seen in Chapter 3, stories can have a spoiling effect on each other, neutralizing each other and destroying each other's meaning, leading to silent incomprehension and confusion.

Secondly, while most researchers have focused on stories of achievement and heroism as a repository of cultural values and symbolism, we are equally interested in stories of suffering and misfortune. As was seen in the previous chapter, each of the four poetic modes represents a distinct way of making sense of misfortune, making misfortune bearable. Achievement itself was found to represent a means of coping with and transcending misfortune. In his classic discussion of fairy tales, Bettelheim (1976: 147) argued: 'Consolation is the greatest service the fairy tale can offer a child; the confidence that, despite all tribulations he has to suffer . . . not only will he succeed, but the evil forces will be done away with and never again threaten his peace of mind.' In our view, consolation is a major psychological function not only of all stories, but of all culture including organizational culture (Gabriel 1983, 1984, 1991b, 1995). In this chapter we shall juxtapose two ways in which consolations for misfortunes and adversities incurred by people in organizations are sought—one relies on idealizing the organization while the other relies on exactly the opposite, reducing the organization to an absurd caricature. We shall argue that the majority of stories in fact tend to diminish or vilify organizations instead of idealizing them. We shall not be surprised if some of the richest narratives and 'strongest' cultures are found not in 'excellent companies' but in oppressive, exploitative, no-nonsense organizations. In such organizations, jokes, stories, and gossip are indispensable mechanisms of psychological survival. Having a laugh at the expense of an arrogant manager or an awkward customer is a standard way of defeating boredom, generating solidarity, and restoring justice, albeit in a symbolic way.

We, therefore, view neither an organization's culture nor any wider culture as independent of the social and political conditions that prevail. Culture (including that part of culture that is expressed through stories) does not stand in a mechanical relation to these conditions, but, in different ways, it expresses them, opposes them, justifies them, and seeks to offer consolations and compensations for them. Stories combine the most parochial, variable, and organization-specific preoccupations with larger social and moral concerns. Within two sentences a story can move from the predicament of the young manager whose brash tie gets caught in a paper shredder to social issues of racial and sexual discrimination to eternal concerns for justice and fairness as shaped by specific material conditions.

But, if culture is not independent of social and political structures, neither is it independent of the psycho-structure, a complex mesh of desires, wishes, fantasies, symbols, and anxieties that are part of each individual's conscious and unconscious mental functioning (Carr 1998; Carr and Zanetti 1998; LaBier 1986; Maccoby 1976). Thus a story can at the same time express an individual's deeply private and personal desires (e.g. for revenge, justice, or recognition), a group's shared fantasy (e.g. of salvation or domination of another group), and deeper structural and political realities (e.g. a group's experience of long-term exploitation, insecurity, or privilege). Stories carry cultural meanings, social meanings, as well as personal meanings.[1] As was argued in Chapter 2, unlocking their symbolism requires the work of analytic interpretation, a systematic exercise in suspicion, which seeks to uncover meaning behind meaning.

SURFACE AND DEEP SYMBOLS

Symbolism operates at different psychological levels. Some symbols, such as flags, words, and emblems, stand for particular ideas in a conscious and explicit way. These symbols are no mere signs, since they are capable of carrying powerful emotions and drive action, yet the majority of individuals would be able consistently to identify their meaning as well as the primary emotions they generate. In addition to this level of symbolism, there is an unconscious level, where meanings and emotions are less fixed and less predictable than those of conscious symbolism. The *Titanic*, for instance, may be the name of a ship that had a fatal collision with an iceberg; most people would be able to identify it as a feature of a tragic story in which many lives were unnecessarily lost. Yet, the *Titanic*'s lasting fascination suggests a deeper symbolism, one that possibly links it to the last days of an empire, to human weakness in the face of natural forces, to the fallibility of machinery, to the wilful negligence of capitalists, to the arrogance of size, and so forth. Likewise, words like 'Watergate', 'Dreyfus', or 'AIDS' resonate their unique symbolism among specific groups, acting as the focus for repressed or unacknowledged desires. This type of symbolism, argued Jones, 'arises as the result of intra-psychic conflict between the repressing tendencies and the repressed.' In this type of symbolism, 'only what is repressed is symbolized; only what is repressed needs to be symbolized' (Jones 1938: 158). Thus, deep symbols give an outlet to wishes that cannot directly be put into words, by evading social and psychological censors. The symbol provides a camouflaged expression to repressed ideas and desires or ideas and desires that are socially, politically, or ideologically unacceptable. These ideas and desires can be immoral, irrational, and contradictory, for the unconscious exercises neither moral nor rational controls over its content. In interpreting a symbol, one should not be surprised if one discovers a diversity of sometimes contradictory meanings.

---

[1] Our argument is similar to that of narrative theorist Livia Polanyi (1979), who has distinguished between culturally interesting, socially interesting and personally interesting stories.

STORIES, SYMBOLISM, AND CULTURE

Stories can carry both types of symbolism—surface and deep. Like moral tales or fables, some stories are essentially monosemic—their symbolism is transparent and inflexible; they offer no interpretive possibilities; within them meaning circulates in a single closed loop, much as in proverbs. Other stories, however, are capable of carrying deep symbolism, permitting much greater diversity and mobility of meanings. The narrator offers his or her poetic interpretations which the audience are invited to test, modify or even reject. The audience of such stories is active. By comparison, the audience of the moral tale, the fable, or the 'PR' or 'official organizational story' is passive; they need not search for hidden meanings, for the storyteller has made sure that all the meanings are explicit, uncontested and incontestable.[2] A powerful story has not only a diversity of meanings for different people but also numerous different meanings for the same person. While the central characters of most stories are psychologically simple, they can, nevertheless, elicit ambivalent and complex emotional responses from the audience. A single character, for instance, may elicit admiration, fear, *and* envy, while another may elicit both pity *and* contempt. Like all powerful deep symbols, some stories can fulfil a diversity of unconscious wishes, evade a multiplicity of mental censors, or result from different mental conflicts. In this sense, stories, like dreams, symptoms, and other symbolic phenomena are overdetermined, the result of multiple processes converging in the same direction. Analytic interpretations, therefore, must seek to establish more than a single link between a symbol and what it stands for.

In sum then, we approach stories as cultural elements entailing both types of symbolism, deep and surface. Symbols are not merely repositories of meaning; they are also attempts to conquer suffering. While there is wide agreement among scholars that organizational culture and its artefacts infuse people's action with meaning, sustain value systems, and allow for emotional discharge in shared rituals, our discussion suggests that behind these phenomena loom unsatisfied wishes and frustrated desires. 'Making sense' of our experience may involve not only interpreting events through a symbolic matrix, but offering wishful rationalizations and self-deceptions in an attempt to deal with psychic injuries. The study of organizational culture must, therefore, restore human suffering as a central point in

---

[2] The point is very well argued by Bettelheim in his distinction between fable and fairy tale. 'Often sanctimonious, sometimes amusing, the fable always explicitly states a moral truth; there is not hidden meaning, nothing is left to our imagination. The fairy tale, in contrast, leaves all decisions up to us, including whether we wish to make any at all. It is up to us whether we wish to make any application to our life from a fairy tale, or simply enjoy the fantastic events it tells about' (Bettelheim 1976: 42–3).

the discussion of storytelling. And the stories told in and about organizations must reflect the specific types of suffering associated with these rather recent and far from natural forms of human collectivity.

ORGANIZATIONAL SYMBOLISM

Is there something unique about organizations or are their discontents similar to those of culture as a whole? Do they make different demands on individuals from those of other cultural units? Certainly, when organizations themselves become topics of mass culture in TV shows and popular books, it is often as hotbeds of evil conspiracies or as objects of ridicule and derision. It is difficult not to laugh at bureaucracies. The inanity of their jargon, the unfathomable complexity of their regulations, the self-evident absurdity of many of their procedures, rules, and requirements, and, above all, their uncanny ability to make simple things complicated offer plenty of amusing material for comedies. In a classic and inadvertently funny example, Chester Barnard speculated that, if a telephone company president ordered two telephone poles to be transferred to the other side of the road, the order would involve about 10,000 decisions by 100 individuals in 15 places before being carried out (Barnard, 1938: 198).

What then is unique about the medley of discontents generated by organizations? What demands do they make on individuals? Does organizational culture address issues unique to organizations? Consider the following incident between a security guard and a departmental head arriving for an early start at the head office of a multinational corporation:

GUARD. *Good morning, Joyce. Your security pass please.*
JOYCE. *Sorry, I accidentally left it in my office yesterday.*
GUARD. *Sorry Joyce, can't let you in.*
JOYCE. *But you know me, I am the head of Sales . . .*
GUARD. *Sorry Joyce, a rule's a rule.*
JOYCE. *Can you phone and have someone send my pass?*
GUARD. *Sorry Joyce, you're first in this morning and I'm not expecting anyone for another hour.*

Where but in a modern organization could an incident like this take place? A visitor from a pre-organizational culture would find it more difficult to make sense of it than would Western anthropologists studying primitive cultures. What is more, neither Joyce nor the guard is likely to try and make sense of the incident. 'A rule is a rule.'

Organizations seek to control human behaviour in a unique way, through a multiplicity of highly specific and impersonal bureaucratic rules and regulations (Selznick 1943). Severe restrictions are placed on individuals' freedoms, restrictions that would be intolerable in a different context (Gouldner 1954). Their time is strictly regimented, their performance 'mathematically measured, each man becom[ing] a little cog in the machine' (Weber, cited in Mayer 1956: 126), their emotions virtually banned and their relations to their fellow human beings substantially stripped of spontaneity, affection, and passion. Their private joys, their sorrows, their worries, and their histories are effectively excluded. The objects that they use, the spaces in which they move, the products that they produce are generally not theirs. For a majority of organization members, meaninglessness and powerlessness are compounded by chronic insecurity—the sense that one's fate may be decided in distant boardrooms and offices, by people one has never met, whose preoccupations and priorities entail only a limited concern for one's well-being.

During in-depth interviews employees from five organizations were asked: 'Does your personality change when you come to work?' Here are some representative answers from staff in the head office of Joyce's multinational corporation:

Yes, I tend not to be so free and easy; at the moment, when I come to work I go on a switch off mode, I switch off the emotional side.   (Network controller)

Yes, without a doubt. At work there is a certain image to be kept up, hence the suits and the hair, everything must look alright; this environment is open plan, so you must keep the right image from every angle . . . I don't think that if I came to work in jeans I could do the work the way I do, I'd have a different sort of attitude . . . That's it, not so much the clothes as the state of mind. (Office skills trainer)

Me, of course not [Laughter]. Well yes, I suppose it must, you have to give this impression of calm even if inside you are boiling.   (Personnel officer)

My personality changes completely when I come to work. I am much less easy-going at work; my emotional responses to things are suppressed. I tend to be more level, less inclined to get heated about things.   (Computer operations manager)

If motivation theory has sought to fill the emotional and symbolic vacuum at the heart of bureaucratic organizations (Sievers 1986, 1994), this may signify that organizations function as the precise opposite of culture, as anti-cultures. Such an impoverishment of meaning-systems suggests that major events in the organization's history may hardly register on the symbolic Richter scale. Consider the following example. Some while ago, a fire devastated a section of the university where I teach. The fire happened in the early evening

95

and many students had to spend the night in makeshift accommodation. The next morning the extent of the damage was apparent. The shining surfaces of walls and ceilings had melted away to reveal an ugly mess of broken pipes, molten cabling, and blackened cement. A nasty smell of burnt plastic permeated the university. Nevertheless, essential services had been restored and, while some classes had to be re-roomed, the vast majority of students, administrators, lecturers, and support staff went about their normal businesses. Several times I tried to engage students and colleagues into conversation about the fire, but I hardly managed to raise a comment more substantive than 'It will all be paid up by the insurance.'

The fire was engulfed in narrative silence; no poetic trope could be discovered to attribute meaning to it. This may be read as a sign of people's symbolic and emotional detachment from the institution and also of the institution's inability to mobilize its symbolic resources to address the fire. There are numerous other ways in which this fire might have been symbolically charged as the subject of a collective fantasy, through the use of different poetic tropes. If participants loved the institution, they might have grieved for its violation (attribution of unity). If they hated it, they might have been inclined to celebrate the fire as divine justice (attribution of providential significance). If they felt ambivalent about the institution, they might have seen it as an omen or a warning (ditto). The story might have been used to scapegoat (Hirschhorn 1988) supposed saboteurs and terrorists (attribution of blame), such as anti-vivisectionist groups that might have started it (ditto). The fire might have been used to blame leaders (Kernberg 1980) as a sign of their negligence of anti-fire and other measures, or as a proof of the government's neglect of the universities (attribution of unity, attribution of causal connections). Alternatively, it might have served as the basis for praising the efficient way in which the university met the crisis (attribution of credit). Yet none of these things actually happened. In contrast to the Halon accident discussed in Chapter 2, this fire was not poetically reconstructed into any sort of narrative. It seemed to generate no emotion. The fire remained stubbornly a 'fact' and nothing more, because the organization lacked the cultural resources through which facts are turned into stories and symbols.

Some authors, like Wilkins and Ouchi (1983), have argued that bureaucracies have no culture. Unlike clans that rely on culture for the purposes of social control, bureaucracies rely on the mechanical application of rules and regulations that override morality and, to a substantial extent, rationality, as illustrated in the earlier example of the missing building pass. Far from being held together by emotional bonds, formal organizations, according to this view, are cemented by bureaucratic routines that generate neither loyalty nor commitment and involve neither idealization nor sublimation. Men and women perform their duties as functionaries through a compulsive repetition of standardized ritual behaviour, whose purpose and meaning are mostly unquestioned (Gabriel 1984). For example, the incident between Joyce and the guard may be symbolically hollow, virtually devoid of meaning; neither Joyce nor the guard would regard it as worth relating to anyone. If so, it can be seen as an instance in which a subordinate resorts to ritual behaviour as a defence against anxiety, typical perhaps of bureaucratic anti-culture (Baum 1987; Hirschhorn 1988; Menzies 1960).

'You will find no myths or folklore in this organization. It's all very hygienic around here, everybody's quite like that. It's very quiet, no chatting at all. Then again most of them are very busy, so they haven't got the time to chat,' said a secretary in the multinational chemical company, summing up an image of organizations as anti-cultures. This view echoes the modernist view, which sees stories and storytelling as having no place in contemporary societies, and certainly no place in that epitome of modernity, the bureaucratic organization.

Yet, as we have seen throughout this book, organizations are not devoid of cultural artefacts, jokes, stories, and symbols. In the organization in question, I collected many stories and incidents that had undergone considerable elaboration, some of them recounted independently by more than one respondent. Some of these were discussed in earlier chapters. There were customer stories, senior-management stories, computer stories, ghost stories, retired-staff stories, office romances, practical jokes, cock-up and disaster stories, to say nothing of the considerable folklore surrounding the company's retired chairman who had been a person with a large public profile. Under certain circumstances, Joyce's exchange with the security guard may itself have become charged with meaning, ending up as part of the organization's folklore and traded as 'a good story'. Humiliation of an authority figure always provides good story material for grudging subordinates; gatekeepers, like Cerberus, have always had their place in mythologies.

As noted earlier, the fire afflicting the university failed to generate stories. By contrast, however, a seemingly trifling event that occurred a little earlier generated substantial discussion. The acting head of one of the university's departments, a man who prided himself on his professionalism, was one not generally loved within his department. This individual presented an important paper on strategy, documented with a profusion of statistical data. The air of seriousness and ceremony with which this paper was presented at the meeting in question was broken when a lecturer pointed out that the figures in the paper's main table did not add up. What might have been a rather inconsequential observation was followed by an eruption of generalized mirth and amusement, not unlike that generated by banana skins and pies-in-the-face in silent movies. Subsequently, this incident was widely discussed in corridors, offices, and common rooms at the university, being embellished and ornamented with every repetition and eventually becoming part of what may be regarded as local folklore.

Unlike the fire, the incident of the recalcitrant statistics seemed to address a powerful wish shared by several organizational members—namely, the wish to see a pompous person humbled. This, as we saw in Chapter 3, is the trademark of the comic story, whereby the misfortunes of others confer superiority upon oneself. Poetic justice is amplified by the fact that the victim's nemesis comes precisely from what he prides himself on—in this case, professionalism, precision, and objectivity (attribution of blame: he deserved his humiliation; attribution of fixed qualities: not only is he pompous but he is also incompetent).

So far, our interpretation of this story limits itself to its surface symbolism, which would be apparent to anyone. Yet, in spite of its great simplicity, the story operates at a deep level as well. It feeds on the fact that the paper being presented by the acting head when the addition mistake was noted was a strategy document—the type of document that often generates feelings of anxiety, especially if administered *ex cathedra* with no consultation. When a fault is discovered in the document, the document is defused of its dangerous qualities; it becomes 'yet another' strategy document (attribution of fixed qualities: strategy documents are rubbish). The participants at this meeting had already been presented with strategy documents in previous meetings, each time being assured that 'this time it is for real'. It was possible that the document being solemnly presented at this meeting would meet exactly the same fate as its predecessors, in which case participants resented having to sit through what they regarded as a futile ritual. However, it is also possible that the document did generate some real anxiety. In the unconscious, the thoughts that 'the document = a possible threat to our interests/values/ways of doing things' and 'the document = another half-cooked idea of incompetent managers' can coexist, happily or unhappily. Thus, in addition to disparagement of an unloved person, the incident of the recalcitrant figures, poetically reconstructed as a story, may have come to stand for: 'Do not get terribly worried about managerial initiatives as presented in strategy documents.' The slip in the statistics helped symbolically to kill the document at birth. Different processes, therefore, converged to ensure that this incident found a niche in organizational folklore at the university.

The question of whether stories focus on typical or untypical incidents is one that has preoccupied many theorists. Labov and Waletzky (1967), for example, writing about personal narratives, argued that only incidents that are unusual, unexpected, or unique are capable of supplying story material; Van Dijk (1975) and numerous other authors have agreed that stories can succeed only if they emerge out of 'remarkable' events. Yet, our examples above do not automatically support this view, since the trifle of the errant statistics led to a story whereas the fire calamity did not. Robinson (1981: 63) has qualified this view by arguing that certain classes of stories emerge out of the mundane and the commonplace. He astutely points out three such classes; first, incidents that are presented as 'typical' of a type of event that happens to everybody; secondly, stories told within a relationship of great intimacy, where trifling events may offer opportunity for close discussion; and, thirdly, stories of victimization, where a single incident is held to be typical of what happens to members of a particular class, race, and so forth. The implication of Robinson's argument is that the commonplace becomes remarkable if placed within a particular 'frame', just as a photograph of a domestic item can frame it in a way that becomes uniquely illuminating.[3] Social constructionists would simply argue that the 'remarkable' is itself socially constructed within a symbolic relationship. What is remarkable in a public speech at a trade-union meeting is not what is remarkable in intimate conversation between lovers in bed. In a pioneering paper on organizational stories, Martin and her colleagues argued that all cultures (including organizational cultures) claim to be unique; stories are told that are meant to support an organization's claim to uniqueness. Yet, in doing so, stories rely on themes and incidents that are far from unique either in content or in structure. '*A culture's claim to uniqueness is expressed through cultural manifestations that are not in fact unique.* This is the uniqueness paradox' (Martin *et al.* 1983: 439). The use of the word paradox is entirely appropriate here, for what Martin and her colleagues go on to show is that in organizational stories the untypical is held to be typical and the typical is held to be untypical. This would accord with our two earlier examples. The fire may have been untypical but could not be constructed as typical, hence no story. The errant statistics, trifling though the mistake might have been, were instantly interpreted as typical of a person's incompetence leading to a story.

---

[3] This principle, 'discovered' by the dadaists, whose extraordinary potential was shown by Duchamps, is one that drives postmodern aesthetics, forever seeking to see the extraordinary in the ordinary. See Bourdieu (1984), Featherstone (1991), and Gabriel and Lang (1995).

Using our terminology, the fire remained stubbornly a fact because no story-work was applied to turn it into story—no interpretation could be found that would turn it into a symbol of something. By contrast, with a small amount of story-work, the errant statistics were transformed into a 'typical' example of the acting head's 'unique' incompetence.

From an interpretive point of view, this story of the errant statistics represents a modest challenge, its wish-fulfilling qualities being fairly transparent. As an attempt to reduce anxiety, it belongs to the same type of defence against anxiety as the instances studied by Jaques (1955), Menzies (1960), and writers working in psychodynamics (Baum 1987, 1989; Hirschhorn 1988, 1989; Hirschhorn and Gilmore 1989; Krantz 1989, 1990; Schwartz 1985, 1987b, 1990). Yet, as we saw in Chapter 2, some organizational folklore can prosper around stories that have a highly unsettling effect upon organization members, which generate anxiety instead of allaying it. It is to such a story that we shall now turn, using it as a window into the organizational culture of a military organization.

AN ILLUSTRATION: 'LOWER YOUR TROUSERS'

'In India nearly everybody spoke metaphorically except the English,' wrote Paul Scott (1973: 111), echoing the ancient observation that satire, allusion, and allegory, the raw material of so much culture, grow out of conditions of unfreedom and suffering. For this reason, it seems to me that few organizations could quite match the folklore found in total institutions. This is why I now turn to another example from the naval training camp described in Chapter 2.

The inspection prior to handing out furloughs to navy recruits is a particularly tense occasion, as the conscripts are raring to leave the barracks. But before they obtain their tickets of leave, recruits are inspected to ensure that their appearance will not disgrace the good name of the forces. This is one of the dangerous instances when the barrier between inside and outside (Goffman 1961) is crossed; this crossing takes the form of a ceremonial.

I observed numerous such occasions as a participant and the scene, like that of students before an examination, demonstrated all the familiar symptoms of the anxiety-affiliation syndrome. During the minutes before the inspection, the recruits nervously polish their hats or their shoes, and continuously tease each other. Rumours and stories—regarding the identity or the mood of the inspecting officer, his past history, and so on—travel with fantastic speed.

In many cases, the inspection amounted to little more than a formal ritual; at times, the officer would ask a recruit to straighten his hat or tidy up his appearance prior to handing out his furlough. Occasionally, a recruit's leave would be delayed by his having to shave again and on some occasions a number of recruits would fail the hair test and would be asked to have a haircut prior to leaving. On these occasions, lengthy and irritable queues would build up outside the barber shop. Finally, there were a very few occasions when recruits were denied leave altogether on some pretext or other—the cleanliness of their outfit, the length of their fingernails, or the expression of their faces.

It was on just such an occasion that I first heard a most interesting story. While waiting for the inspection, word circulated that a particularly feared officer had delegated the inspection to one of his deputies. This was greeted with a feeling of relief, as this officer had been known in the past to withhold leave on the most unusual pretexts. On one occasion, I was told, he had asked recruits to lower their trousers while standing to be inspected. He then proceeded to cancel everyone's leave. The motherland, he had explained, went to great trouble and incurred substantial cost in providing each recruit with three full sets of underwear as part of the military uniform. But, he observed, the recruits had seen fit to discard the regulation white boxer shorts stamped with their serial number, in favour of a motley assembly of briefs. This he regarded as a violation of the military code with disciplinary consequences. The recruits needed a reminder that a soldier was to be a soldier through and through—for instance, spending some more time in the barracks.

This story, which enjoyed wide circulation, possesses an amusing, almost theatrical quality. The image of the recruits standing to attention with their trousers around their ankles undoubtedly is a comic one. Yet, like 'Trial by Fire' (Chapter 2), in spite of the light-hearted way in which it was recounted, this story generated discomfort and anxiety, especially among new recruits. It is essentially a traumatic story that, on first appearance, has no redeeming features and shows little evidence of the wish-fulfilling character of consolation. If anything, the story accentuated anxiety and generated paranoia. It is easy to imagine the utter helplessness of the story's victims as they stand with their trousers down, and it is easy to sympathize with the new recruit's anxiety that a similar fate may befall him. He imagines himself standing there, trousers down, not knowing what will come next—will he be asked to lower his underpants as well? Is there some worse humiliation to come? For a second, he may feel relief that his ordeal is at an end; then, the shock that his leave has been cancelled for a most absurd reason.

Why then should such a disagreeable story become part of organizational folklore? Assuming that the trousers-down incident described actually occurred (and this is by no means certain), would it not make more sense for the recruits collectively to repress it and to pretend it never happened? Alternatively, could it not be seen as a tragic story built conventionally around undeserved misfortune? This may have occurred had the incident been one of routine bullying. Yet, the traumatic quality of this story is mitigated by its undeniable humorous aspects. This is what makes it a telling story, embeds it in the organizational culture, and (over many tellings and retellings) turns it into an item of organizational folklore. 'Si non e vero e ben trovato', goes the Italian saying. It is a good story, even if not true; even if rather unpleasant, we may add.

A good story

But why exactly does the trousers-down incident make a good story? What is the point it is trying to make? In the first place, it presents the good soldiers as victims of their officer's malice—a classic theme in virtually all military satire. Eventually, in such lore, the underdog turns the tables on the top dog. If this story was to be part of a theatrical script, the follow-up is self-evident: just as the officer (who predictably is fat) is about to cancel the recruits' leave, his own trousers split to reveal an even more colourful pair of underpants than those of the recruits! Such an embellishment of the original story could, under some conditions, become part of the narrative. At the stage I encountered this story, however, the underdogs did not turn the tables on their tormentor, at least not dramatically. Symbolically, however, the diversity of underpants by itself may be seen as proof that, underneath the uniform, each soldier is still an individual. His underpants are a symbol of selfhood, the part of himself that he did not surrender to the authorities in spite of all their attempts to eliminate individuality (attribution of fixed qualities: individuality).

The story now displays the seed of consolation. 'Don't worry, good soldier,' it says, 'the army's blinding uniformity is just for the show; underneath, each person retains a part that is uncompromised.' Certainly, the conscript has to pay a price for maintaining his individuality, but this is justified by the story's subversive effect: not only are the rules not rational (what possible reason can be found for requiring the recruits to wear uniform underpants?), but their administration is not consistent. Rules are to be bent and broken. They are part of a contested terrain. Operating in such a minefield, as we saw in Chapter 2, is dangerous. The crafty recruit may evade punishment on numerous occasions; equally, he may be punished when he thinks that he is operating safely within the bounds of the rules. 'Lower your trousers' reminds him that in this contested territory there are unpredictable dangers. The officers have ample ammunition, in the shape of dormant regulations, weird interpretations, and *ad hoc* enforcement to keep recruits in their place. The recruits, for their part, can profit from the very profusion and irrationality of rules, not all of which could possibly be enforced simultaneously. In my experience at the camp, trying to live by the rules and regulations was as futile as trying to make sense of them (attribution of fixed quality: organization is absurd). To go from A to B a recruit had to traverse C, which was officially designated a 'No Go' area. Alternatively he could go via D, but that took longer than the time he was allowed for getting from A to B. The result was that recruits routinely crossed C without punishment, until an officer decided to enforce that particular regulation. Similarly, to be ready for the morning's first assembly at 6.10, a recruit had to wake up, get dressed, and shaved long before the official reveille at 6.00. As a result, recruits would wake up and start getting ready long before the sounding of the bugle. I have distinct memories of shaving with cold water in virtual darkness, surrounded by shadows of other conscripts doing likewise. I can also recall the day when the officer in charge rounded up a random motley of recruits shaving before daybreak and cancelled their leave.

Anyone familiar with military outfits and procedures knows that misfortunes, such as having your leave delayed or cancelled, befall people more or less on a random basis—an officer intent on finding fault with the recruit's behaviour, appearance, or posture will have no difficulty in doing so. If the new recruits experience anxiety when confronted with a story like 'Lower your Trousers' or other alarmist stories, like 'Trial by Fire', the anxiety generates 'watchfulness' and serves a useful prophylactic function. 'Don't think that just because you keep your nose clean, you are safe,' the story seems to say. 'The dice are weighed against you; playing the game by the rules will not get you far.' The new recruit soon realizes that survival in such a total institution requires more than adherence to the rules, it requires cunning. Even then he must be prepared for disappointments and injustice. At the same time, the fact that the dice are unfairly weighed gives him the moral superiority of the victim and justifies the use of devious means to re-establish parity (attribution of blame and credit). I believe that many similar stories that proliferate in organizations in conditions of acute insecurity may serve similar psychological functions, lowering expectations, partially inoculating against suffering, giving the moral upper hand, and highlighting the critical import-ance of cunning against force.

In all these ways, the story can be seen as a perfect vehicle for socializing the new recruit—the perfect counterpart of the fairy tale in the development of the young child in Bettelheim's conception. The story reassures the new recruit that just as previous generations have endured and survived the hardships of camp life, so too will he. Moreover, the story gives in a highly condensed form as much in-formation about military life as virtually any manual could. In this respect, then, it functions exactly as a map of what lies ahead, as Wilkins (Wilkins 1983, 1984; Wilkins and Ouchi 1983) has aptly argued. The young recruit then goes psychologically prepared for the dan-gers and injustices. Yet, in addition to this prophylactic effect, the trousers-down story enables the recruit to laugh at the organization, whose claims to rationality or legitimacy are 'proven' to be paper thin.

I recall a particular scene that had a profound effect on me when contrasted to the strictures of the hero of our trousers story regarding the costs incurred by the motherland. The scene, imprinted in my mind without movement or action, entails a truck loaded with cab-bages, parked in a prominent point in the camp. Two conscripts are standing at the edge of the truck and slicing each cabbage into four segments, which they then proceed to throw into large garbage cans in front of them. This scene seems to me to epitomize the senseless waste and irrationality of the organization in question. But if the con-script's experience in such an organization (as portrayed in such mil-itary satire as *MASH* or *Catch-22*) can be summed up as mystifying absurdity, stories like 'Lower your Trousers' enable the recruit to make light of his bafflement and to laugh both at himself and at the organization.

Tricksters

Far from being invested with all the positive qualities of an 'organiza-tional ideal' (Schwartz 1987*a*), the image of organization that emerges from such stories is precisely the opposite, an 'organizational malig-nant', a caricature of undesirable or laughable attributes. In such cases, one derives satisfaction from deriding the organization and distancing oneself from anything tainted by it. The character who reveals that the tiger is made of paper is the trickster, an archetypal and much loved character of military satire, from the good soldier Schwejk to Yossarian (Kets de Vries 1990)—the soldier who continu-ously outsmarts the blind and corrupt forces that stand in his way.

Our trousers-down story, however, transposes the roles so that the trickster is the officer. This displacement does not contradict the earlier interpretation but, if anything, strengthens it, by over-determining the fantasy. As stated earlier, what makes the story a telling one is the fact that the officer is not merely a bully. If the officer had arbitrarily cancelled all leave, the event might have generated a very different type of story, possibly a tragic story, or no story at all. However, by constructing the bully as a prankster, the story transforms the officer from an object of raw fear into something quite different—possibly a mischievous child, or even an object of admiration and identification.

During my time in the naval camp, I heard numerous stories centring on tricksters. Among the enlisted men, tricksters violated the regulations, systematically avoided hard work, extricated themselves from apparently irretrievable situations using cunning against force, and played a number of more or less unpleasant pranks on their colleagues. Equally, however, certain officers (like the hero of the trousers-down story) were sources of rich folklore, frequently celebrated for their open disregard of military decorum or for their taste for naughty and often infantile pranks. The exploits of such individuals underwent continuous embellishment and elaboration.

What I found interesting is that, as recruits (including myself) turned from wide-eyed novices in need of socialization into seasoned veterans, stories like 'Lower your Trousers' increasingly lost their traumatic quality; the comic quality came to predominate. Instead of identifying with the story's victims, older recruits identified with the officer, thus obtaining a vicarious if malicious type of satisfaction by scaring the new recruits, not unlike older children who gleefully frighten their younger siblings with terrifying stories. This identification with the aggressor has been widely observed in such settings (A. Freud 1936; Kets de Vries and Miller 1984). The seasoned recruit symbolically switches sides—his narrative virtuosity in spinning a scary yarn directly echoes his hero's perversity in conceiving colourful ordeals for his victims. In virtually all of these ways, the polysemic qualities of this story parallel those of the 'Trial by Fire' story discussed in Chapter 2.

The trickster figure may not be quite as prominent in stories drawn from business or other organizations that lack the oppressive uniformity of total institutions. Nevertheless, it still featured prominently in many of the stories I collected in non-military organizations. Tricksters populate many of the world's great myths, stories, and folklore. Jung (1969: 144) viewed the trickster as 'a primitive "cosmic" being of *divine-animal* nature, on the one hand superior to man because of his super-human qualities, and on the other hand inferior to him because of his unreason and unconsciousness'. In a highly original article, Kets de Vries (1990: 758) has developed Jung's insight, viewing the trickster as 'a person with magical powers. He is both underdog and culture hero, a mirror to man, who provides order out of chaos by connecting the unexplainable to the familiar. He is a person with uncanny powers of insight and prophecy.'

In our view, if the figure of the trickster emerges as a protagonist in many modern organizations, this may be due less to its archetypal origin and more to its relevance to specific discontents and privations generated by such organizations. As humanity's champion against the blind forces of bureaucracy and technology, the trickster enables us to make light of these discontents. The trickster provides a narcissistic consolation for the many psychic injuries that we sustain (Hirschhorn 1988; Sievers 1994, 1998). It is certainly consoling to know that humanity will prevail against machines, that the world chess champion still has the measure of powerful computers, or that a trickster figure can cut through red tape with the aplomb of Alexander the Great cutting the Gordian knot.

It would be unreasonable to expect a single story to display all the variety and complexity of the artefacts that make up organizational culture. Clearly, few organizations display the extreme features of a total institution such as the military. However, 'Lower your Trousers' contains the germ of several features of organizational stories generally. First, it has an informative function, conveying to the new recruit something about the character of the organization, its rules, and its officials, and helping the recruit to 'learn the ropes' (Schein 1988). This resembles the 'epistemological function' (Campbell 1976). Secondly, the story warns the recruit of imminent dangers through the signal of anxiety (McDougall, 1908/1932); this prepares him for the worst and cushions the blow when the worst happens. Thirdly, it offers the recruit a narcissistic consolation, by reassuring him that he may be able to outwit the forces that oppose him and to maintain a part of himself intact. Fourthly, the story gives the recruit a moral superiority that justifies the use of deviousness on his part. Fifthly, it offers him a symbolic avenue for swapping camps and overcoming victimhood. Finally, the story enables the recruit to laugh at his tormentor, to laugh at the organization, and to triumph symbolically over the hardships that he is forced to endure. In doing so, the recruit may be deceiving himself (Schwartz 1985), for the organization and its officers usually have the last laugh, as the recruit may come to recognize. His illusion has a patently wish-fulfilling character and, as Demosthenes argued, 'where the wish is the father of the thought, the truth is often different' (*Olynthiac* 3. 20).

The sacrifice of the truth is both the secret and the price of the individual's symbolic triumph. To imagine that organizational symbolism banishes forever the bureaucratic iron cage would be mistaken. Stories like the ones presented in this chapter provide individuals and groups within organizations with a poetic space in which fantasy prevails over reality, where spontaneous, unplanned activity temporarily replaces regimentation, and where pleasure temporarily overshadows expedience.

Can interpretations of stories like the ones offered here be corroborated? Like works of art, some stories permit numerous different and even contradictory interpretations. How can we distinguish between valid and spurious interpretations? What corroborations may be offered to strengthen specific interpretations? Since the work of Barthes (1964/1972, 1973) and postmodernist theorists (e.g. Baudrillard 1983a,b; Bauman 1992; Fiske 1987, 1989), we have learned that we can read meanings not only in stories but in virtually any cultural artefact, from particular advertisements to blue jeans and from businessmen's grey suits to AIDS. Are all interpretations equally valid? I do not believe so. As Ginzburg (1980) has shown, interpretation lies at the heart of all semiotic processes in which one seeks to paint a general picture from individual signs or clues. While specific interpretations may not be proved or disproved by conventional criteria of logical consistence and factual verification, this does not mean that every interpretation is equally meaningful or valid. An interpretation may be original, clever, perceptive, incomplete, misleading, or even plain wrong.

Martin (1990) has offered a helpful codification for the deconstruction (her term for what amounts essentially to interpretation) of organizational stories. She has proposed nine specific techniques for opening up the text.

1. dismantling dichotomies, seeking to discover whether they are false distinctions;
2. examining silences or absences in the text;
3. examining disruptions or collapses in the text;
4. focusing on the most alien feature of the text;
5. interpreting metaphors;
6. analysing double ententes;
7. iterative substitution of key features of the discourse;
8. reconstructions—unexpected ramifications of small changes;
9. identifying the limitations of reconstruction.

Martin's techniques greatly facilitate interpretation, though I doubt that interpretation can ever be reduced to the application of uniform rules and procedures. As Ginzburg has noted, interpretation relies as much on 'rule-of-thumb', makeshift, and *ad hoc* inferences as on systematic generalizations. In the last resort, what makes interpretations convincing is their ability suddenly to shed light on what seemed opaque, to make sense of something that seemed senseless, to explain the unusual and unexpected. Yet, in all these respects, a clever but possibly false interpretation can seem more convincing than a dull but true one. In determining the validity of interpretations, it is important to differentiate once again between poetic and analytic interpretations. The former cannot be said to be 'false', no matter how self-contradictory, implausible, or ignorant of facts they are. Poetic interpretations aim not at truth but at effect—they either work or they fail to work. Analytic interpretations, on the other hand, aim at truth, at a deeper but ultimately testable and contestable level. Different interpretations can compete against each other, reinforce each other, or remain oblivious of each other. On the basis of the interpretations offered in this chapter I would argue briefly that there are four general corroborating techniques that may be used to enhance the robustness of specific interpretations.[4] First, the consistency between parts and whole. In a strong interpretation, the interpretation of parts is consistent with the interpretation of the whole, different signs or clues pointing in the same direction. A strong interpretation does not disregard signs that oppose it, but, on the contrary, seeks to incorporate them, account for them, or discredit them. Secondly, in strong interpretations specific outcomes are overdetermined—that is, not only do different signs point in the same direction, but different mechanisms can be established leading to the same outcome. These mechanisms can operate at different levels, such as narrative, psychological, or political, but they converge in a certain direction. Thirdly, strong interpretations, although not falsifiable on the grounds of individual signs or pieces of evidence, do, nevertheless, make clear what evidence would lead to their refutation. They are not content to defend themselves against straw men, but engage the most awkward adversaries. Thus, strong interpretations will generally address, account for, and supersede less strong ones.

It may be argued that the interpretations offered here, especially that of the trousers-down story, proceed from a negative portrayal of organizations—the organization presented as an oppressive force, devoid of legitimacy or value. The soldiers may have been stripped of their trousers, yet they can still believe that the emperor is not wearing any clothes. The organization, with all its powerful accoutrements, its bureaucracy, and its technology, is an 'absurd farce'. Like the emperor's new clothes, the symbols of the organization's power—the machines, the rules, the offices, the buildings, and the

---

[4] For a more extended discussion, see Gabriel (1999).

'official stories'—are all revealed as phoney. 'The organization is a madhouse,' stories of this genre are proclaiming; 'let's laugh at the absurdity of it all, instead of trying to make sense of it'. For his part, the emperor may tolerate such innocent pleasures; having a laugh at him may be permissible, so long as we continue to obey his orders, pay our taxes, and convey our respects. We may even forget that only a few minutes earlier we were reverently bowing in front of his imperial majesty. What the story enables us to do is overcome our resentment, our suffering, and our dependence. At the same time, the story has helped us to deceive ourselves: the emperor's new clothes may be phoney, but his power is not. It is to politics that we must now turn.

5

Stories, Culture, and Politics

Following Maxim Gorky, the Russian folklorist Vladimir Propp (1984: 14 ff.) argued that folklore is fundamentally the genre of the oppressed classes. Dominant social classes may spawn literature and art through which they express their concerns and sensitivities. For their part, oppressed classes, the peasantry and the proletariat, generate folklore. Folklore expresses protest and defiance. Folk songs and folk tales, ballads, stories, anecdotes, jokes, dances, and rituals are expressions of discontents against oppression, exploitation, and social injustice. In addition to oppressed classes, all victimized and vulnerable social groups, ethnic groups, races, minorities, and nations find their voices in folklore. These voices, collective, anonymous, and transient, sustain long-standing traditions and oppositional forms of consciousness that challenge and resist the culture of the dominant classes and groups. Folklore then is in a true sense a form of counter-culture and cannot by its very nature become institutionalized or domesticated into a hegemonic culture.

This Marxist view of folklore has been contested by Western folklorists, who have argued that any group, including accountants, bankers, surfers, and net-surfers, may have their own specific folklore. A clan or a family may have its particular folklore, as can a group sharing an office or a table. Folklore, according to this view, may express protest but does not have to. In fact, folklore is the shared legacy of any group that can be characterized as folk. Thus, Dundes (1980: 7) defines folk as

any group whatsoever who share at least one common factor. It does not matter what the linking factor is—it could be a common occupation or religion—but what is important is that a group formed for whatever reason will have some traditions which it calls its own . . . With this flexible definition of folk, a group could be as large as a nation or as small as a family.

A THEORY OF ORGANIZATIONAL STORYTELLING

Dundes argues (1980: 36) that different folk groups utilize different folklore genres, such as superstitions, proverbs, recipes, dances, etc.; many of these express not opposition, conscious or unconscious, but rather shared fantasies:

It is my contention that much of the meaning of folkloristic fantasy is unconscious. Indeed, it would have to be unconscious—in the Freudian sense—for folklore to function as it does. Among its functions, folklore provides a socially sanctioned outlet for the articulation of what cannot be articulated in the more usual, direct way. It is precisely in jokes, folktales, folksongs, proverbs, children's games, gestures, etc. that anxieties can be vented. If a person knew exactly what he was doing when he told a joke to his boss or to his spouse (or if the boss or spouse knew what he was doing), the joke would probably cease to be an escape mechanism. Man needs such mechanisms. That is why there will be folklore, and also incidentally why there is always new folklore being created to take care of new anxieties—I refer, for example, to the folklore of bureaucracy transmitted so effectively by the photocopier.

In contrast, then, to the Marxist view of folklore, Dundes's Freudian view does not regard political oppression as a precondition for folkloric creation. Folklore can express political opposition but may equally express a wide range of fantasies and their underlying emotions. Instead of being of necessity part of a counter-culture, folklore is a feature of overlapping subcultures that often take little notice of each other. Individuals are 'part-time folk', in Dundes's view, belonging to different folk groups in different spheres of their lives, and exchanging one folkloric discourse for another as they move in and out of social groupings.

In this chapter, we shall locate stories and storytelling within an organization's politics. We will show that both the Freudian and the Marxist positions can contribute to an understanding of storytelling as embedded in organizational politics but also organizational politics embedded in storytelling. I will propose that there is within every organization an uncolonized terrain, a terrain that is not and cannot be managed, in which people, both individually and in groups, can engage in all kinds of unsupervised, spontaneous activity. These activities occasionally engage with the practices of power, in unpredictable or indirect ways. I will refer to this terrain as the *unmanaged organization*, a kind of organizational dreamworld dominated by desires, anxieties, and emotions. The chief force in the unmanaged organization is *fantasy* and its landmarks include various folkloric elements, jokes, gossip, nicknames, graffiti, cartoons, and, above all, stories. All too often fantasy in organizations is seen as either a form of escapism reinforcing conformity or as a primal form of opposition leading to full-scale resistance. Both of these interpretations steer fantasy and its products back to a core control-resistance dialectic and the privileged domain of the managed organization. Instead, I will argue that fantasy can offer a third way to the individual and groups, which amounts to neither conformity nor rebellion, but to a symbolic refashioning of official organizational practices in the interest of pleasure, allowing a temporary supremacy of emotion over rationality and of uncontrol over control.

STORIES AND CONTROL

As narrative constructions, stories have been seen as part of a panoply of controls that have been at the centre of discussions of postmodernity and postmodern subjectivity. Following the work of Foucault, post-structuralist scholars have argued that various discursive practices in and out of the workplace have transformed today's people into self-policing subjects constitutionally unable to turn their despair into resistance, subjects who do not merely have a psychological, material, and social dependence on their organizations but who are actually derivative of them. Today's consumer no less than today's employee is controlled through a variety of unobtrusive surveillance techniques, spatial design, and above all, highly sophisticated, pervasive, and invasive uses of language. Classifications, badges, labels, assessments, tests, observations, appraisals, plans, programmes, recipes, measurements, lists, and leagues are among the wide-ranging discursive techniques through which the postmodern subject is constituted as a pliable, self-controlled, and self-disciplined subject, even as he or she imagines him or herself free to pursue careers, build fortunes, and achieve happiness through highly idiosyncratic consumption patterns. Stories are highly efficient methods of control—they indoctrinate without the subject being aware of being indoctrinated. In Chapter 2, 'Trial by Fire' was a typical example of a 'warning story' whose fierce if flawed logic ('*if* you break the rules, *then* untold of punishments follow') allowed no room for discussion or argument. At the other extreme, the stories of today's advertisements deceive not through brutal rhetoric but through the seduction of shining surfaces and initially resisting but ultimately yielding objects.

Long before the invasive controls of postmodernity came to prominence, the disciplinary potential of different types of stories was clear. Certain narratives, like the cautionary tale, the parable, and the fable, have an express purpose of imparting a moral lesson, generating fear and guilt in cultivating conscience. Stories of terrifying punishments that await those who lie, steal, or lust, those who sin in deed or in thought, were as effective at blunting rebellious tendencies as they were at turning forbidden pleasures into overwhelming temptations. Readers of Joyce's *Portrait of the Artist as a Young Man* get a good sense of the disciplinary force of the priest's story—at its worst, it is as terrifying as witnessing the most terrible physical punishment. Throughout the twentieth century another type of story has proved invaluable as a means of social control. This is the media story, whose use as a propaganda weapon has been recognized by every political regime, since tales of rapes of Belgian women by German soldiers fuelled British appetites for war in 1914. The media story can assume many forms but usually involves an exposé of an injustice or an outrage, which generates indignation, quelling opposition and diverting public attention from other possibly worse outrages nearer home. As we saw in Chapter 3, a different form of social control is exercised by jokes and comic stories that rely on chastising, drawing group boundaries, and offering a permissible expression to aggression. Fear of public ridicule, embarrassment, and exclusion act as powerful instruments of conformity and self-policing.

In addition to such rather evident uses of stories for social control, more subtle modes of control have been signalled by theorists of organization (Martin 1982; Martin and Powers 1983; Wilkins 1983, 1984; Wilkins and Ouchi 1983).[1] One of the most original illustrations of how deeply a story's disciplinary function can become lodged in the text is offered by Martin (1990), who sets off to deconstruct the text of a particular story told on national television by the Chief Executive Officer of a multinational. The story was offered as an example of the company's concern for the welfare of women employees with children:

We have a young woman who is extraordinarily important to the launching of a major new (product). We will be talking about it next Tuesday in its first world wide introduction. She has arranged to have her Caesarean yesterday in order to be prepared for this event, so you—We have insisted that she stay home and this is going to be televised in a closed circuit television, so we're having this done by TV for her, and she is staying home three months and we are finding ways of filling in to create this void for us because we think it's an important thing for her to do. (1990: 339)

Martin skilfully unpacks the text of this story, its lacunae, silences, slips, and non sequiturs to show 'how organizational efforts to "help women" have suppressed gender conflict and reified false dichotomies between public and private realms of endeavour, suggesting why it has proven so difficult to eradicate gender discrimina-

---

[1] For a good review, see Boyce (1996).

tion in organizations' (Martin 1990: 345). Martin displays how, behind the proclaimed company benevolence, lies a profusion of discursive devices. These are aimed at suppressing the conflict between individual and organization, constructing the difficulties faced by working mothers as personal problems for which the organization has no moral responsibility and, yet, at the same time displaying the company's benevolence for taking responsibility for decisions normally left to doctors and patients. Martin (1990: 346) summarizes her analysis thus:

Beneath the surface of the company's apparently benign concern with the employee's well-being are a series of silences, discomforts, and contradictions. These difficulties arise because the Caesarean operation exposes conflicts of interest between the organization (for example, to have the product released on time, to have the employee perform her job) and the individual employee (such as, to rest and let her incision heal). Although the president ostensibly was claiming wholistic concern for the employee's well-being, the text's disruptions reveal that concern is expressed, not as an end in itself, but rather as a means of maintaining some level of employee involvement and productivity during a leave. The primary beneficiary of this company's attempt to 'help' a working woman is the company, not the woman.

It is telling then that, through Martin's analysis, the very story that is meant to publicize the company's progressive qualities and concern for its employees is revealed to be quite the opposite—a disciplinary mechanism that ties even a woman who has recently undergone surgery and is nursing a newborn baby to the omnipotent eye of the company. The story is emblematic of the new postmodern controls that seek to discipline the employee from the inside, so that even at the moment of bringing a new being into the world she is not allowed to forget that she is a member of an organization. The controls embodied in the story can be appropriately described as totalizing, to denote their scope and intrusiveness: they aim for complete control of the employees, their hearts and minds (including their emotions and ways of thinking), as well as their bodies (the physical space that they occupy, their movements, appearance, and exposure); they seek to colonize individuals from within rather than from above or from the outside, making them incapable of conceiving of themselves outside the unique organization of which they are part. Any conflict between individual and organization or any other conflict within the organization is simply obliterated. The story then becomes one of the machines that tie the individual's uniqueness as an individual to the uniqueness (as expressed in power, beauty, glory, glamour, and even caring) of his or her organization.

In this argument, the individual remains in a permanently dependent and infantile state, bonded to the organization, which combines the omnibenevolence of the primal mother with the omnipresence and omnipotence of the primal father (see Gabriel 1999). It is not surprising, therefore, that the organization is endowed with all the qualities with which these primal figures were endowed during the child's early stages of dependency. All positive qualities, competence, excellence, and devotion to their members, are represented through stories, which emphasize their uniqueness. It is not then merely the deep and surface symbolism of stories, but the framing of some elements and the obfuscation of others, that turn them into powerful carriers of dominant organizational ideologies. Martin (1990: 340) again: 'In a text, dominant ideologies suppress conflicts of interest, denying the existence of points of view that could be disruptive of existing power relationships, and creating myths of harmony, unity and caring that conceal the opposite.'

How effective are stories as mechanisms of organizational control?

Martin's arguments present a formidable demonstration of the variety of ways in which a story seeks to reinforce organizational controls. Does this indicate that folklore, the domain in which stories become crystallized, becomes itself part of an organization's disciplinary apparatus? Hardly. It is unlikely that the Caesarean section story could become part of the organization's folklore, celebrating the company's caring and progressive qualities. *Poetically*, of course, this would be quite possible. 'What a wonderful, caring, progressive organization we have! And how well our CEO represents us in the media! Even when some smart interviewer tries to trip him over with a dumb question on the company's concern for family values, up comes the answer which puts him firmly in his place. Would the company drag a woman who has just had a Caesarean out of her home to launch a new product? Of course not? Would it launch the product on which she put so much hard work without her? Of course not. Through the miracles of modern technology (a trademark of our company) the company enables her to be at the launch without leaving her baby. Family and work in perfect harmony. There are no insoluble problems for us.' *Politically*, however, it is not. Stories do not waft smoothly in an unpolitical textual domain. Instead, as soon as they are uttered, they enter the contestable, unpredictable world of politics. Martin informs us that the CEO's story in the TV studio received three types of response, nods of approval, baffled expressions of puzzlement, and hisses of disapproval. She informs us that, had she been in the audience, she would have joined the hissers.

How surprising then that the hissing does not feature in her analysis, which, to use her preferred expression, silences the audience and gives undivided attention to the emperor. In an appendix, we learn that one of the hissers later said, 'Not only was it an outrageous statement, it was stupid. It didn't occur to him to ask, "Where are our values here?" . . . Didn't it occur to him that this kid deserves his [sic] own timing?' (Martin 1990: 358). This response indicates that the story held a rather different political message for at least part of the audience than the ones that Martin painstakingly extracts through her analysis. The hisser views it, not as a sophisticated discursive practice that reveals by concealing and deceives by silencing, but as the performance of a bigot and a fool. She will certainly not be fooled by the emperor's much trumpeted new clothes.

The story of the Caesarean section may be about to embark on one career, or many. The least likely career is one that turns it into a proud achievement; more likely is one that views it as a cynical attempt at manipulation in which the narrator gets hoisted by his own petard—for the CEO of a great multinational the text represents a fairly pathetic performance. More likely still is the telling of the story in a way that presents it as paradigmatic of the callousness of large companies in dealing with the private lives of their employees, especially women. Even a favourably disposed audience is unlikely to turn it into an epic and more likely to turn it into a tragic story— one in which the CEO is heckled by a bunch of feminist extremists having been set up by a perfidious anchor man. This analysis does not seek to devalue Martin's untangling of the story's condensed and coded disciplinary messages; it merely seeks to question the uncontested effectiveness of these messages. Who ultimately controls the story? The answer is nobody. Once told, the story becomes contestable. Attempts by the CEO to appropriate the story's meaning— for instance by explaining that he had not intended to offend anybody and that the woman employee was truly delighted to have the closed-circuit TV intrude into her house—may simply add fuel to the fire; few things are more ridiculous than seeing someone who has committed a *faux pas* seeking to retrieve the situation by digging him or herself deeper into a hole.

In their research, Martin and her colleagues (1983) found that there was another type of story—one that accentuates the negative rather than the positive in organizations:

Positive versions of the common stories portray the organization and its starring employees as uniquely good, a sanctuary in an otherwise difficult world. The negative versions also endow the organization with a special distinction. Rather than being the best of all possible organizations, however, it becomes the worst. (Martin *et al.* 1983: 452)

My own research revealed a very small minority of stories accentuating the positive. Uniquely good organizations did not feature extensively, unless as objects of nostalgia, in which case they were used to highlight the deficiencies of the present. Occasionally an organization featured as an object of affection in a story, notably if it had been falsely accused or taken advantage of. Poetically, such stories fell into the romantic mode, in which the organization as a whole stood symbolically for the ill-treated lover or the lover in need of support. Alternatively, in a few instances the organization or its senior executives stood as the delivering hero (as in the Caesarean example above), performing heroic deeds in the epic mode. However, the vast majority of stories treated the organization either in neutral or in negative terms.

Even when individuals were asked directly of incidents that made them feel proud (inviting them to respond with an epic story), the organization featured overwhelmingly either as a force to be overcome or as a neutral arena for individual heroics. Here is an epic–comic story, told by an executive of a company manufacturing printers which treats the organization in neutral terms:

We were carrying out a demonstration for a major contract which we were really hoping to win. One of the features of the test was dropping a printer to the floor from the height of a desk. The test did not require that the printer should be printing when it was dropped. The amusing thing is that the demonstrator started the printer and dropped it while it was actually in full swing. The printer continued printing without missing a single character. The firm were very impressed by this. 'We didn't require that the printer should be running when you dropped it,' they said. 'This is a standard test for our printers,' I replied, 'you should definitely require it from all the other printers competing for the contract. After all, when printers are dropped accidentally, you can't first switch them off, can you?' None of the other printers passed this test and IDK got the contract. The funny thing is that, although we tried this test again with different models of printer, none of our printers ever passed this test.

In such stories, the organization is not an important feature of the narrative, and we scarcely can tell the narrator's feelings towards it. We are in no doubt, however, about his feelings towards himself and his quickness of mind which gained the company a major contract.

The absence of stories in which the organization was treated in the idealized way noted by Martin et al. and other theorists especially in the 'excellence literature' was initially puzzling to me.[2] I had cer-

---

[2] Wilkins (1983: 87) reports that as many as 33% of the stories told by participants in the company he refers to as Z were 'used to illustrate or legitimate the management philosophy . . . These stories were concrete symbols of how management applied their philosophy.' This finding is at variance with my research in five organizations and

tainly not gone out seeking to elicit stories with a negative image of the organization, yet this is what most of my stories seemed to do. It is possible that my choice of organizations—an old manufacturing company, a publishing and research organization, a hospital, a public utility, and an academic organization—lacked the qualities of youthful enthusiasm and pioneering spirit that might have spawned some epic stories, featuring the organization as a ideal entity. It is possible that such epic stories might emerge in organizations or parts of organizations that take themselves rather seriously in the pursuit of their objectives and manage to imbue their members with the same seriousness. On closer look, it seems that every single story depicting the organization in idealized terms cited by Martin *et al.* (1983) is in fact drawn second-hand either from corporate literature or from authors setting out to tell the story of particular organizations, not from people telling stories directly in an organizational setting. My own findings are consistent with Watson's, who carried out a one-year ethnographic study of management at a British telecommunications company. He too discovered that stories portraying Ryland (the organization) in positive terms were almost exclusively those focusing on the past, which sought to paint the present in bleak terms. 'The bulk of Ryland tales were negative ones. Almost totally dominating the stories told to me, when I asked the managers I interviewed to pass on stories they thought were typical of the ones told on the site, were anecdotes, myths and jokes with Ted Meadows [CEO] as the villain or butt' (Watson 1994: 193).

Unlike the CEO's Caesarean-section story, which sought to silence conflict, the vast majority of stories I collected (like Watson's) highlighted conflict at every level—intrapersonal, interpersonal, departmental, gender, group, generational, and organizational. In fact, with the exception of some romantic stories, it hardly seems possible to imagine a worthwhile, telling story that does not entail conflict. Stress, tension, and conflict are essential in ensuring that a story crystallizes as part of organizational folklore, instead of being dismissed as a PR exercise or subverted into a different story. Most people seem to maintain a healthy suspicion of rose-coloured narratives and, certainly, organizations in the larger culture are not treated with unalloyed trust as conflict-free zones with the welfare of individual employees foremost in their priorities.

I have increasingly come to view stories that become part of folklore as treating the organization either in neutral or in negative terms. Undoubtedly many individuals in different organizations

some 404 stories. A tiny minority of stories in each organization express management philosophy and the overwhelming majority are either neutral or oppositional. For details, see Chapter 6.

harbour some warm positive feelings towards them and undoubtedly many cultures find means of expressing these feelings. Schwartz (1987*a*, 1990) and many others have argued strongly that some individuals forge their own identities out of idealized images of their employing organizations, whose prestige and power become sources of personal prestige and power. However, it seems to me that storytelling is not the major cultural means for doing so. Communal rituals, choreographed festivals, vast and luxurious offices, official organizational brochures, advertisements, and so forth may celebrate the positive. Stories, on the other hand, to the extent that they find a poetic place for the organization itself, treat it fundamentally in neutral or negative terms.[3] They grow overwhelmingly out of misfortune and adversity and, in their different poetic modes, seek to make light of it. Far from celebrating organizational achievements and successes, they tend either to celebrate and laugh at the negative (cock-ups, failures, and reversals) or to bewail the tragic (traumata and injustices).

STORIES, COUNTER-CULTURE, AND RESISTANCE

While individual stories may represent attempts to proselytize, to neutralize, and to bolster organizational controls, stories can also represent resistance. Not only can they celebrate acts of resistance, but the very telling of a story can be an act of resistance, challenging, dodging, or subverting management power. This is most obviously the case with comic stories and jokes. In a classic essay, Mary Douglas (1975: 98) has argued that, 'whatever the joke, however remote its subject, the telling of it is potentially subversive. Since its form consists of a victorious tilting of uncontrol against control, it is an image of the levelling of hierarchy, the triumph of intimacy over formality, of unofficial values over fixed ones.' In a similar way, Zijderveld (1983) has observed that 'freedom is the prerogative of humour'. Gregor Benton (1988: 33) has analysed the political joke and found that 'the politically powerless use it as a tribunal through which to pass judgements on society where other ways of doing so are closed to them'. It is not accidental then that jokes become part of a counter-culture in political dictatorships. 'Every joke is a tiny revolution,' wrote George Orwell in 'Funny, but not Vulgar'; 'you

---

[3] It is interesting that even prefatory comments that announce a story, such as 'Guess what happened to me', treat the events as happening to the protagonist rather than being initiated by him or her. This contrasts to the more neutral 'Once upon a time . . .' preamble of folkloric narrations.

cannot be memorably funny without at some point raising topics which the rich, the powerful and the complacent would prefer to see left alone.' Joking subverts taboo subjects and exposes an organization to criticism; above all, joking undermines the sanctity and legitimacy of authority. It does not necessarily rebel against authority, but it certainly casts authority as something conditional and precarious.

Joking subcultures have been examined in street societies (Liebow 1981; Whyte 1943), among football supporters (Robins 1984), medical professionals (Coser 1959, 1960; Goffman 1961), professional thieves (Steffensmeier 1986), college basketball players (Golenbock 1989), police officers (Holdaway 1988), dustmen (Perry 1978), high steel ironworkers (Haas 1977), and many other occupational groups. Some of these accounts approach joking predominantly as a safety valve or even as a mechanism of incorporation and control; some, however, have analysed it predominantly as an attempt to subvert conventional values and generate resistance. One of the most vivid of such analyses has been offered by Willis (1979) in his study of a working-class English school. Willis focused his study on a group of 'lads' who represented a highly vocal counter-culture. The most important feature of this counter-culture was a generalized opposition to all authority.[4] Willis goes beyond most other authors who have studied joking and horseplay in establishing that it does not merely generate solidarity but it represents an attempt to wrest moral, political, and even spatial control from the school authority, above all an attempt to defeat the institution's main perceived purpose, to make them 'work' (1979: 26). Thus the joking counter-culture is no mere symbolic resistance, but actually represents a refusal to act in the ways prescribed by the organization. In a similar way, Linstead (1985, 1988) has observed how joking and horseplay represent an attempt by workers to colonize space (canteen, toilets) and time (breaks), seeking to establish pockets outside management control. Like Willis, he locates joking within a nonconformist, highly masculine counter-culture, which celebrates manual work and the strength of the physical body and disparages middle-class values that are seen as effeminate, soft, career oriented, and weak. These authors recall Propp's view that folklore is the genre of the oppressed, the genre through which the oppressed can express their opposition and defiance, venting their discontents and resistance.

---

[4] The major way in which opposition to everything is expressed is by 'having a laff', through constant teasing, joking, testing, and talking (Willis 1979: 29). Interestingly, Willis's fine ethnographic account of school counter-culture includes few stories, although it includes numerous other folkloric elements, especially jokes, pranks, nicknames, insults, swearing, proverbs, and opinions.

One author who has criticized this approach is Collinson (1988, 1994), who has argued that it tends to romanticize joking subcultures and to disregard their self-defeating and self-destructive qualities; ultimately such subcultures tend to reinforce the oppression of subordinate groups. Willis's 'lads', for instance, for all their proud machismo, defiant swearing, and celebration of working-class values and freedom, are merely preparing themselves for dead-end manual jobs and a life of severely restricted freedom. Through detailed interviews with manual workers in a heavy vehicle factory in north-west England, Collinson argued that the joking subculture (1) built collective solidarity and defeated boredom, (2) exercised heavy pressure on individuals to conform to working-class norms of macho-masculinity, swearing, and being dismissive of women, and (3) exercised considerable control on behalf of the company, ensuring that potential shirkers 'pulled their weight' in production. Collinson is impatient with theorists who seem intent on celebrating every gesture of recalcitrance or bravado as representing resistance, no matter how self-defeating it may be in reality. Collinson's argument that token symbolic resistance (which he terms 'resistance through distance') must not be confused for 'real material' resistance ('resistance through persistence') has been rehearsed by various authors. Benton (1988: 44), for example, who has linked the political joke to political oppression, is categorical that

political jokes are revolutions only metaphorically. They are moral victories not material ones . . . The political joke is not a form of resistance. Revolutionaries and freedom-fighters are engaged in a serious and even deadly business, and are reluctant to make light of the enemy or fritter away hate through laughter. To permit jokes against the state is therefore a clever insurance against more serious challenges to the system.

In contrast then to writers such as Douglas, Linstead, and Willis, Collinson and Benton favour the view that joking acts as a safety valve, which in the long run reinforces the official controls. The temporary reign of anarchy under the regime of joking is as short-lived as the laughter it generates.[5]

But, if a joking subculture can be seen essentially as defusing potential conflict by offering an acceptable outlet for discontent, so too can a 'griping subculture', whether the griping is jocular or not. In her study of patient jocular griping at a hospital, Coser (1959: 180)

---

[5] The conservative function of the joke as a reassuring mechanism for the containment of anxiety is similar to that served by the child's attachment to transitional objects, such as dolls and pieces of cloth (Winnicott 1964, 1980). By contrast, the anarchic and potentially transforming quality of jokes is captured by Bakhtin's (1929/1973: 88) concept of the carnival: 'The carnival attitude possesses an indestructible vivacity and the mighty, life-giving power to transform.'

argues that it 'performs integrative functions for the social structure of the ward', by offering a 'safety valve, i.e. it provides institutionalized outlets for hostilities and for discontent ordinarily suppressed by the group'. A similar conclusion is reached by Bate and Mangham in their study of a chemical plant, where moaning and complaining went on non-stop as part of what they refer to as the 'futility script' (Bate and Mangham 1981: 85). Whether proud and defiant or cynical and withdrawing, subcultures and their associated folklores can be seen as escapist consolations that ultimately reinforce organizational controls. However, the view that a subculture must be seen *either* as escapism reinforcing social controls *or* as subversion and resistance may be a false dichotomy. Resistance and conformity are all too frequently presented as opposites, as indeed they can be. But this is not always the case. As Fineman and Gabriel (1996: 87) have argued,

people may be rebelling even as they appear to be conforming. Pupils who wear the regulation uniform may be conforming to the rules, but by leaving the top shirt button undone, they express their resistance to them. Compliance and resistance are not either/or responses. Orders may be obeyed willingly or unwillingly; they may equally be obeyed grudgingly, inaccurately, ritualistically or sarcastically. In all of these cases, compliance and resistance can coexist in the same form of behaviour.

Rebellion rarely assumes the form of total and irrevocable revolution; nor does compliance regularly involve the total paralysis of critical faculties and questioning spirit. Even when token or ritualistic, resistance establishes the limits of control and reminds those in power that they may not take consent for granted. Control is, therefore, constantly tested through various tactics of resistance, which may range from the purely symbolic to the material. A simple 'No' can sometimes represent a successful challenge to authority, as in the following example told by a clerical supervisor.

If you are a supervisor, you can tell who is not doing anything, just by wandering around. The question is whether you do anything about it. I mean most people go for an easy life, why push themselves. [Do you feel like that?] No, because I have to push myself at the moment because I have an awful lot to do. But if I'm honest, I do, when Pam [the manager] is away, and I'm in charge, I think, 'Thank God for that, I can have the day off!' I mean it's a completely different atmosphere when she's not there, we all get involved, we all get the job done and go home. But I have an attitude where people want to do things for me, rather than because I am their supervisor. I enjoy making a team, I don't like saying, 'Do this, do that'. This, in fact, was what I said to someone when I was younger and they said 'No' and I thought 'Now, what am I suppose to say?' and this did teach me something. I mean alright, you can say, 'I'll go to personnel', but all that creates an even worse atmosphere. Who wants to come to this kind of work every day?

The story described here is the essence of all political resistance. A superior asks a subordinate to do something, and the subordinate says 'No'. The superior then realizes that his or her power is being contested and that an attempt to enforce his or her command raises the stakes and threatens a humiliating retreat. Sometimes a small 'No' can lead to a bigger 'No' on a subsequent occasion. At other times a 'Yes' may in reality amount to a 'No', signifying a token compliance, a poorly executed job, and the start of a subsequent bout of control and resistance.[6]

Thus compliance and resistance need not always be mutually exclusive.[7] By evading various social and organizational controls, stories, jokes, and anecdotes sustain a critical and subversive commentary against dominant values, especially when these values are underpinned by authoritarian, rigid regimes. By themselves, such phenomena may not threaten a regime or an organization, but they do establish the legitimacy of criticism. They also act as a reminder to those in authority that conformity cannot be taken for granted, that commands, rules, and regulations are contestable if not constantly contested. What they achieve, in other words, is to puncture the impression that the organization is an 'uncontested terrain', a unitary, family-like, harmonious entity like those that are promulgated by corporate culture.[8] The very telling of a story or joke can be a political gesture, since it brings conflict, opposition, and legitimacy back within the discourse. One of my undergraduate students was struck by the number of posters bearing the slogan 'Making friends is our business' at his internment in a financial institution. He asked his manager about them, and instead of an answer he was shown a cartoon of a rugby scrum, surrounded by dust, from a flurry of blows. Most of the blows were directed at teammates. His manager grinned meaningfully and said 'The management!' The joke expressed in a telling way what the manager may have felt inhibited to express in words; yet, it instantly drew the wide-eyed student into a little conspiracy of understanding that all was not what it looked. Such a conspiracy is unlikely to bring down the organization's management; it does, however, create a space within which different conversations can be had, different experiences can be acknowledged, and different desires can be recognized from those allowed in the spaces of the

---

[6] Different forms of material and symbolic resistance have been explored by contributors to a volume edited by Jermier *et al.* (1994), who have studied oppositional strategies including sabotage, whistle-blowing, ritualism, bloody-mindedness, legal recourse, pilfering, output restriction, counter-ideologies, and refusal of discretion.

[7] Schein (1988) refers to the middle path between conformity and rebellion as 'creative individualism'.

[8] See e.g. Burawoy (1979, 1985), Edwards (1979), Gabriel and Lang (1995), Sturdy (1992, 1998), Thompson (1990), and Willmott (1990, 1993).

controlling, managed organization. It establishes the fact that 'even' managers can joke with their subordinates about the organization.

THE UNMANAGED ORGANIZATION

In his study of contemporary consumption, Michel de Certeau (1984) has used the metaphor of colonial domination to transcend the opposition between resistance and control. De Certeau has likened contemporary consumers to native Americans responding to Spanish colonization; while appearing to capitulate to the colonizers' rule and acquiesce to their religious and political practices, indigenous peoples 'subverted them not by rejecting or altering them, but by using them with respect to ends and references foreign to the system they had no choice but to accept' (de Certeau 1984: p. xiii). In a similar way, consumers are often seen using products and places in unorthodox ways, replacing the stories of script-writers and advertisers with their own stories, reasserting that, even in the area of consumption, management and control are problematic. De Certeau refers to the unmanaged terrains of consumption as 'spaces'. Stories are identified by de Certeau as the instrument through which 'places', organized, planned, and policed by 'clamorous production', are reclaimed, at least temporarily, and converted into spaces. Places, argues de Certeau, are determined by objects and laws that are simply there. Spaces, on the other hand, are specified by the actions of historical subjects, temporal, ephemeral, full of meaning, emotions, and ambiguity (de Certeau 1984: 117–18).[9]

Unmanaged spaces do not exist only in shopping malls, streets, and houses; in fact, unmanaged spaces need not be physical spaces at all. My argument is that such spaces exist also in organizations, spaces where all kinds of organizational controls (including ideological, administrative, spatial, and technical) are evaded, dodged, or sidestepped, spaces in which desires and fantasies take precedence over rationality and efficiency. Within these spaces, all types of spontaneous uncontrolled activities happen, which may involve clever

---

[9] See also Fiske (1989), and Hetherington (1992). The idea of unmanaged organization is one that I have drawn from two unrelated works by friends of mine. Born (1979) has offered a powerful portrait of unmanaged spaces within which lepers living inside, outside, or at the margins of institutions reclaimed vestiges of their dignity and pride; Gott (in press), in his massive survey of over 200 years of opposition, rebellion, and recalcitrance against the British Empire, has documented very well the diverse tactics of opposition across the globe, the continuous attempt to create unmanaged territories by the colonized, as well as the methodical and unflinching determination of colonizers to eliminate such territories.

ruses, privately coded texts, noise, silence, the unorthodox uses of established objects, and so forth. Just as the native Americans developed skills of communicating with each other in ways that were either invisible to the disciplinary gaze or meaningless, so too members of organizations learn to talk in code. Their narratives and stories may appear incomprehensible as stories or frustratingly opaque. Whispers, nods, smiles, secrets, gossip, subterfuge, occasionally stories, jokes, and laughter mark these spaces as at least temporarily unpoliced. Of course, such spaces may soon be brought back under control, through incursions and raids, new commands, new rules, and new regulations. They may then be replaced by different ones. At times, this cat and mouse game turns into guerrilla warfare or rebellion, where tactical strikes and retreats are undertaken; victories and defeats are short-lived. At other times, engagement with the practices of power takes place through the medium of fantasy. Fantasy offers to individuals and groups a third way, one that amounts to neither conformity nor rebellion, but a symbolic refashioning of official organizational practices in the interest of pleasure, allowing a temporary supremacy of uncontrol over control and spontaneous emotion over the organization's emotional scripts. While such spaces may be marginal much of the time, they are not unimportant as spaces where identities are fashioned, tested, and transformed. In these terrains a critical commentary on the symbols of the colonizers is maintained, chinks in their armour are discovered, and alternative, less docile, more recalcitrant identities can be fashioned. These are the spaces to which I refer as the unmanaged organization (see Gabriel, 1991*a*, 1993, 1995; Gabriel and Lang 1995).

The colonizers, for their part, are ambivalent about these unmanaged terrains, living both in ignorance and in fear of them. Some rulers may flatter themselves to believe that their rule is absolute. Leaders may enjoy thinking that peace and prosperity reign in their territory, that their followers are full of love and loyalty, and that all enemies and threats are external. In organizations, such leaders are likely to believe their own rhetoric of the organization as one big happy family, without secrets, conflicts, or contradictions. As Kets de Vries (1990: 755) has argued, leaders are liable to the hubris of believing their rule to be both ever-popular and absolute, the hubris being a 'predictable off-shoot of unbridled narcissism'. The role of the 'fool' in royal courts was that of an antidote to this hubris. 'The fool becomes the person who through various means reminds the leader of the transience of power. He becomes the guardian of reality and, in a paradoxical way, prevents the pursuit of foolish action' (Kets de Vries 1990: 757). The court fool, as Kets de Vries recognizes, represents a pocket of anarchy, irrationality, and disorder in the leader's most private domain. 'Thus, the fool, using humor, can do the unthinkable, trespassing on otherwise forbidden territory and satirizing leaders and followers. Through his actions, he provides a vicarious outlet for the most basic antisocial feelings' (Kets de Vries 1990: 760). The fool represents the unmanageable within the leader's own court and, in doing so, he must play a delicate and dangerous game. If blindness to the unmanageable is the narcissistic ruler's hubris, the paranoid ruler imagines himself surrounded by traitors and conspirators, constantly threatened to be overwhelmed by the unmanageable, in the form of rebellious crews, deceitful and disputatious subordinates, vast criminal underworlds and seething underclasses. Such rulers need no fools in their courts, relying instead on elaborate networks of spies, henchmen, and thugs to maintain control, as illustrated by Kapuscinski's (1983) brilliant portrait of the Ethiopian court. They have no delusions of ever being loved or ever converting their subjects into law-abiding and loyal citizens. Instead, they rely on bribes, raids, deception, terror, division, exclusion, and banishment to maintain their overall control.

The unmanaged terrains in organizations should not be thought of as synonymous with the informal or unofficial organization. For the greatest part, these are part of the managed organization, patrolled and policed in more or less subtle ways. Nor should all fantasies, individual or shared, be thought of as part of the unmanaged organization—such a view would fly in the face of the massive resources devoted to the creation and propagation of *corporate fantasies* for both internal and external consumption. Disneyland, the culture and heritage industries, public relations and advertising firms, a substantial part of the mass media, as well as companies' own PR departments and consultants, all those individuals and agencies that Sievers (1986: 347) labels 'merchandisers of meaning' are busily engaged at devising fantasies for consumption by customers or members of organizations. These find expressions that range from official stories, like those mentioned earlier, to escapist television programmes and advertising slogans as well as whole arrays of cultural artefacts. While many of these fantasies belong firmly to the realm of the managed organization as tools in the management of culture and meaning, they too can be subverted, altered, or embroidered in ways that draw them into the domain of the unmanaged organization. This unmanaged organization is composed of spaces that can transmute from the political to the psychological, from the social to the narrative, and from the physical to the electronic.

Because of their plastic nature, stories make perfect inhabitants for the unmanaged organization. They slip furtively in and out of sight, they evade censors, they are easily camouflaged, and they can rapidly join forces with each other to provide mutual reinforcement and support. They are notoriously difficult to suppress, since the result of doing so is to add to their currency and appeal. Managers have been known to comment that 'It's easier to slay a dragon than to kill a myth' (Berg 1985: 292; Ingersoll and Adams 1986: 365). Additionally, stories often cross the boundary between unmanaged and managed organization in different guises. The stories about the man inventing adhesive tape in his spare time, or the loyal employee who discharges his or her mission against all odds, may be adopted as parts of official organizational discourse. These may crystallize into organizational myths, which may then generate pride, cynical derision, or indifference among different groups of people. These, in turn, may reappear in the unmanaged organization with a new twist, such as that the erstwhile hero was subsequently fired or fell foul of management. Other narratives may cross the boundary in a different manner, not as potential supports for organizational practices but as open, visible challenges to such practices. Victimized employees who dispute management decisions (Collinson 1994), morally outraged individuals who become whistle-blowers (Rothschild and Miethe 1994) and criticize their organization in public (Jackall 1988), or individuals who have the fortitude directly to confront their superiors (like Gill, in Chapter 2) intervene in the control-resistance domain of their organization and risk bringing its organized power upon themselves by their stories. Their narratives are no longer treated as stories, but they become claims, allegations, 'lies', and 'facts'.

Stories continuously test and redraw the boundaries between the managed and the unmanaged. In telling a story, one is busily making assumptions about what can properly be discussed under the circumstances, the audiences' likes and dislikes, their interests, the meanings they are likely to read into different images, their tastes, their sense of humour, and so on. While, in analysing stories, one concentrates on the text, stories rarely emerge out of people's heads already fully shaped. The telling of stories requires minuscule judgements depending on how the narrative is being received and engagements with questions, suggestions, and hints from listeners (as in the cases above when the interviewees were being prompted by the interviewer). It is sometimes aborted altogether, killed when hardly born, when one of the listeners or even the teller him or herself quickly steers the narrative back to verifiable facts or to official stories, the precincts of the managed organization. At times, the mere presence of a certain person or a particular look may be enough to put an end to a venture in the unmanaged terrain. Alternatively a story started by one individual may be finished by another, or different variants may be discussed and compared. Stories in the unmanaged organization are far more plastic than their counterparts embedded in official 'mythologies', and frequently tend to mutate into other stories and merge with them. The unmanaged organization can then be seen as a kind of organizational dreamworld, where fantasy obtains a precarious advantage over reality and pleasure over work.

Identity and the unmanaged organization

As we saw earlier, one of the distinguishing features of postmodern discussions of organizational controls is the view that they do not constrain or limit a pre-given subject, but rather that they are responsible for a unique constitution of the subject. Various writers have examined different ways in which management practices such as job interviews, performance appraisals, career advice, corporate culture packages, job titles, and so forth do not merely affect individuals' identities but are the places where subjectivity is forged (Barker 1993; Clegg 1981; Collinson 1982, 1994; Jermier 1998; Knights 1990; Knights and Morgan 1991; Knights and Vurdubakis 1994; Marsden 1993; Sturdy 1998; Townley 1993; Willmott 1990).

The argument developed in this chapter suggests that subjectivity at the workplace must also be examined outside participation in or rejection of control practices, in a different set of constructions. It would be wrong to see the managed organization, with its practices of power, its strategies, its tactics, and its mass-produced fantasies, as the exclusive source of the sets of meanings and identities of people, whether as members of organizations or as consumers of their output. The unmanaged spaces of the organization do not generally directly challenge organizational controls, but allow individuals and groups through their stories and other narratives to affirm themselves as independent agents, heroes, survivors, victims, and objects of love rather than identifying with the scripts that organizations put in their mouths. They also allow them to cast others into different roles, such as heroes, villains, fools, tricksters, and so forth. Whether constituting the subject as hero, as survivor, as victim, or as object of love, stories treat organizational realities, not as parcels of information, but as poetic material, capable of being infused with meaning. Events are moulded according to wishes and desires, evading organizational controls, giving vent to fantasies in which the pleasure principle prevails over the requirements of veracity and accuracy. In this way, organizational storytelling allows people to try out and develop identities for themselves that are not available through official organizational practices and discourses.

This does not invalidate the much-debated Foucauldian link between control and subjectivity (Clegg 1990; Foucault 1980; Knights 1990; Knights and Morgan 1991; Knights and Vurdubakis 1994; Willmott 1990), nor does it imply a sovereign subjectivity that can take off in its Quixotic adventures with no regard for power practices of organizations. Imagining oneself in the role of rebel or victim or trickster does not automatically dissolve other identity determinations. It does, however, highlight how fantasy and dreaming can supplement fictions of self created by management and control.[10]

Contemporary identities are fragmented, tentative, experimental, and ever-changing. They are cobbled together in numerous fields—homes, offices, shopping malls, in front of television sets, factories, hotels, universities, and so forth—distilled from numerous narratives, featuring different truths, half-truths, and wishful fantasies. A bewildering variety of objects, images, practices, and symbols can come in and out of focus as individuals pursue their projects of identity: clothes, myths, communities and peer groups, tattoos, body piercing, relics from the personal and family past, role models, relationships and friendships, and above all stories and other narratives can be transiently incorporated into self-identities to be discarded later in favour of other ingredients. The workplace may not be as fecund a source of stories and narratives as other fields; in the view of many postmodern theorists, it is increasingly less important as the sphere where identities are fashioned as compared, say, to consumption (Bauman 1988, 1992). Compared to a time when a career or a job fixed an individual's identity virtually for life, identities at the end of the twentieth century are for the most part discontinuous, fragmented, full of tensions and ambiguities (Baumeister 1986; Brown 1997; Carr 1998; Du Gay 1996; Erikson 1968; Gabriel and Lang 1995; Giddens 1991; Lasch 1984; Warde 1994). The stories through which individuals seek to make sense of their daily experiences in organizations add tensions and discontinuities to these precarious identities. Accidents and mistakes, bold deeds and cowardly duplicity, insults and injustices, successes and failures, fortune and misfortune—these are not things that simply happen to pre-given characters, like those that feature in folk tales; instead, they are poetic constructions through which contemporary identities emerge, develop, and

---

[10] Identity involves numerous conscious and unconscious elements. An individual's identity grows out of idealized images drawn from role-models and symbolically important objects; these mostly unconscious images make up an individual's 'ego-ideal', against which each individual compares his or her ego. The ways in which individuals cast themselves in the stories that they tell are very revealing about the content of their ego-ideal.

change, identities that make it possible for people to live with their frustrations and passions.

In locating stories within an organization's political universe, we set off with two highly compelling but contrasting ideas of the relationship between folklore and politics: the idea that folklore is the genre of the oppressed classes in channelling their discontent and their defiance, and the idea that folklore is an expression of shared unconscious fantasies of any group, dominant or subordinate, that constitutes a folk. We examined different ways in which stories become embedded in an order's disciplinary apparatus, either by occluding conflict and celebrating an organization freed of tensions and contradictions or by acting as a warning for those who transgress against the order's norms. We argued that purely disciplinary stories are unlikely to become embedded uncontested in an organization's folklore unless they simultaneously fulfil deeper psychological needs. More generally, we noted the paucity of stories spontaneously extolling the organization in organizational folklore. Official stories, stories without conflict, contradiction, or criticism, can be seen as glossy images and slick clichés that invite defacement and subversion. We then examined different ways in which a subculture rich in joking or griping folklore can express opposition. For the most part, such folklores may not directly challenge the organization and its values and may act as safety valves for the containment and defusion of discontents. Yet, by allowing for a poetic refashioning of reality that expresses deeper emotions and desires, they generate spaces within organizations that are sheltered from direct controls and from mainstream values of rationality, subordination, efficiency and work, an unmanaged organization. Within these spaces, individuals and groups discover new ways of experiencing their organizations, which amount neither to rebellion nor to conformity, and which allow them to fashion identities that are more complex than those deriving from official organizational practices.

II

WORKING WITH STORIES

6

Using Stories in Organizational Research

Stories are emotionally and symbolically charged narratives. They do not present information or facts about 'events', but they enrich, enhance, and infuse facts with meaning. This is both their strength and their potential weakness. Stories will often compromise accuracy in the interest of poetic effect, itself an expression of deeper fantasies, wishes, and desires. They may focus on the incidental details, remaining stubbornly silent about what a researcher may regard as vital clues; they may contain inconsistencies, imprecisions, lacunae, non sequiturs, illogicalities, and ambiguities. Ultimately, as was seen in Part One, the truth of a story lies not in its accuracy but in its meaning—and paradoxically the inaccuracy, the distortion, or even the lie in a story can offer a path towards the deeper truth it contains, at an individual or collective level.

Part Two examines the use of stories in organizational research. This chapter introduces some general issues of methodology, explaining how stories may be generated, analysed, and classified. As an illustration, one particular piece of field research is presented, the source of most stories in this book. Each of the subsequent chapters examines one particular aspect of organizational life through the medium of stories—the folklore surrounding computers and information technology, an organization's past, leader–follower relations, and insults. Throughout this part, we shall argue that researchers who want to use stories as a research instrument must be prepared to sacrifice at least temporarily some of the core values of their craft and adopt instead a rather alien attitude towards their subjects and their texts. They must rid themselves of the assumption that quality data must be objective, reliable, accurate, etc. and must be prepared to engage personally with the emotions and the meanings that reside in the text. Faced with distortions and ambiguities, researchers must resist the temptation of 'setting the record straight'; instead, they must learn to relish the text, seeking to establish the narrative needs, and through them the psychological and organizational needs, that distortions, ambiguities, and inaccuracies serve. At the same time, researchers must not lose sight of the relation between stories and facts: facts are not dissolved by stories but re-created through them. We shall argue that this approach represents not merely a valid and useful way of doing research, but can also be highly engaging and enjoyable.

STORIES—HOW TO GET THEM

As was seen in Part One, stories may be used to pursue different research agendas. They can be used to study an organization's culture and politics, the psychological wishes and needs of its members, the nature of its surface and deep symbolism, the effectiveness of its structure, and the pervasiveness of its values. They can also be used to study the process of storytelling itself, at a dramaturgical, morphological, poetic, narrative, or psychological level. The overall purpose of a study will dictate the precise methodology used, the type and range of stories sought, and the ways the stories are analysed. Yet, any research making use of stories must first address itself to the question of where and how to find them.

'How do I get stories?' is a question frequently asked by researchers keen to experiment in their use, but unsure on how to start. In finding stories, researchers must be aware that they are furtive, fragile, and delicate creatures. They can easily be driven away, they can emerge without being noticed, they can rigidify into descriptions or reports, and they can be killed. The researcher's demeanour, attentiveness, and reactions play a decisive role in the generation of stories. Any display of a judgemental or critical orientation is likely to discourage storytelling. A researcher perceived by his or her respondents as a cold figure of scientific authority or as a forensic investigator interested in facts is unlikely to elicit many stories. The stance advocated here is that of a *fellow-traveller* on the narrative, someone keen to engage with it emotionally, displaying interest, empathy, and pleasure in the storytelling process. The researcher does not risk alienating the storyteller by seeming to doubt the narrative or by placing him or her under cross-examination, but conspires to detach the narrative from the narrowness of the discourse of facts, guiding it instead in the direction of free association, reverie, and fantasy. Contradictions and ambiguities in the narrative are accepted with no embarrassment. While the researcher may ask for clarification of particular aspects of the story, the story-teller must feel that such clarification is asked in the interest of increased understanding, pleasure, and empathy rather than in the form of pedantic enquiry. The metaphor of the researcher as fellow-traveller on the storyteller's narrative suggests an inquisitive quality that combines passivity with activity. Like a traveller, the researcher is subject to the narrative's momentum, never seeking to control it or derail it, yet constantly and attentively engaged with it, encouraging it, sometimes nudging it forward, sometimes slowing it down. Like a traveller, the researcher must be prepared for disappointments, for long hours of waiting, and for dead ends. At times, the researcher can be afflicted by doubt and anxiety—is he or she still *on* the narrative, still following the story, missing important clues? This must be accepted as part of the price one pays for doing this type of research, one that is amply compensated for by the narrative delights one unexpectedly encounters. At other times, the researcher discovers that he or she is no free-rider, but is expected to reciprocate the storyteller's favour, either by offering a story of his or her own or in some other way.

Within this general approach, researchers are still presented with numerous choices. One of the first decisions is whether to elicit the stories by asking appropriate questions and explaining the point of the research or whether to collect them as and when they occur. Eliciting stories generates larger amounts of field material, the stories 'framed' for the benefit of the researcher. Different accounts of the same story may be compared, as can the story profiles of different organizations in a relatively economical manner. The researcher knows when to switch the tape recorder on and off and may easily transcribe and process the material later at his or her leisure. This approach is favoured by many of the systematic researchers into stories. The main disadvantage of eliciting stories is that the researcher risks imposing his or her definitions of what is important, meaningful, or enjoyable. The stories are not encountered in their natural state—that is, as part of organizational talk—but are pre-sented and performed for the benefit of an outsider. They are part of the dyadic research relationship rather than of organizational dis-course proper. Nevertheless, in as much as certain stories become embedded in an organization's culture or subcultures, they may be re-created for the benefit of the researcher in a very telling manner, as though they were significant artefacts or heritage figures, unchanged by the circumstances of their presentation.

In carrying out this type of research, the management of the dyadic research relationship is vital. Respondents must have a clear understanding of what the researcher is seeking, what uses will be made of their material, what undertakings (of confidentiality, of sharing and respecting the material, and so on) are offered. Researchers may explain to their respondents that they are studying one particular feature of their organization through the medium of stories, or may (after the manner of journalists) explain that they are seeking to give 'a voice' to those whose stories are inadequately heard, understood, or appreciated. In my own research, I found that people rarely had a difficulty in understanding why a researcher is interested in stories (rather, say, than in answers to questionnaires, accounting figures, or, generally, other 'information'). As with other types of research, research involving stories requires a degree of trust. The researcher must put him or herself in the position of the respondent as storyteller and appreciate the latter's vulnerability— will his or her story be believed, will it be understood, will it be respected, will it be appreciated, will it be twisted or misrepresented, will it be misreported or reported to the wrong people? These are causes of genuine inhibition and tension and can be overcome only through sincere and unpatronizing explanations.

Researchers may elicit stories by asking questions such as:

- Can you recall any incident that was widely discussed among yourself and your colleagues?
- Can you recall an incident that made you laugh/concerned/sad/proud/angry, etc.?
- Are there any special characters in this organization? Any stories about them?
- Are there any special days or functions?
- Are there any special stories about the organization's leaders/founders?
- Are there any parts of buildings or other locations you associate with specific incidents?
- Can you think of an incident that sums up to you what it means to be part of this organization?
- Can you think of an incident that sums up the stresses and strains of your job?
- Can you think of an incident that you discussed outside the workplace, with your partner or your friends?

It will be noted that many of these questions may generate factual answers rather than stories. Undoubtedly there are some individuals who, at least in the early parts of an interview, stick to the facts, either because of defensiveness or for other reasons. Skilful researchers can sometimes overcome such inhibitions, steering the conversation in the direction of story and fantasy, with questions like:

- What exactly did this incident mean to *you*?
- Did anyone read the situation differently?
- How did you feel at the time? How do you feel about these events now?
- What did the incident show about the way this organization treats its members?
- What would you have done if you were in the position of that person?
- What is the moral of this story?

Collecting stories *in situ*

The alternative to eliciting stories is collecting stories when and as they occur as part of a broader ethnographic approach; this is more time- and money-consuming. It has been used with notable success for studying humour (Collinson 1988; Coser 1959, 1960) and is especially important if the emphasis lies in approaching stories as performance rather than merely as text. Boje (1991), whose work was extensively discussed in Part One, observed that, in their 'natural' organizational settings, stories are fragmented, terse, discontinuous, polysemic, and multi-authored—most renditions omit large amounts of information that is taken for granted. Observers who are not familiar with such taken-for-granted information may miss the point or the catch or may not be aware that a story is actually being performed at all. This is similar to the situation depicted in the joke about an outsider who overhears a conversation of friends in a train compartment. Each time one of the company shouts a number, the rest burst out in lively laughter. Eventually the outsider asks what the fun is all about and is told that each number corresponds to a previously agreed joke—the number evokes the joke, which generates laughter. The outsider shouts a number, but generates no laughter. On enquiring why, he is told, 'You didn't tell it right.'

The researcher who pursues storytelling as part of a broader ethnographic project, without specifically seeking to elicit stories, may be charged with pursuing research agendas hidden from his or her subjects. Besides ethical questions, this raises both practical and methodological questions. Does the researcher use a tape recorder? This risks intimidating or unnerving potential storytellers. The presence of a tape recorder may seriously inhibit organizational participants from telling tales that may not be factually backed up or that may compromise them with colleagues, subordinates, and superiors. If no tape recorder is used, the researcher must rely on either handwritten notes or recollection. Written notes have a less disturbing effect than tape recorders but nevertheless slow down the story-telling and undermine the naturalness of the setting. It is often not possible to keep written notes if a story is told in a bar or a corridor. Recollection is not regarded as a very reliable method of recording research data. For the purposes of some types of research, recollection would be virtually useless. In the case of stories, however, recollection is quite a legitimate method, especially if stories can be committed to paper, tape, or electronic medium shortly after they were heard. Some stories may be remembered years after the researcher first heard them (Mangham 1995) and occasionally their meaning becomes clearer after the researcher has assumed a certain distance from the subjects (see Chapters 2 and 4). Like myths, some stories may be timeless and able to cross organizational and linguistic frontiers with modest distortions (Lévi-Strauss 1963*b*, 1958/1976, 1978). In spite of all these justifications, however, there is no denying that stories recorded, interpreted, and analysed from recollection will bear the marks of the researcher's own conscious and unconscious elaboration and embellishment. Facets of the story that resonate with the researcher's own desires, interests, and research agendas are likely to be highlighted. Other features, which the researcher finds uninteresting, incidental, or distasteful, may be omitted or reduced.

The unit of analysis

While collecting stories, researchers must reflect on the fundamental unit of analysis of their research. This may be the individual story, the individual storyteller, specific incidents in an organization's history (e.g. an accident or a crisis), specific story themes (for example, the breaking of rules or meeting the organization's top leader), or particular types of story. Alternatively, a particular organization may be the unit of analysis either as a space where stories happen (how many stories, what types of stories, and so on) or as the topic of stories (for example, what kind of stories are told *about* IBM or McDonald's).

As with many types of qualitative research, the unit of analysis of story-based research tends to be frequently redefined in the course of the research; yet it cannot be disregarded altogether. If the unit of analysis is the individual, the research must focus equally on individuals who are good raconteurs and those who are not; by contrast, if the unit of analysis is the individual story, the researcher will spend more time with those individuals who will supply many stories. If the researcher wishes to explore a specific incident, he or she will seek to elicit accounts of the incident by both direct and indirect means.

The role of the researcher and the practicalities of research

Granted that researchers become fellow-travellers on the narratives that they encounter rather than collectors of facts, they must still decide how much of the researcher's role they are going to project. Will they prompt their respondents with questions on areas that interest them? Will they seek clarification when they do not understand something? Will they invite the tellers to give their interpretations of the meaning of their narrative? Will they offer alternative interpretations? Will they ask questions regarding the feelings that the narratives evoke? The more interventionist researchers risk undermining the spontaneity of the storytelling, yet when they come to analyse their material they can speak with greater confidence and authority about the tellers' own sensemaking processes.

Should the researchers reciprocate by joining in the storytelling? This may increase the reciprocity of the research relation and may further encourage the respondent in his or her storytelling. The risks of this approach are numerous. The researcher's own stories may fall flat with the respondent, trivialize the research activity, or generate a particular type of counter-narrative on the part of the respondent. The stories may then become specific to the research dyad and lose all organizational referent. So, the same respondent may tell anti-management stories to a researcher who appears interested in them and anti-union stories to a different researcher. This may or may not be a serious drawback, depending on the research agenda being pursued.

A further set of questions that researchers must address concerns the locale, timing, and context of the research. Such research can take place during working hours in a separate room, at a company restaurant over coffee or lunch, or after working hours. There are advantages and disadvantages to different arrangements, which must be weighed in the light of the specific concerns and agendas of the research at hand and the researchers' own needs and aptitudes. What researchers investigating stories must bear in mind, however, is that what matters is the quality rather than the amount of material that they collect. In the excitement of fieldwork, it is easy to fetishize quantity, seeking at all costs to fit in an extra interview or an extra session. Such efforts are usually counterproductive—tired, over-stretched researchers, overloaded with information, lack precisely the qualities of attentiveness, patience, empathy, sensitivity, and, at times, frivolity that are necessary for this type of work.

Access

The use of organizational stories as a research instrument is fairly time-consuming and researchers interested in this type of field research make considerable demands on the hosting organizations and on individual respondents. In my experience, few organizations are likely to provide access to researchers who are interested simply in exploring organizational stories. While those with the power of granting access may see the point of *using* stories to analyse some vital organizational issue, such as the management of change, stress, departmental rivalry, and so on, they would not generally see much benefit in a researcher interested in collecting and analysing stories. In gaining access, therefore, researchers are faced with the issue of 'framing' their research agenda in ways likely to interest organizations. This is both a difficulty and a challenge. Researchers must resist the temptation of couching their research agendas in rhetorical forms acceptable to managers or using subtle deception and subterfuge in collecting their material. In gaining access, I believe that two strategies are viable: first, to hitch this research onto another piece of research that is of greater interest to the organization and, secondly, to make research on organizational stories relevant to the interests or the requirements of the organization where access is requested. These strategies treat stories both as the vehicle of the research and as a topic of the research itself.

AN APPLICATION EXAMPLE

I shall now offer an illustration by outlining the results of a six-month field study, entitled 'An Exploration of Organizational Culture through the Study of Stories',[1] my first systematic field research on the subject and the source of most of the stories in this book.

Initially, I approached some organizations in which I had carried out research earlier and asked for permission to study organizational storytelling; their responses ranged from indifference and hostility to mild interest. It was suggested to me by a colleague willing to introduce me to a company that access would be facilitated if I focused on stories dealing with something of practical interest, such as computers and information technology. The idea of collecting stories about computers (and machines in general) quite appealed to me;

---

[1] This fieldwork was undertaken in 1992, with the aid of a grant from the Economic and Social Research Council (R 000232 627).

machines (especially mechanical breakdowns and magical devices) have always played important parts in stories, and as a relatively unthreatening topic of discussion they could provide a useful opening area of investigation before possibly exploring stories of a potentially more threatening nature.

Letters were sent out to ten organizations requesting access and five of them responded positively. They represented a broad spectrum of organizations, including one of Britain's largest manufacturing companies, a research and publishing company, two district headquarters of a privatized utility, a hospital, and a consultancy unit attached to a university. Eventually, 126 individuals were interviewed by myself and one associate,[2] as shown in Table 6.1. Four additional *ad hoc* interviews were conducted with computer analysts to obtain a sense of the type of stories favoured by computer experts. These yielded a further twenty-seven stories. In all 404 stories were transcribed and entered into a database.

Table 6.1. Programme of field research

Organization	Interviews	Number of stories collected[a]
Manufacturing company	24	138
Research and publishing company	24	48
Privatized utility	47	112
Hospital	25	60
Consultancy unit	6	19
TOTAL	126	377

[a]Numbers include narratives that were later classified as proto-stories and reports.

The interviews

The interviews were loosely structured, seeking to evoke stories the respondents had heard recently or memories of critical events, which were then presented as stories. Initially the interviews explored information technology and especially computers as a feature of organizational stories. The findings suggested that these generate their own unique brand of folklore. Later other types of story were explored.

The respondents were given an explanation of the research purpose (which included an explanation of the idea that through stories we often express our deeper feelings), and were asked a small number of questions:

[2] The associate was David Robins, a distinguished criminologist and urban ethnographer.

- Do you see computers as your friends or as your enemies at the workplace?
- Can you recall an incident that was widely discussed among yourself and your colleagues?
- Are there any other incidents, not necessarily involving computers, that were widely discussed?
- Can you recall an incident that made you laugh/concerned/sad/proud/angry etc.?
- Can you recall any practical jokes?

Respondents were also asked to try and describe their organization in terms of one of a list of metaphors (which included family, madhouse, well-oiled or creaky machine, castle under siege, conveyor belt, dinosaur, football team, etc.) and then asked to think of a critical incident that supported their preferred metaphor. The list of metaphors had been piloted with a group of undergraduate students returning from internships, and provided a light-hearted topic of conversation, frequently leading to stories. Initially the respondents were not prompted to recall specific incidents; however, in certain organizations where particular incidents or individuals were widely discussed, later respondents were asked on occasion if they had any recollections of them.

Most interviews lasted between forty-five and seventy-five minutes. All but a handful of interviews were recorded. During the interviews, brief handwritten notes were kept to facilitate later transcriptions and analysis.

Processing

The interviews were then transcribed from tapes, yielding 404 organizational stories. The stories were analysed with the help of a special version of a computer database package, Cardbox-Plus.[3] Each story was entered on a separate record and the following information was recorded on a distinct field on the record:

- serial number;
- author;
- organization;
- type of story;
- theme (a one-line summary of the events described);
- the full text of the story;

[3] Cardbox-Plus (Version 4) is supplied by Business Simulations Limited, 30 St James's Street, London SW1A 1HB.

- the emotions described in the story and the emotion generated by the delivery;
- the moral of the story (if any);
- the main characters;
- keywords;
- a subjective assessment of the story's quality.

The software permits the selection of stories sharing specific qualities, or having particular words in common. For example, it instantly retrieves all stories that involve a disparaging comment about one's supervisor, or all comic stories involving computers or animals.

FINDINGS

Density of folklore

The number and quality of stories drawn from different organizations varied enormously. For example, twenty-four interviews at the manufacturing firm yielded 138 stories, whereas the same number of interviews at the research and publishing organization yielded a mere forty-eight. This variation is not a product of the methodology but reflects, at least in part, the vitality and strength of folklore in different organizations. This appears to be linked to the length of service of those interviewed in their organization and the wider culture of the organization itself. The research and publishing organization had an ethos of factual precision and accountability that seemed to inhibit the making of unsubstantiated claims and the spinning of elaborate stories. The median length of service of those interviewed was less than two years. By contrast, the manufacturing company had many older participants who had known and worked with each other for a number of years; their median length of service was five years, with ten having been with the company for more than fifteen years.

Types of stories

The classification of stories into different types was the hardest part of the processing. Some stories instantly fell into a well-established type, such as comic or epic, or were hybrids of two or more types (e.g. comic–tragic); yet several were not easily classifiable in spite of several iterations. Several things gradually became clear. First, that the same 'events' may feed different types of story. Secondly, that certain narratives described events purely as facts, devoid of emotional or symbolic content. These were often responses to the question regarding the most significant event an individual had witnessed during his or her service with an organization. After trying different alternative labels, these narratives were eventually classified as 'reports' or 'descriptions'. Thirty-eight such narratives were found among the 404. A third classification issue arose in connection with those terse narratives that had a very thin plot. As has already been mentioned, these were eventually classified as 'proto-stories'. There were 119 proto-stories among the 404 narratives in the database.

After several iterations, the main types of story were identified; these were substantially the types analysed in detail in Chapter 3. In brief, these included four main types, as follows:

- *Comic stories* had emotional qualities that encompassed amusement and mirth but also disparagement. The majority of these stories had a critical quality—that is, they were at the expense of an individual or group of individuals, for instance, experts disparaging non-experts or vice versa. Specific groups in different organizations were targeted for special types of disparaging comic stories—for example, lawyers at the manufacturing company or central management at the utility. Comic stories also included jokes and humorous stories, characterized by their higher and finer qualities noted earlier (see Chapter 3).
- *Epic stories* focused on struggle, achievement, and victory. Their chief emotional qualities were admiration, approval and especially pride. About one-quarter of epic stories had comic qualities as well.
- *Tragic stories* focused on undeserved misfortune and generated the classic mixture of fear and pity for the victim. These were variously mixed with bitterness, horror, guilt, and anxiety.
- *Romantic stories* expressed gratitude, appreciation, and love. Many of these stories involved gifts and acts of unsolicited kindness and marked the triumph of love and humanity over all other forces. Some romantic stories involved love affairs and office romances, without turning romantic attachments into occasions for disparagement or ridicule. These were subclassified as *romances*.

In addition to the above primary types and their combinations, some stories were classified into three additional derivative types:

- *Gripes* were less sorrowful than tragic stories and usually focused on personal injustices and injuries experienced. A few of them had a jocular quality. They were generally associated with feelings of self-pity, disapproval, sadness, and resentment.

- *Traumas* involved much deeper psychic injuries than gripes and were associated with feelings of anger, outrage, and despair. In many cases, these stories were so powerful that they coloured the storyteller's total emotional outlook towards his or her organization. In effect, these were tragic stories in which the narrator was the protagonist/victim, and their numbers may legitimately be added to the tragic stories.
- *Practical jokes* are accounts of events that were organized and conceived as such. They generally generated amusement, although they often expressed hostility or disparagement. Because of the nature of the research, twelve of the twenty-three practical jokes involved tampering with other people's computers. While all of these were comic stories, some contained epic or tragic elements (see Chapter 3).

This classification proved quite effective; eventually only five stories remained unclassified, calling for different categories, such as morality tales, horror stories, ironic tales, etc. The numbers of stories in the different categories are shown in Table 6.2.

Table 6.2. Types of organizational stories collected

Type	Total number	Total number excluding proto-stories
Comic	146	125
Epic	82	59
Tragic	53	42
Romantic	32	21
Gripes	40	25
Traumas	22	19
Practical jokes	23	23
Reports/descriptions	38	32

Note: Sums exceed the total number in each category as several stories were hybrids of more than one types (e.g. both epic and comic) and were double counted.

The distribution of story types varied in the five organizations surveyed. Clearly, the methodology of the research was not geared towards establishing the 'story profile' of each organization, as conditions had not been standardized. This comparison of the story profiles of different organizations suggests an interesting line of investigation for future research.

Thematic distribution of stories

In each organization, a small number of events generated a large number of stories; for instance, the imbroglio over the introduction of a new information system, the disturbance during a Christmas party, an office romance leading to marriage, the death of a colleague, and a practical joke involving a horse were recounted by more than three interviewees in each case, with a minimum of prompting. Comparison of the different accounts reveal wide variations in matters of fact, substance, and meaning. If one were to try and reconstruct 'what actually happened' from these accounts it would be very difficult. The retired chief executive officer of the manufacturing company, a man of considerable public profile, had generated many stories within the company. With little prompting eleven such stories were collected, several of which presented him as a 'hero' or at least as a leader admired by his 'troops'. Favourite themes of stories (not including proto-stories) were as shown in Table 6.3.

Table 6.3. Favourite themes of collected stories

Theme	Number
Computers (prompted)	90
Leaders	30
Senior managers	28
Personal traumas or emotional injuries	32
Accidents	30
Special characters in the organization	26
Crises	23
Practical jokes (prompted)	23
Cock-ups	21
Nostalgia	14
Sex and love	17
Sackings and redundancies	14
Death	10

Raconteurs

The narrative ability of different individuals differed greatly, as did their willingness to share a story with a stranger. There were some respondents who displayed great facility in spinning a good yarn on almost any topic without any prompting; some failed to bring to life vivid scenes that they had experienced and that obviously had meant much to them; some reported events in a highly factual, 'objective' way, quite unwilling to sacrifice accuracy for effect; finally, there were some who simply offered opinions and were unwilling or unable to link them to any type of narrative. Characteristically, one respondent provided fourteen high-quality stories (with virtually no prompting), while several others provided no stories at all, in spite of considerable prompting.

Most of those who related several stories seemed to have one or two preferred types of stories—for example, jocular gripes, personal traumas, cynical jokes, romance—that accorded with their personality and their experience at work. I repeatedly felt that each respondent's stories appeared to have a sense of continuity or coherence, converging on various points of plot or characterization.

Narrative complexity and emotional richness

Very few of the stories collected combine the emotional, symbolic, and narrative complexities and wide dissemination to be comparable with folk tales and fairy stories. Only twelve of the 404 stories exceeded 300 words when transcribed and only thirty had more than three distinct characters or groups of characters. Yet, the emotions generated and communicated by these stories were quite powerful, and go some way towards reinforcing the view of organizations as emotional arenas (Fineman 1993). In fact, the stories provide a fascinating window onto a wide range of emotions that one might not normally associate with organizations.

It is not possible to analyse and bring to light every emotional nuance present in a story—the same story may evoke different emotions in different listeners, and the narrator may have ambiguous or confused feelings about his or her material. The emotional content of a story comprises the emotions recollected by the narrator, the emotions that the story seeks to communicate to the listener, the emotions that the listener experiences while hearing the story, and the emotions that he or she later feels on recollecting it. Thus, a comic story that generates mirth and amusement for the teller may be based on events that generated horror and panic at the time, and may be received by the listener with disgust. The complications resulting from any attempt to classify stories solely in terms of their emotional content are, therefore, formidable. Nevertheless, a preliminary exploration of the emotional tone of the stories in my database identified as the most frequent emotions amusement (resident in 114 stories), disparagement (82), pride (70), disapproval (57), relief (20), anger (19), pity (19), reproach (17), sadness (17), satisfaction (15), affection (14), approval (14), frustration (14), nostalgia (14), derision (13), worry (13), bitterness (12), horror (11), admiration (10), disappointment (9), diversion (9), panic (9), irony (8), mockery (7), anxiety (6), fun (6), guilt (6), scorn (6), and self-disparagement (6).

It will be noted that certain important emotions, such as embarrassment, happiness, hope, and hate, are conspicuous by their absence from the list. Doubtless, by scrutinizing the stories in the database, one could discover numerous stories in which such emotions are present or at least latent. This illustrates the shortcomings of using quantitative techniques in analysing *en masse* what is highly subjective, delicate material. Different readers, reading the same story will read different emotional nuances in the text; a person not sensitized to hate or embarrassment may pass by several stories in which someone else would immediately identify these emotions. Chapter 8 uses this database as the starting point of an investigation into organizational nostalgia, an emotion infrequently encountered in organizational literature but not uncommon in organizational stories. Initially, nostalgia was recognized as present in six stories, but on a closer reading a further eight nostalgic stories were identified.

The quality of the stories

An attempt was made to assess the quality of each story on a scale of 1 to 10. This is a highly subjective measure of how interesting, memorable, repeatable, meaningful, and telling each story seemed to me. The measure is evidently inadequate as an analytic device but permits the easy selection of 'the best' stories of each genre for the purposes of analysis, discussion, and illustration. Eleven stories were given a 10 rating, twenty-four were given 9, seventy-nine were given 8, seventy-one were given 7, fifty-nine were given 6, and the rest were given 5 or less. Good stories were characterized by happy ends, comeuppance, coincidence, and above all unpredictability, the ability to hold the listener suspended. Another feature noticed is the seemingly insignificant detail that forms part of the story's backcloth and adds to its credibility and vividness. The following is an example of a story rated 10. Told by a computer analyst, it combines a self-deprecatory sense of humour with a sense of sexual dare:

I had an office next to the girls in the legal department, and they were talking about the sexiest man in the building and came up with all these men I'd never heard of before, so I said, 'Sorry about this ladies, I thought that I was the real myo-star, the hulk', and they cracked up laughing and said, 'We had a vote and you were voted the most boring old fart in here.' So, I'd say definitely not, they do not wolf-whistle as I walk down the corridor.

This story combines a sexual dare with a humorous self-deprecating quality and vivid language that maintain the listener's attention and interest.

DANGERS OF STORY-BASED RESEARCH

The most evident danger of story-based research is the selective use of organizational narratives to amplify or reinforce the researcher's preconceived ideas or assumptions. Organizational narratives then become ingredients in the researcher's own agendas. They are especially pernicious because of their plastic and memorable qualities. As every journalist knows, through selective presentation, editing, headlining, and framing, a narrative may be put to work within virtually any overall story. This danger is ever present in ethnographic research and does not imply any conscious malfeasance on the part of the researcher. Researchers who are pursuing a particular line of investigation may focus on those stories or story interpretations that support their ideas and disregard or underestimate the importance of others. Researchers must exercise constant vigilance, asking themselves questions such as, 'What evidence stands or would stand in the way of my interpretation?', 'What would be the most unwelcome finding that would undermine my analysis?', and 'What feature of my data makes me feel most uncomfortable?'

A second danger of story-based research is the risk of regarding stories as facts, especially if a storyteller insists that the events described in the story 'actually happened' or that he or she actually witnessed them. In many stories, the idea that something 'actually happened' or that it was 'witnessed with one's own eyes' is itself part of the poetic elaboration, or what I have referred to, in analogy to dreamwork, as story-work; in virtually all instances such assertions have great political significance. Yet philosophers of science, especially Kuhn (1962) and Feyerabend (1975, 1978), have established very persuasively that even scientists talking about 'facts' are often making use of inferences, assumptions, and frames of reference, presenting plausible stories rather than describing 'objective' observations.

The opposite danger, however, is to regard everything as narrative and to lose sight of the importance of actual events in organizations. Some postmodern approaches have tended to reduce everything, including organizations, to discourse and narrative, this tendency, which denies any difference between text and context, narrative and meta-narrative, fact and fantasy, views all social reality as mediated by language and existing through language. Numerous writers have challenged this approach, which has nevertheless acquired something of a *succès de scandale* (Parker 1992, 1995; Thompson 1993). It seems to me that postmodern approaches have made considerable contributions to elucidating the role of language in organizing, structuring, and occluding our understandings, without for one moment convincing us that everything *is* language. Between the unmediated externality of an objective world and the denial of all externality that is not discursively constructed, this book advocates the use of organizational stories as poetic elaborations on actual events, as wish-fulfilling fantasies built on everyday experience, and as expressions of deeper organizational and personal realities.[4] The remaining chapters of this book present four aspects of organizational life through the medium of storytelling. Chapter 7 examines the folklore surrounding computers and information systems, making use of the material generated by the research analysed in this chapter. Chapter 8 focuses on the emotion of nostalgia in discussing how an organization's past is constructed in relation to the present. Chapter 9 examines stories inspired by encounters of ordinary organizational members with their company's supreme leader. Chapter 10 looks at the rarely discussed topic of insults as an avenue into organizational and interpersonal politics.

---

[4] This is most immediately apparent in stories of criminal acts. A story of fraud, rape, or child abuse may be the focus of legitimate scientific enquiry, whether the incident took place or not; yet the meaning of the allegation cannot be detached from the events. Two very similar stories may have quite different meanings if one stays close to actual events while the other does not.

7

Heroes, Villains, Fools, and Magic Wands

I used to work for a company where we had regular bomb practice. The security chief would hide a package with a sign saying 'BOMB', to see how quickly people got out of the building and how quickly his boys would locate the 'bomb'. They carried out this exercise many times and were pleased with their response times. Until eventually the bomb was hidden under the mainframe, where it proved impossible to locate; for hours they searched all over the building, but nobody thought of looking under the machine!

This story, recounted light-heartedly over lunch by a computer executive, generated much amusement. It is interesting to speculate why the security staff failed to check under the mainframe. Was the machine seen as being above suspicion or was it a taboo object? Did the men perhaps fail to see the computer altogether, regarding it as a fixed part of the building, in the same way that our untrained eyes fail to distinguish the dozens of types of snow apparent to an Eskimo? It is also interesting to speculate about what made it a good story. Does the story try to tell us something more general about computers and organizations? Is there some meaning, some significance, in the seemingly trivial fact that the security men failed to discover the 'bomb' under the computer?

The meaning of the story (at least as far as the storyteller was concerned) becomes clearer when we learn that it was recounted in response to a casual comment to the effect that, to the non-expert, computers are mystifying and threatening. The story came as an amplification and embellishment of this rather trivial point, as if to say that even security men, hardened men who will go after bombs, share in the general malaise when confronted with computers. They did not dare touch the computer or even get close to it, as if that was the real bomb. The image of computers as potentially dangerous objects generating anxiety is one of the factors that made them rich sources of organizational folklore, throughout the 1980s and 1990s, as they became part of the daily work reality of ever-increasing numbers of people. An analysis of ninety stories involving computers[1] suggested three main ways in which they were embedded in narratives:

1. In some stories, the computer featured as a physical object, as a machine, which gets stuck in lifts, falls off trolleys, or 'crashes' to the basement. In these stories (some of which are extremely funny or unpleasant), the role of the computer could be taken by some other machine, like a photocopier, without drastically changing the meaning of the story and will not be addressed directly in this chapter.

2. In other stories, the computer was treated as a 'living being', whose strange and unpredictable behaviour puzzles, amuses, threatens, and dismays. In these stories, the computer appeared as a true character in the narrative, most frequently as the villain or the fool of the piece, occasionally as the innocent scapegoat, now and then as the hero. In such stories, the computer becomes anthropomophically a 'character' in the plot, fully attributed with agency. It can also become part of a wider net of attributions, which include attribution of blame and attribution of fixed qualities (especially 'dumbness').

3. In the largest number of stories, the computer featured as a unique resource or tool,[2] often a priceless one, which can be used or abused, which may be mastered, and whose control conferred great power to its owner. In these stories, the computer functioned in a way reminiscent of magic rings or golden keys in folk tales. The commonest presentation of computers in such stories was as a valuable but dangerous tool or resource. In such cases, the principal attributions are those of fixed qualities (magical powers) and providential significance (magic powers of the computer restore justice or prove fateful).

COMPUTER FOLKLORE

Like organizational stories in general, much computer folklore revolves around human error and technical malfunction. Cock-ups and disasters are favourite themes of organizational stories espe-

---

[1] These were part of the 404-story database discussed in Chapter 6.
[2] This is what Burke (1945/1969) refers to as 'agency', one of his five fundamental terms of dramatism.

cially when they can be interpreted as the result of human foolishness or mechanical breakdown. Computers multiply the cost of errors and malfunctions many-fold, as the following story illustrates.

A friend of mine worked for a market research organization, writing reports which were published just as she submitted them. So once she typed 'Oh my God, how I hate this word-processing system' in a moment of complete fury and forgot to take it out, and it was not spotted until the finished version was about to go out to 10,000 subscribers, so they had to reprint the whole thing.

Fully two-thirds of the stories analysed relate to errors, malfunctions, and cock-ups. Another story in this vein was related by the chief librarian of a large manufacturing company:

A nice one we had recently. Someone who was not very well informed on how to use the system, went into a database and was looking for information on China. Fair enough, but they forgot to put the country code for China, so they got hundreds of abstracts on the china and pottery industry, all totally useless. They could have pulled the plug quite easily but they didn't even do that. So when I saw the bill coming from the system, from £20 or £30 a month it had shot to £1,000, it flashed red lights in me. The person involved didn't think it would get any further, they hadn't even told their supervisor that they had done this, and it was only when I started to inquire that they nearly broke down in tears and admitted it. There was a happy ending to this because I rang the database and explained what had happened. They had a good laugh and said, 'Oh we'll put this in our book of all the funny jokes we've had and we'll reimburse you.'

'To err is human, but it takes a computer really to mess things up', proclaimed the inscription on the mug of a software executive, who explained, 'Nobody would think twice about a mega cock-up; these days we are into giga cock-ups.' The magnitude of disasters, actual and imagined, resulting from the dangerous cocktail of human error and computer failure is mind-boggling. Days of work can be wasted, priceless data destroyed, vast expenses incurred. Merchandise can be sent to the wrong destination, bills to the wrong people, money to the wrong accounts. Even these, however, may pale in comparison with nightmare scenarios of aeroplanes sent crashing or even wars being started accidentally, which suggest that, at the symbolic level, computers are indeed as dangerous as bombs.

EXPERTS AND NAÏVE USERS

A second and related message inherent in many of the cock-up and error stories is that computers reveal human foolishness, that they are especially dangerous in the hands of stupid users. Most of these stories tend to be funny ones and include numerous examples in which experts ridicule non-experts. The quality and detail of these stories varied enormously. Some were very short, with the computer playing a rather minor role:

A funny one. Somebody, I don't know how they managed to do it, but they had a tube of glue on a shelf and they managed to knock it off and all this glue dripped down all over the computer monitor, all the way through it, all into the keyboard, there was glue everywhere, sticky horrible stuff, you couldn't do anything about it. So, you do get all sorts of funny stories about what people do with computers.

I picked up a story about a woman. One of my colleagues came in and said, 'I don't believe it, I don't believe it'; he'd been to see this lady whose hard disk had failed and he said, 'Have you got a back up?', and she said, 'Yes, I make a back up regularly, every week, I've been doing it over the past four years.' 'So, where do you keep your back-up disks?' 'In this folder here.' She opened the folder, and she had hole-punched all her disks into a ring binder! We roared with laughter at this one.

And another woman, funnily enough most of these stories are about women, but that's not a sexist comment at all, ha, ha, another secretary got a new PC. She'd had an old style PC, with 5.5" disks and she was told that she had to use 3.5" disks with her new PCs, so what she did was that she cut down the 5.5" with her scissors and tried to slip them into the drive.

Over half of all the stories that I collected fall into this category of disparagement comic stories. In many of them, like the three noted here, the male expert ridicules the ineptitude or stupidity of the non-expert, frequently female, with things technical, thus reinforcing negative gender stereotypes. The computer plays, in such stories, a part directly comparable to the banana skin of slapstick comedy as an instrument of humiliation and embarrassment, revealing the stupidity of the users. As Thomas Hobbes (1651/1962) noted long ago, stupidity and its attendant misfortunes are a favourite theme of jokes, because such jokes confer a sense of superiority on the teller and the listener: 'We wouldn't do such a silly thing, would we?'

COMPUTER JARGON

If many of the funny stories involving computers highlight human folly, these stories (as in the case of banana skins) appear to be funnier when the victim is a pretentious or pompous one, the kind of person whom we would not mind to see humbled (Davies 1984, 1988;

Powell 1988; Zillmann 1983; Zillmann and Cantor 1976). Two executives of a major computer company recounted with relish how they had made a long presentation to a government department, demonstrating a package called DRS-PWS, colloquially referred to as Doris Pughes. The presentation went very well and the officials said that they were very impressed with the system, only they could not understand who Doris Pughes was, the woman whose name kept cropping up throughout the presentation. This gave away the fact that they had understood very little indeed.

This story highlights another feature of many computer stories, technical jargon. Jargon often serves like the magic words of folk stories, enabling its master to control the resource, often achieving almost miraculous results (Cleverley 1971; La Barre 1979). By contrast, people who get the magic words wrong, like sorcerers' apprentices, either come unstuck just as they think that they are about to enjoy mastery of the resource, or unleash its power in totally unpredictable and uncontrollable ways.

Computer jargon comes in two varieties, both of which feature in stories. On the one hand, there are obscure acronyms and highly technical terms, like RAM, ROM, cache, etc. Routine users discover that no sooner have they mastered one generation of these terms than a new one has appeared. More disconcerting to the uninitiated is the second type, which includes apparently ordinary words, like virus, corrupt, default, floppy, fatal failure, environment, and so forth, used in unorthodox ways. Mastery of both types of jargon, like the ability to understand a language or a joke that excludes others, creates a strong sense of union among those in the know and a barrier to those left out (Bloomfield 1989). It is perhaps the biggest divider between 'the expert' and 'the non-expert'. Jargon stories are based on the *double ententes* that result when the expert uses such a word in the technical sense, while the non-expert understand it in the conventional way (as in the Doris Pughes story above).

Language serves as a barrier between expert and non-expert; it equally serves as a barrier between experts from different cultures, who may share command of the technical jargon, but not of the vernacular. This is illustrated in the following story told by the same executive who supplied the 'bomb' story of this chapter's opening.

I had been doing some consultancy for the UK launch of a US software product called Soft-tool. 'With a name like this you don't stand a chance,' I told the manufacturers, 'you have to change the brand-name.' No luck, it was company policy to use the same name in all its geographic divisions. My job was to come up with a logo for this product. Imagine now, 'Buy Soft-tool to increase your performance'. When they realized their gaffe, they changed the name to . . . Hard-tool!

In spite of its very light-hearted nature, this story is especially telling, in many different ways. The *double entente*, stemming from the sexual connotation of the word 'tool' which is evident to a British person but entirely lost on an American, creates an imaginary conspiracy between the teller of the story and the listeners at the expense of the American company, which thought naïvely (and with a degree of imperial disdain, perhaps) that it could force its brand name on other people, disregarding their culture and language. The imaginary logo 'Buy Soft-tool to increase your performance' strengthens the conspiracy with its implied questioning of American virility as well as the patently inadequate recipe for restoration of the ailing virility.

Would the story be as good if the object in question was unrelated to computers, if 'Soft-tool', instead of being a piece of software, was a photocopier or a new lighting system? The story could probably stand such transpositions, if a connection was made between the products and 'softness'—for instance if the lighting was meant to be 'soft' as against the hardness of neon. Even so, however, the story would lose much of its punch. I would argue that the reason for this is that computers (software and hardware) are far more plausible 'tools' for increasing company performance than lighting or photocopiers.

The story's quality then seems to rest on the fact that 'Buy Soft-tool to increase your performance' sounds like an eminently plausible logo for a computer program, to someone who does not understand the innuendo in the word 'tool'. It plays on the widely accepted and yet problematic notion that information technology is a key, or even the key, to performance and competitive advantage (Ciborra 1991; B. Jones 1982; Zuboff 1985, 1988). The story's subtle irony (which runs in parallel with the coarse sexual allusion) seems to be something like 'Here is an American company which preaches high-tech recipes to competitive advantage and then proceeds to shoot itself in the foot through a brand name, whose absurdity would be evident to any simpleton in England.'

MANAGEMENT, COMPUTERS, AND THE EXPERTS

Understanding of computers and their language is not only the preserve of the expert. It is also a symbol of modern management, generating an aura of competence, efficiency, and success. Nevertheless, keeping up to date with bewildering developments in the area of information technology is not easy. The computer-literate manager of yesterday is occasionally revealed as the technological dinosaur of today.

HEROES, VILLAINS, FOOLS, AND MAGIC WANDS

The director of a research organization prided himself on his computer literacy, had four computers in his office, and insisted on being the first to test new packages. In my presence, he severely reprimanded his personal secretary for typing the address on an envelope rather than having it printed off a program. Yet one of his support staff reported a story that both questions the director's real competence and also illustrates how criticism is more acceptable when couched in the terms of a story:

The great story about computers is the common belief that the director doesn't really know anything about computers at all; one of my friends . . . was always getting called into his office to sort things out on his computers, and she would say, 'You know, it was only a simple matter, and he pretends he knows all about it, but in fact he knows bugger all, and he's just showing off.' He had these computers as a symbol of how important he was and all that, but he actually didn't use them.

Computers represent a special challenge to managers. If keeping up with the technology is hard, maintaining some control over the experts is often harder. Some of the managers I interviewed were evidently highly versed in computers and their language, experts in their own right, and often spent much of their private time keeping up to date with developments. Their stories were substantially like those of computer specialists, laughing at the naïvety of users or joking about those of their subordinates who were seen as 'unteachable'. Other managers felt less confident and knowledgeable. While realizing the value of modern information technology, they also felt that they depended on experts whom they did not especially trust.

This uncomfortable dependence is reflected in numerous stories, including two related by the telecommunications manager of a large manufacturing company. The first story describes some of the ingenious tricks he employed to break the resistance of his subordinates to computers, while the second describes his continuing difficulties in controlling the 'experts':

I said to Val [his deputy], 'That is it, we are running everything on the computer.' 'No, no, you're not bringing any in here' and there was a terrific argument. So I had to write the most stupid prompt screens and help screens with the most silly comments, little men walking on the screen saying, 'I'm now working hard backing up your files, so go and get a cup of coffee.' I eventually had to get her to try it, play with the keyboard. The silly men would pop out of the screen bearing messages on banners and she would laugh, so she tried a bit more, and as a result of that she got used to it. The same with others of my staff. The only trouble is that I had an absolute bollocking from corporate computing when I gave them the programs to check that they were clean. 'Get all those prompts off,' they said, 'we don't want any funnies.'

This is the one that drives me around the twist, the telephone system, and this is the bloody computer department again. You put in a new telephone system. In the old days, it was a mechanical system; you couldn't do anything with it. Now of course it is totally computerized. Put in the new telephone system and for the first ten days, it was going wrong all the time, and it was the computer guys trying to see if they can wreck it—you know, 'let's be clever', messing about with the software. We had things like the chairman's phone got extended to a lift and oh! they are absolute menaces.

Val, the subject of the first story, had another interesting story, regarding the computer boys and their tricks:

It is my responsibility to give people authorization codes with which they can make long-distance calls. This is where the computer boys often start to come up with their tricks. A few weeks ago I found that my personal code had been used 700 times in a single week! I went and told them 'I resign!' [laughter]. [What happened then?] They laughed! I found out on the computer records that most of the calls had been made from an exchange outside the computer room.

While many of the stories recounted by managers are in a light-hearted, comical vein, the stories of managers regarding the experts reveal considerable anxieties. In a publishing organization, the replacement of its antiquated information system by an up-to-date one had been a five-year process, during which vast sums of money were spent on consultants' fees and dead-end 'solutions'.

This process was invariably described as 'traumatic' by five different executives, who, in spite of eventually installing a successful package, could not bring themselves to laugh at the events. Instead, they described the long saga, its devastating impact on morale, and, in the case of two of the protagonists, the deep personal impotence and despair that they experienced during that period. In all the accounts, the expert consultants featured as the villains of the piece, out to make as much money for themselves while ruining the organization in the process. The events of the transition from the old system to the new were a major organizational drama, which became central to the organization's history (Pettigrew 1979).

LAUGHING AT THE 'EXPERTS'

We have seen how naïve or incompetent users and people (including managers) who pretend to know and understand more than they actually do are the butt of numerous stories by experts. We have also seen how experts feature in managers' stories, essentially as a group difficult to control, at times temperamental, at times unscrupulous, generally awkward, but also as a group with whom it is necessary to do business.

While computer experts attracted negative nicknames from non-experts, such as 'zombies', 'androids', or 'the zoo', they were rarely the direct target of disparagement humour by non-experts. Out of fifty-five stories expressing derision and/or disparagement, I found only the following two in which users deride the experts:

Occasionally we have near disasters with disks 'dying'. On one occasion, one of these disks curled its toes and died, the service engineer said to the shift leader: 'Right, I'm going to change the Hard Disk Assembly,' so the operator said, 'OK, fair enough,' so the engineer changed the HDA, tested it, went away, and nobody could imagine that he had actually taken away the disk with all the data on and replaced it with a blank disk. This went unnoticed, until we came back the following morning and everyone went around flapping: 'What happened, what happened?' The idiot factor!

We had a computer with a great big disk-drive which used to make a lot of noise. It went wrong on one occasion, it sounded like an aircraft circling, so I got on to the engineer and explained to him, and he said, 'Yes, that's an exact description, you've got a bear with a sore head, just hold the phone in front of him.' So the next time when it happened, I rang up and told him we had a bear in the computer . . .

These two stories turn the tables on the 'expert', who either lacks common sense or seems unduly patronizing. There were other stories told at the expense of experts, but they were invariably told by other experts. In the first of the two examples that follow, the targets are the experts who designed the original programme:

The butt of the jokes in this department are the people who wrote the system that we have to maintain. There's a couple of names of authors which keep cropping up, Eileen Stanley is a classic. She stopped putting her initials on her work when she started getting embarrassed about her work. But she's left her signature all over the system. These people . . . put in an awful lot of code which is pretty unmaintainable . . . They are people who left the organization long before I joined but they've left such chaos behind.

Although there is not much action in this story, it is quite revealing. It highlights how difficult it is to evaluate the quality of the programmers' and analysts' work as well as the long-term havoc that poor-quality work causes if it goes unnoticed early on. Another story at the expense of a programmer was told by a woman analyst, who uses it as an opportunity to describe her own relation to computers:

I never forget going to a party and there was one of the most eccentric programmers that I've ever met in my life, sitting on a sofa with a bottle of gin, and he proceeded to tell me that he preferred computers to women because they didn't answer him back and he was serious! He was totally serious. His whole life revolved around computers. I just think it's sad. It's funny but it's sad. And I think that a lot of people become obsessed with it. I think I was, when I first started learning about computers, oh I loved it! It was exploration, there was always something you didn't know, there were always things to find out, but it was always achievable, you'd get there in the end. Whereas I don't feel like that any more!

This story echoes the views of some of the interviews with home-computer enthusiasts reported by Turkle (1984). She argued that mastery over a difficult but ultimately controllable part of life, computers, is used to compensate for inadequacies and low self-esteem in other spheres. It is, however, significant that none of the respondents displayed the extraordinary obsession observed by Turkle among 'amateur' enthusiasts, and I did not collect any stories of computer heroics or wizardry that are the sign of the true fanatic. Among my respondents, even the experts approached their work as a job rather than as a calling, though a handful, including the teller of the last story, had once been true fanatics.

THE GHOST IN THE MACHINE

The last story also highlights another feature of computer folklore, anthropomorphism, referring to the computer as if it were a person (Bloomfield 1989; Frude 1983). This was also in evidence in some earlier stories. Phrases such as 'curled its toes and died', 'a bear with a sore head', and 'preferred computers to women' indicate familiarity and closeness, and suggest that computers must claim pride of place among machines within organizational folklore. Unlike cars, lifts, and other machines, computers feature in some stories not as tools or resources, but as characters.

Everyday language has given up trying to treat computers as it does other tools and machines and routinely attributes agency to them. The computer 'works out the answer', it 'makes forecasts', it 'invests money', it 'beats us at chess', or, more ominously, it 'keeps watch on us'. If the computer has earned its place in language as an honorary human, it is also seen as having human qualities, such as responding to praise and threats like a human. Most of my respondents confessed that they talked to their computer, encouraged it, and ticked it off, and not a few physically assaulted it. 'This machine is so temperamental!' commented a frustrated student trainee to her boss, who quipped back with relish: 'She is obviously female!'

Unpredictability and temper are regular features of computer stories, especially those told by non-experts. Their behaviour is at times so perplexing that people, including experts, suspend disbelief altogether. This makes them excellent instruments for playing practical jokes. Although most organizations these days severely disapprove of such jokes, because of the evident risk of viruses, I did hear of a number of pranks played on other people's terminals, such as the machine pretending to delete someone's files on the screen, the prompt command being replaced by unusual messages, or the machine 'pretending' to crash when a particular sequence of keys was entered. Some of these pranks were played by experts on their colleagues, to see whether the other would fall for it.

Suspension of disbelief was a prominent feature of a story, in which the computer was seen as a supernatural source of mystical messages:

There is one thing I will never forget about this organization. Somebody in the library, you must have heard this already, she is a Star Trek fanatic, she is obsessed, every day she wears a different Star Trek badge. When I first came here I was working in user support, and she had a problem with her PC, which was flashing some error numbers, and the numbers happened to have some association with Star Trek, and in all sincerity she turned around and said, 'I think that somebody is trying to tell me something.' I'll always remember this incident, because we were all rolling around on the floor with laughter. This woman had absolutely no sense of humour; she was dead serious.

This was the only story in which the machine is endowed with metaphysical qualities. Much more commonly, it is the villain of organizational stories, especially those related by non-experts. While it is rare for the non-expert to laugh at the expense of the expert, it is more common to laugh at the expense of the computer. In fact, the non-expert enjoys computer failures almost as much the expert who is amused by the naïvety of the users. In this type of story, the computer emerges as 'a dumb machine, pretending to be smarter than it is', whose humbling is similar to that of pompous and pretentious persons discussed earlier. As was seen in Chapter 3, numerous organizational stories revolve around staff having to fall back on their traditional skills and use their cunning and experience every time the computer crashes or fails. Even in highly automated organizations, such stories seem to proclaim, the computer does not have the last word. People cannot and must not become mere servants of the computers; they must maintain their skills and aptitudes and remain in control of the machines.

CREATIVE AND ROUTINE USERS

We have seen some of the main themes of computer stories, related by three groups of organizational participants, computer experts, managers, and users. Among these three groups, users provided fewer and less interesting examples than the other two. Most of the stories came from users whose work can be described as 'creative', such as journalists, library staff, and researchers. Some of them developed an interest in computers, experimented with different packages, and, in spite of frustrations and irritations, found that the computer enhanced their satisfaction and creativity.

By contrast, very few stories came from staff using computers in a routine manner, such as receptionists, clerks, telephonists, and typists. They did provide stories on numerous aspects of organizational life, but computers were not a common ingredient of these stories. 'We talk about everything under the sun in this office, except for the computers, what is there to say about them?' I was told time and again. When pressed to talk about computers, many of these people gave opinions or made comments (at times very revealing, about, for example, how they 'cheated' or 'tricked' the machine), but did not provide stories. These workers rarely thought of themselves as users of computers, even though many spent the largest part of their day in front of VDUs.

Among these users, lack of interest in computing went hand in hand with inadequate training, ignorance of any technical terminology, and only rudimentary understanding of the systems used. The majority of them did not know the name of the software or hardware they were using. Interviewing a hospital secretary, I asked her if she had a special system for naming files on her PC. 'Oh, yes,' she said, 'I name them all Jackie.' 'Surely, every time you create a new file named Jackie, you delete the earlier one on the hard disc,' I said innocently, taking as a given what is in effect a technical limitation of DOS.[3] 'I don't use the hard disc,' came the answer. 'Those of my files I will need later, I save them on floppy discs.' I realized to my surprise that Jackie had an entire library of floppy discs, each containing a single file named Jackie. Interviewing several of her colleagues, I quickly discovered that none of them had received any training in the use of the operating system or in the organization of their files.

Computers are powerful tools and those who control them have power. To control them, one needs to speak their language. Many

[3] This along with all the other stories in this chapter pre-date the widespread use of Windows as the standard personal-computer 'environment'.

people find these languages forbidding. As systems become increasingly 'user-friendly' or 'idiot-proof', many routine users operate systems that they hardly understand and over which they have very limited control (Linn 1985; Zuboff 1988). Weaving stories around them would generate neither pride nor amusement, neither derision nor diversion. For these users, computers, like filing cabinets or pencils, are part of a daily reality that is symbolically hollow or emaciated. The bump on the boss's car, a new hairstyle, or the latest office romance are infinitely more exciting story materials than the fact that the computer was out of action for the best part of the day.

Even though the computer is symbolically hollow for routine users, in two of the organizations surveyed that had recently installed electronic mail, it functioned not as the message but as the medium of organizational lore. It was used extensively for disseminating information, gossip, and stories. For example, the registry clerks of a manufacturing firm had been asked to go on courses to improve their standard of English, following complaints from some of the firm's lawyers. The following e-mail message was circulated to fourteen clerical staff, all female.

Subject: eggication
Well folks, today it has become essential to be stuck up and pretentious. So let's form a kind of 'freemason' club for women. Only Latin will be spoken. This involves greeting each other with the words: 'ave nauta' (hello sailor). And reciting old Macdonald had a farm in latin thus:
Senex Macdondaldus habuit fundo,
E-i-e-i-o
Et in hoc fundo habuit boves
Cum moo moo hic, cum moo moo ibi . . .
Salve

I encountered several such items of e-mail lore, which has been generated by the use of computers, and which is similar to what is known as xerox lore, the widespread duplication of cartoons and caricatures, which resulted from the widespread use of photocopiers. Occasionally, the e-mail became itself part of a story, as in the following example:

One girl sent a message on the e-mail to everybody's account saying, 'I'm going to be in my bikini getting a suntan in the park,' including the Chairman's and the directors', and they all sent messages back saying, 'Right, we'll all be there in our trunks,' and she got hundreds and hundreds of messages.

In stories like this, the computer is not part of the message but purely the medium. My experience suggests that introducing e-mail into a system has, initially at least, a favourable impact on the users, helping them overcome their inhibitions, offering some scope for being creative or playful, and humanizing a work environment in which much of the information that people handle as part of their jobs in front of VDUs is stripped of a symbolic dimension.[4]

The kinds of computer stories favoured by different organizational participants and the symbolism that stories reveal differ. Four main types of participant were identified.

1. Non-creative users generally do not talk much about computers or incorporate them in their stories; for them, computers are symbolically insignificant, they do not form part of their identity, and, provided that they have mastered the essentials, they do not generate especially strong emotions.

2. Creative users have rather ambivalent feelings towards information technology and computers. Many are apprehensive about the disappearance of traditional 'professional' aptitudes and skills as a result of computerization. At the same time, they enjoy the benefits of access, speed, and range afforded by modern information systems. In their stories, they very occasionally laugh at the experts, while more commonly they blame the machine for everyday difficulties and problems; at times they laugh at themselves, for 'silly' mistakes that they make, and at others times they gripe at the complexity or rigidity of the systems that they use. In spite of these reservations, most of them cannot envisage doing their work without the help of computers.

3. Managers face different dilemmas. In their stories, they laugh at naïve users' blunders as well as at experts' lack of common sense. Yet, they also express discomfort at having to control the experts and to depend on them without always having the knowledge or expertise. Some seek to promote an image of themselves as computer competent or indeed as experts, yet in many of their stories information technology is a territory full of promise but also full of danger. Few of them feel very secure operating in this territory.

4. The experts, on the other hand, see themselves as the masters of this territory that they seek to mark and protect. Their stories, celebrating the naïvety of users and highlighting their indispensability for the organization, strengthen their sense of pro-

---

[4] Weick (1985) offers a highly insightful account of the symbolic impoverishment that accompanies the dominance of computers in the office. People absorbed in front of computer screens have not the time, the inclination, or the raw material for moving into a poetic type of engagement with the information they handle. One has the impression that the high hopes for greater and more direct personal contact initially raised by e-mail have been quashed as e-mail becomes the medium for vast amounts of impersonal information.

fessional unity and of being special. Their stereotypes of users are invariably disparaging. Some expert stories are at the expense of fellow-professionals, but on the whole these tend to be part of what have been termed 'joking-relations', i.e. relations in which mutual baiting and teasing are a sign of respect and affection.

While managers and users often attributed agency to the computer, either to deride it or to blame it, in the experts' stories the information system featured primarily as a resource or a tool over which they had privileged access and control. Perhaps, a weapon might be a better metaphor. A DOS veteran in a consultancy organization put it quite aptly in describing DOS, the standard operating system in most PC environments:

DOS is, I wouldn't say part of a conspiracy, people are not organized or intelligent enough to perpetrate such a large conspiracy, but I think that it conspires in a way that gives people power. Because it is difficult to operate, difficult to understand, difficult to work with, those people who can work with it have power, they have influence and they are respected for their knowledge. In this organization, DOS is the source of my power.

If power is one of the hidden agendas of computer stories at the workplace, especially of stories recounted by experts and managers, discomfort and apprehension are the underlying message of many. It is interesting that in no stories did the computer feature as the friend of the user ('my old and trusty PC') nor as party to heroic deeds (Kidder 1982). At the heart of these apprehensions may lie the sense that computers are already too clever and too powerful to be controlled by humans, while at the same time we have become too dependent on them to be able to function without them.

8

Studying Emotion through Stories

I came here at a time when there was very little bureaucracy and a much more laid-back approach, but also a dedicated approach. People knew what they were doing, where they were going, why they were here, and bureaucracy was to be avoided. People were friendly, generally got on well together, it was an organization, a place worth working for. Today, frankly at times it's . . . like something out of 1984. It's a cross between George Orwell and Kafka; this is my point of view.

They used to go out on great day-trips like to Leeds Castle and the whole company, like 500 people, would have a medieval style of banquet or a summer party or something. Pete who I work with said that he'd been on two of those, whereas the only summer party I've been here was a picnic across the road in Hyde Park. I think that it was all a dreadful waste of money taking the whole company to Leeds Castle, I mean it's the customers' money after all. The older ones think about the good old days, but I don't think they mind too much; it was just a nice time that has passed now.

These statements come from two employees of a publishing and research organization. They highlight a generational divide, a divide between old and new. Where the young man sees but waste and irrationality, the old man sees true purpose and value. The divide is cognitive and normative, but above all it is emotional. The older man fails to comprehend how the younger one may actually enjoy what he sees as a *1984*-type nightmare; and the younger man is unable to appreciate the depth of the older man's attachment to the organization that was, his yearning for the past, his nostalgia.

This chapter is an exploration of nostalgic stories in organizations. It also offers a systematic analysis of one particular emotion, nostalgia, through the medium of storytelling; in so doing, it presents one particular mode in which organizational members seek to make sense of their daily experiences—namely, by juxtaposing them to an organizational past and comparing them to it. Choosing to discuss nostalgia in organizations may seem idiosyncratic. It may be countered that nostalgia is not an emotion at all, at least not one to compete with driving emotions, such as love, hate, envy, or anger. Alternatively, it may be suggested that organizations are not a natural habitat for nostalgia, that one feels nostalgic about one's childhood, early loves, or youthful indiscretions, but hardly about one's place of work. This chapter presents a view of nostalgia as encompassing a range of distinct emotional orientations in organizations. I will argue that organizational nostalgia is not a marginal phenomenon, but a pervasive one, dominating the outlook of numerous organizational members, and even defining the dominant emotional complexion of some organizations. It feeds organizational folklore about 'characters' and events, engraved in the collective memory. In addition, nostalgia for an organizational golden age exercises a considerable influence on the way present-day events are interpreted, acting as a rich source of symbolism and meaning. More generally, I will try to show that the study of nostalgia provides a powerful approach to the study of feelings and fantasies, revealing some of the fundamental complexity and ambivalence of emotional life in organizations.

BACKGROUND

The study of nostalgia has grown in recent years, as nostalgia itself has assumed a dominant place in Western cultures. Whole sectors of the economy are fuelled by nostalgia. The heritage and tourist industries, a large section of entertainment, music, and the arts continuously strive to feed people's yearning for a golden past. In the hands of advertisers, nostalgia has become a tried and tested if overused device for promoting anything from potato crisps to insurance policies. The film industry has become dominated by endless recycling of themes and archetypes from the past, full of references to classic movies and sequels to not-so-classic ones which then come to be seen as classic. Television forever repeats its own golden oldies. Politicians, such as Thatcher and Reagan, built substantial support by mobilizing nostalgia for an earlier era, a mythologized past of authentic values and heroic achievements. The celebration of this past, uncomplicated, innocent, and thoroughly sentimentalized, has found its spiritual home in Disneyland, whose consequences reach far beyond the leisure sector (Kaplan 1987; Schwartz 1988).

Under this onslaught, academics have abandoned their highbrow disparagement for the concept of nostalgia and have addressed it

along two main paths that have occasionally crossed.[1] Cultural critics have approached nostalgia as a social phenomenon whose causes
and functions must be sought in contemporary culture. Most (Davis
1979; Williams 1974; Wright 1985) have criticized nostalgia as the latest
opiate of the people, a collective escape from the complexities of the
present in times of trouble and change in an idealized vision of the
past. A few, however, have tried to defend the way nostalgia resurrects the past (which our culture would otherwise banish) as a 'political and psychological treasury from which we draw the reserves to
cope with the future' (Lasch 1980: p. xviii). As a militantly anti-
modern current, nostalgia has more recently found a more hos-
pitable environment in postmodernism.

A second line of enquiry has been pursued by depth psychology.
While Freud recognized that loving memories are a central ingredient of psychological maturity, most of his successors noticed nostalgia as an abnormal condition akin to melancholia, which leads to
serious disturbances including guilt and self-reproach for the loss of
loved objects (Daniels 1985; Kaplan 1987; Kleiner 1970; Sohn 1983;
Werman 1977). In its acute forms, nostalgia amounts to a total inability to accept the present and a morbid determination literally to live
in the past, as embodied in persons long dead, old movies, and old
radio programmes.[2]

Organizational theorists, for their part, have steered clear of the
concept. This is paradoxical, given that ethnographic research has
not been slow in revealing 'nostalgic feelings' in the first-hand testi-
monies of organizational participants (Terkel 1985). In my own
research I had frequently been impressed by the cognitive and emotional gulf that separates old from young organizational members
(Gabriel 1988, 1991c), yet I never thought of nostalgia as being part of
this gulf. Along with many other theorists no doubt, I felt an instinctive dislike for a term that has been sentimentalized and trivialized to
the point where it can hardly qualify as a concept.

It is ironic then to discover that the word 'nostalgia' originated in
medicine, as one of those terms that sought to medicalize a complex
of emotional and behavioural disturbances. It was first used by the
Swiss physician Johannes Hofer in 1688 to describe the morbid
symptoms of Swiss mercenaries who spent long periods away from
home. The term derives etymologically from the Greek words *nostos*

---

[1] Cf. Lasch (1984: 65) on 'fear of nostalgia'; this describes well the intellectual's aver-
sion to the concept.
[2] There is a third path, which has little to offer the present discussion, that of marketing. Marketing has taken the nostalgia of the masses as a fact and has sought to understand how specific products may be planned, packaged, and presented to maximize
their nostalgic appeal. See e.g. Moriarty and McGann (1983) and Unger *et al.* (1991).

meaning homecoming and *algia* or pain; it initially signified acute or pathological homesickness, a meaning that it still maintains in some European languages.[3] Until the Napoleonic Wars, nostalgia was seen as a peculiarly Swiss sickness, at times attributed to sudden changes in altitudes or the quality of breathing air. It was only in the early part of the twentieth century that nostalgia was demedicalized, losing its link with the military, and later still that the link with home as a place was weakened. Gradually nostalgia found its own anchor in the past—that is, *a time*—coming to signify a warm feeling of yearning and longing towards that time.[4]

In spite of its connection with the past, nostalgia is not the product of the past itself. 'Almost anything from our past can emerge as an object of nostalgia, provided that we can somehow view it in a pleasant light' (Davis 1979: p. viii). People can feel nostalgic for trying, hard, and disagreeable times, such as the Great Depression of the 1930s or the Battle of Britain. Experience in Eastern Europe has revealed nostalgia for the communist past, as a period of security, togetherness, and survival in the face of adversity. *In this sense, nostalgia is a state arising out of present conditions as much as out of the past itself.* Its attitude towards the past is highly plastic, growing not out of mere recollection, still less out of a historical inquisition. Instead, the nostalgic past is highly selective, generally idealized, and infused with symbolism and meaning. Nostalgia, therefore, creates a retrospective mythology, something that is at once part of us but not part of the present world, evoking a glowing emotional response and inviting further idealization and embellishment, but resisting historical elucidation. In all of this, nostalgia is crucially a feature of a poetic rather than a historical construction of the past.

To this idealized picture of the past, nostalgia compulsively juxtaposes the present, which is almost invariably found emaciated, impoverished, and lacking (Davis 1979). In this sense, nostalgic feelings can profoundly affect our construction and interpretation of present-day phenomena and mould our emotional reactions to them. Within organizations, the current leaders, today's buildings, or even today's products may be compared unfavourably with the past ones. One outstanding feature of nostalgia is that it always selects the terrain so that the past, dressed up and embellished, will triumph over the present. If, for example, the past leaders of the organization are generally discredited and the present ones admired, nostalgic feeling will focus on some other feature of the past.

[3] This is *Le mal du pays* magically recreated by Liszt in one of the pieces of his *Années de Pèlerinage: Première Année, Suisse.*
[4] For etymology and history of the term 'nostalgia', see Kaplan (1987) and Davis (1979).

But, if nostalgia approaches the past in this glowing manner, it also affirms that the past is irrecoverably gone; it is part of a 'world we have lost'. In organizational nostalgia, the past is frequently separated from the present through a *radical discontinuity*,[5] a symbolic watershed, which cannot be undone.[6] In some organizations this is referred to as 'the changes' (Gabriel 1988) and may include the move to a new building, the introduction of computerized technology, a corporate takeover, privatization, or a new managerial regime or ethos. Employees who experienced the change from old to new see themselves as radically different from those who joined later, and at times may see themselves as 'survivors' from an earlier age. Their past is a shared heritage that binds them together, and excludes those who never tasted life before the fall.

There are forms of nostalgia which are intensely private (Daniels 1985). They draw on intimate moments of our personal histories, as we remember ourselves, little boys or girls lost in a bewitching world. This chapter does not focus on this Proustian variant of nostalgia. Instead we will approach it as a social phenomenon, whose expressions are often shared with others. People who have shared a past experience, and have a nostalgic disposition towards it, will generally feel close and will tend to reinforce the features noted earlier.[7]

Some ambiguities of nostalgia

Nostalgia is not an unproblematic concept. Is nostalgia a pleasant or an unpleasant experience? In some European languages (including Russian, German, and Greek), the word 'nostalgia' never shed its disagreeable associations with homesickness. Yet, in English, the word has come to signify a predominantly pleasant experience. Although some people comment on its 'bitter-sweet' quality, the majority

---

[5] Bakhtin, following Goethe and Schiller, argues that a radical discontinuity is one of three core features of the epic as a genre: 'The epic past is called the "absolute past" for good reason: it is both monochromatic and valorized (hierarchical); it lacks any relativity, that is, any gradual, purely temporal progressions that might connect it to the present. It is walled off absolutely from all subsequent times, and above all from those times in which the singer and his listeners are located' (Bakhtin 1981: 15–16).

[6] It could be that the greater the discontinuity that separates us from the time that forms the object of nostalgia, the more recent that time can be. For example, some individuals in Eastern Europe are nostalgic about a very recent past, because of the magnitude of discontinuity that separates it from the present.

[7] The question of whether a person who did not partake of the initial experience may partake in the nostalgic feeling towards it is an open one. My view would be that there is a considerable overlap between fond and yearning feelings for situations we experienced first hand and those we experienced via the descriptions of our parents, great authors (such as Homer or Scott), and great artists. For example, Homer may create in his readers, whether young or old, an acute nostalgia for the heroic times.

indicate that they view nostalgia as a positive, pleasant experience. In spite of the recognition that the past is irrevocably lost, nostalgia, at least in its English usage, refuses to collapse into despair or grief even if, at times, it is tinted by feelings such as self-pity or what the French call *tristesse*. A major paradox presents itself, which I will call the *nostalgia paradox*. In a famous passage of Dante's *Divine Comedy*, Francesca da Rimini, tormented in hell for her illicit passion for Paolo, greets the poet with the immortal words:

> Nessun maggior dolore
> Che ricordarsi del tempo felice
> Nella miseria
>
> There is no greater pain
> than to remember, in our present grief,
> past happiness.
>
> (Canto V, ll. 121–3)

The truth of this statement seems overwhelming, and yet nostalgia somehow evades the painful consequences of such recollections. The paradox suggested here, which existing literature has failed to raise, is this: how can the memory of a past irredeemably lost be experienced as pleasant?

A further question concerns the status of nostalgia as an emotion. The common identification of nostalgia with a yearning, or a longing (Davis 1979; Kaplan 1987), would place nostalgia closer to desire than to feeling. There are indeed times when nostalgia has a motivating edge—for example, when we visit places with significant earlier associations. This is what advertisers seek to exploit, whether to entice us to visit heritage parks or to attract us to the 'old-fashioned' taste of Brand X.

Desire *demands* satisfaction, as do the driving emotions associated with it, such as love, hate, jealousy, or rage. The same cannot be said about nostalgia, which cannot be frustrated in the same way that desire can. There is general agreement in literature that the emotional tone of nostalgia is not a loud one, but a contemplative, quiet one. This would place it at the opposite end of the spectrum from those above, an emotion resulting from desire already fulfilled, as if the fact that one has lived through a golden past is by itself the fulfilment of the yearning. Kaplan (1987: 471) has, therefore, suggested that nostalgia may be closer to a mood than an emotion, a psychological orientation that affects the entire person, lending a uniform colouring to the world, and combining a repertoire of emotions and behaviours. In the pages that follow, we shall retain the concept of 'nostalgic feeling' to describe a warm and loving orientation for the past or features of the past, a tender yearning towards it, as well as a resigned acceptance of the impossibility of bringing that past back.[8]

NOSTALGIC VOICES FROM ORGANIZATIONS

In spite of these ambiguities, most of us have no difficulty in understanding intuitively what nostalgia is or when someone is experiencing nostalgic feelings. While some of us may still find it distasteful or 'ideologically suspect', we must recognize that the very dislocation of the word from its original meaning of melancholy resulting from long absence from home indicates that it has filled an important semantic space for which no other word is suitable. What forms then does nostalgia take in organizations? In my fieldwork, nostalgic stories were sometimes evoked by a list of metaphors, from which respondents were asked to choose one that aptly depicted their organization. The list included family, madhouse, well-oiled or creaky machine, castle under siege, conveyor belt, dinosaurs, football team, etc. (see Chapter 6). The responses varied across different organizations, but one type of response was common among older respondents, who, on seeing the list, would say, 'It used to be a family, but . . .'. Consider, for example, the response of a personnel officer in a large chemical company, who had been with the company for twenty years:

I've seen a lot of changes in the company since I came . . . This is confidential . . . Today we are told we are world class, and we go for this unified image, that we are all one, one big happy family, and in my earlier days with the company I'd have said, 'Yes, we were wonderful.' It doesn't seem that way now. People are not quite as friendly as they used to be [long pause]. I mean we had, years ago, we had more time to, FOR people. I mean, I suppose, it's the old con trick. Someone in the management decides that we have far too many staff and they start to cut staff and they cut it to the bone and lose an awful lot of people who had all the experience, who really knew. And the sort of history of the company . . . is lost.

The image of the organization as a *family* seemed to be at the heart of many nostalgic feelings. Not all of the references to family were prompted by my list of metaphors. A hospital training officer, who had previously worked as a telephonist and a receptionist, said,

---

[8] Nostalgia, as a form of yearning for the unattainable, which combines idealization with abasement, has much in common with the now obsolete form of 'courtly love', dated from the twelfth-century troubadours. This combined idealization of the beloved lady, the inferiority of the lover, a recognition of the unattainability of the quest, as well as the refusal to collapse into despair and anguish. See Lindholm (1988).

when asked to describe some memorable incidents of her working life:

The most significant thing since I started working for the NHS was the closure of the old hospital, because that marked a complete change. They closed it down in 1974. It used to be like a small community, being small, everyone knew each other, everyone helped each other, and if a doctor went out he'd say, 'I'm going out, if a patient comes, just sort it out.' The nurses would say, 'Do you want a cup of tea?', just like a family. When we came to this big place here, all those same people were spread across the site and when you pass each other, you don't have the same contact. That was quite a change. You walk along the corridor and very often you speak to no one because you don't know anyone; in the old hospital you would have asked who they were.

This respondent later went on to describe the present hospital as a 'sort of machine, well-oiled but still creaking', further highlighting the distance between what was seen as a bureaucratic present and the warm personal atmosphere of the past.

At the time of the interviews, nostalgia was not part of the research programme, and was not consciously raised with any of the interviewees. It was while analysing the research material, attempting to classify the stories that had been collected, that the theme of nostalgia emerged. Listening to the taped interviews I was first struck by a handful of respondents; virtually everything they said was tinted by nostalgia. The emotional tone of what they said, present in voice timbre and tone, pauses and sighs, as well as the words that they used ('lost', 'gone', etc.), was closer to reverie than to recollection. Whenever they talked about the present, whether about the catering, the furniture, the buildings, the leaders, their colleagues, or the general ethos of the organization, they drew unfavourable comparisons with the 'good old days'.

In addition to those interviewees whose nostalgia was overpowering, the majority of interviews with older employees displayed some nostalgic qualities at some point. These employees would not merely recollect important incidents in the organization's history, but would seek to incorporate them in an idealized image of the organization's and their personal past, charged with a fond feeling of affection and warmth. This contrasted sharply with the exceptional few, who sought to demean and devalue the past, and suggested to me that nostalgia may be studied not only as an individual phenomenon but also as an organizational one—that is, as an emotional and symbolic attribute of some organizations, growing organically out of organizational processes. Many organizations, like societies, are seen by their members as having a golden age, belonging to the mythological prehistory rather than to documented history. People with first-hand experience of this age treat it as a personal and a collective heritage, against which they perceive, interpret, and judge the present.

SOME ELEMENTS OF ORGANIZATIONAL NOSTALGIA

The five organizations under investigation differed in the extent as well as the nature of their members' nostalgic feeling. One organization, the small consultancy firm, which had been in existence for only a short while before the research, had none that was detectable. In the publishing and research organization, nostalgia was a marginal phenomenon; few of those interviewed had been with the company for more than five years. Nostalgic voices in this organization (like the one in the opening text in this chapter) tended to get lost in the buzz of everyday life. In the remaining three organizations, however, the chemical multinational, the utility, and the hospital, nostalgia played a pivotal role in the emotions and perceptions of the numerous older and longer-serving employees. As nostalgia was not part of the planned research, it is not possible to compare its representations at the corporate level. What can, however, be done is to identify certain elements that act as focuses of nostalgic feeling.

Buildings

First, the physical buildings of the company. The experience of the chemical firm is instructive. This company had moved away from its historic building in the centre of London for a number of years, while the building was radically refashioned. When the company moved back, while the building remained outwardly the same, its interior was unrecognizable. A senior executive said:

The old building was like a gentlemen's club, long dark corridors, heavy oak doors, but during the 70s recession we had lost a lot of staff and the rest were rattling like peas in a pod. When we moved out, I found people I didn't even know existed and I'm supposed to know everyone in the building. Everyone at that time worked in their distinct little cells, and the idea was to make the culture of the organization much more open; we would have an all-glazed environment, so that it would appear more open. I have my own personal views on whether it happened, but I'd rather not risk them . . . As for my staff, a lot of them don't like the modern architecture, can't open the windows. We have a high incidence of sickness, headaches. Don't know if this is psychological, psychosomatic, or the 'sick-building syndrome', but the staff personalize their

*work environment a lot more than they did in the old building. They didn't
used to have all these fluffy toys around.*

The old building acted as a powerful source of nostalgic feeling for
those staff who had lived and worked in it. A supervisor who had
worked for the company for twenty years said:

*When we moved back, I liked the cleanliness of it, the smell, the new desks. I
still like the building concept but I find it difficult to work in . . . I think that
the ceilings are too low. The old building was a 1920s building, very elegant; it
was a shame to lose a lot of that.*

Another supervisor, with thirty years' service, had more extreme
views.

*I hate it [the building], I loath it. It's a lovely building to come in and walk
around and say 'Isn't it wonderful!' To work in it it's hell, nothing goes right
. . . The idea was that there should be an atrium, where there used to be just a
light well, sort of white lavatory tiles on it, an unused space, just open. They
decided to turn it into usable space, originally they were going to have trees,
then they said it was going to be too noisy. So they carpet it, it's quite stunning
if you look from the eighth floor, but from the working point of view it's no
good. The idea was that we'd all feel part of a whole, you could see everybody,
but you don't. All you can see is the people in the corridors, or you look at the
fishtanks, the offices that line up the atrium, half of the time they are empty,
so that's depressing!*

In addition, however, to the difficulties of living and working in an
exposed environment over which one has little control, employees in
some corporate buildings experience another source of dissatisfac-
tion. Corporate culture theory has viewed the ostentatious lavishness
of corporate headquarters as an emblem of corporate might, much
as the cathedrals of the past stood for the might of God and His representatives on earth. For those who have to work in such environments, there is a contradiction between the outward opulence of the
buildings and their lifeless, spiritually impoverished qualities.

In the chemical firm in question, the new building carried a potent
symbolism, but for many the symbolism was very far from that
intended by the architects and the corporate image-makers. Far from
corporate splendour, the new building came to stand for a corrup-
tion of the old values. Although the building was outwardly the same,
its new interior affronted people's sense of authenticity and epitomized the hollow rhetoric of PR. The atrium, intended to symbolize
corporate openness, came to stand for what many of the older staff
felt to be the spiritual void at the heart of the organization. Under
such circumstances, the old building's dark corridors, ironically,
came to symbolize authenticity and community.

I liked the look of the new building when I first walked in, very impressive. But the offices, the way that they are organized, you don't see an awful lot of people. Where we are you might not see anyone all day. It is quiet. Conducive to work, but not conducive to gatherings or anything like that. The old building, well it was antiquated, but it had character, while this has no character, and this is also how I feel about people. There used to be birthday parties in our offices, Christmas parties, whereas now, they don't have impromptu get togethers any more.

Leaders

If the physical set-up of an organization acts as a powerful symbol evoking nostalgic feelings, so do the organization's leaders. In two of the organizations I studied, earlier leaders had left a powerful legacy against which present leaders were assessed and found lacking. The old leaders had been heads of the family, in contrast to the technocratic or even macho styles of management of the current ones. The following quote interweaves two nostalgic themes to reinforce a comparison with the present: disaffection with the physical premises (absence of bar in the new building) and affection for the departed leader:

He'd come to the bar most days and have a pint and he might have a packet of crisps and a pork pie or something like that. And he would come and sit down with anybody, it might just be a secretary, someone who'd just started that week. He would put himself in their shoes. He probably learnt more about what went on in the company from these conversations . . . you never see the current chairman, he never comes down. There is no bar anyway. It was a place where you socialized. So we've lost this these days.

Similar feelings for the retired chairman were expressed by numerous members of that organization:

The nice thing about Sir Roy, I didn't have many dealings or any dealings in fact, but he was always around. He was quite visible in the dining room having egg and chips for lunch, or in the bar having a pint and people would go and talk to him if they wanted. No matter what he did while he was in power, he always seemed a very human person. Sir Roy was different from all the other chairmen I've known. Although I didn't see him everyday, someone would say, 'Oh yes, I saw him in the bar having a sandwich,' so yes, that made me feel different, just the fact that he was around. The current chairman, I wouldn't go back home and say, 'The chairman was having egg and chips today.' He doesn't. I don't feel I know him at all.

I collected no fewer than eleven stories (and seven proto-stories) about Sir Roy, a Falstaffian figure, nearly all of them having him talking to people in bars, lifts, or dining rooms. A sense of bonhomie and familiarity characterizes these portraits. Sir Roy was by all accounts a character and *characters* form focal points of nostalgia.[9] They readily come to embody the whole spirit of the golden past, become its champions and its emblems. Characters are memorable, they are unpredictable, they stand out from the crowd and provide a key for a temporary escape from bureaucratic uniformity, predictability, and order.[10]

Other characters and departed colleagues

But characters who attract nostalgic feelings are by no means always leaders. Colleagues who departed often form the subject of fond reminiscences, as if their departure was equivalent to their having died. These are instances when nostalgic feeling is most tinted with sadness, melancholia, or even mourning.

Julie was a caring person and would take time to listen to me and then a few days later she'd pop round and have a chat. These days there is not so much time around to have a chat with somebody. She'd organize things. She was secretary of the social club and organized events, making sure that everyone got involved. A lot of people felt like I feel about her. The space is not available now for recreational activities in this building. There are just two squash courts.

I've been here for a long time and I've seen the atmosphere change. In the old days, ten years ago say, I have still some friends now that I made here then. But the numbers of friends I have now, I can count them on the fingers of one hand. One of the women that used to work here, she is someone who I always look back on, when I look at how it used to be here when it was good fun. She plus another girl are the two people I think of when I think, 'It was good in those days when such and such a person was around.' If I look back at the company when it used to be fun to be here, they are the sort of people I think of.

Such quotes weave the departed characters with other nostalgic themes, such as the building and the social functions. In spite of their different emotional content, they highlight *caring* and *altruism*

---

[9] Note how the old building in earlier quotes was seen as having character.

[10] This is not to say that some current organizational leaders are not seen as characters. Two of the organizations I studied were led by individuals whose eccentric behaviour and unusual foibles attracted much gossip and fuelled organizational folklore. What, however, makes 'old characters' different from 'current characters' is the unequivocally warm feeling they attract, which is evident in the stories recounted about them, like the ones above. By contrast, stories about current leaders seen as characters usually present them as faintly ridiculous or threatening figures. This theme will be explored more fully in the next chapter.

as central features of the organizational golden age. These features are prominent in most nostalgic stories, often contrasted to the contractual, cash nexus of the present.

Consider the following two accounts, which focus on this theme. They come from two women working in the same department of a utility, dealing with telephone enquiries from customers. Jackie Simpson painted a positively Kafkaesque picture of the present situation in the office, but throughout the interview maintained a cheerful and defiant attitude summed up in the comment: 'It's funny really but when everything is really low, then people decide to have some fun. You are treated like dirt, and you say "Sod it, let's enjoy ourselves, even if we just make fun of each other." ' Jackie's proud and outspoken attitude left little room for nostalgia. But when asked for an incident that summed up her experience in the organization, she replied thus:

I used to work for a man, he is at head office now, I was a lot younger then, but to me working, it was my first job, and to work here it meant . . . giving a bit and taking a bit. And with him you had that feeling, and I would work a couple of minutes [sic!] over. I didn't mind if you had somebody on the phone, you wouldn't get rid of them abruptly just because it was time to go. You wouldn't mind. That sums it up for me. Then you wouldn't mind helping. But now I just don't like it at all.

This text illustrates the quality of mutuality that was seen as a central feature of the past. This theme recurs in the testimony of Mary Crighton, Jackie's supervisor, a woman who spoke with frustration but also with affection for her subordinates. She had herself been promoted from being a telephone clerk and now found it difficult to generate much cooperation among her staff.

Everybody now has that selfish streak; my team is alright, but if you ask them to do something, 'Ooh!' We talk about the past, we say to the young ones, 'You should have been here, when we all used to do this job together and it was good and we used to have good spirit, and we had loads and loads of work, but it had nothing to do with the work, that was loads and loads, but everyone seemed to want to help each other and you would look out for each other and be sympathetic. It was a different sort of thing.'

The power of such feelings and their familiar quality make it remarkable that nostalgia has been so little noticed in research on organizations. Space does not permit an illustration of some other focuses of nostalgic feeling in organizations, but two should at least be mentioned. In contrast to chaotic and irrational rules and procedures of the present, the organization's golden past is seen as one of order and reason; it is as if all the bureaucratic absurdities and the vexations that result never existed at that time. Secondly, the technology of yesteryear is seen as permitting individualism and creativity in contrast to today's deskilling and routinized systems. This applies especially to pre-computerized information systems, which often attracted nostalgic feelings in my research.

To summarize. A number of objects have been identified that attract nostalgic feeling in organizations; these include the physical buildings of the organization, the leaders, departed colleagues, and social functions. In all cases, these are compared favourably with their equivalents of the present time and found to be richer, more authentic, more meaningful. However, the nature of what I have until now referred to as nostalgic feeling is not constant. The emotions, though generally contemplative, range from pride to self-pity, from sadness to joy; most are tinted with some melancholy, at times verging on mourning. In most cases, nostalgia appears to make the present more bearable, but in some cases it puts today's realities in grim relief. What is constant is idealization and simplification, the experience of the past as a personal heritage, an emphasis on community, and harping after a quality of authenticity. Nostalgic stories may entail pleasure and sadness but never sorrow or grief. From a poetic point of view, they mostly eschew agency, causality, and responsibility, in favour of three kinds of attribution—namely, attribution of unity, attribution of fixed qualities, and attribution of emotion. As we shall see presently, these converge on an idealized image of the family, as a cohesive, caring, utterly authentic unit, free of conflict, tension, and irrationality.

NOSTALGIA AND IDENTITY

Organizational nostalgia combines a powerful but variable affective component, a cognitive reconstruction of the past—its idealization— and a symbolic enrichment—mythologization. Psychologically, it is most accessible as a component of *self*, that valuable but precarious web of truths, half-truths, and fictions that surround the entity that we familiarly refer to as 'I'. Davis (1979: 34) recognized that, as a dimension of identity, nostalgia increases our sense of self-worth. No matter how low, infirm, or powerless we are now, we take heart from earlier glories and grandeurs. The world may have changed but no one can deny us our past. We too were there and experienced the golden age. Having met a famous person, having participated in a historic event, having tasted life before the fall all become treasured possessions. Kaplan (1987: 473) has rightly pointed out that the memory of such experiences is treated with devotion and veneration.

This gives us a clue to what we called the nostalgia paradox—namely, the pleasurable recollection of a past irredeemably lost. The rarer, the more unique the experience, the greater its value. Just as collectors of stamps take greater pride in the rarest items they possess, or even the rarest items they *once possessed*, in nostalgia we take special pride in our most unrepeatable experiences. Consider the football fan who saw England win the 1966 World Cup, the opera enthusiast who attended Maria Callas's last historic performances of *Tosca* in London, or the ageing hippy whose identity was shaped at the famous Woodstock pop festival. Being able to say that they were present on these legendary occasions becomes all the more valuable a part of their heritage, the less likely it becomes that they might be repeated. Idealization is comprehensible in this context. The details of the events may be less significant than the fact that one was 'there'. The discontinuities that separate those experiences from the present become psychologically beneficial by enhancing their uniqueness and therefore their value. The experiences above become all the more powerful as sources of identity, when juxtaposed to the 'dire state' of English football, operatic singing, or youth culture of today.

Nostalgia then provides a vicarious fulfilment of what Schwartz calls the 'ontological function', the individual's need to see him or herself as someone of value, summed up in 'being somebody is good, being a "has been" is bad' (Schwartz 1987a: 329). Nostalgia enables a has-been to become somebody again. Nowhere is this clearer than in the example given by Schwartz's mentor, Ernest Becker (1962: 84): 'Anthony Quinn in his great role in *Requiem for a Heavyweight* earned his inner sense of self-value by constantly reminding himself and others that he was "fifth-ranking contender for the heavyweight crown". This made him somebody.'

What types of experience become the focuses of nostalgic feeling? Though they may have the qualities of rarity and uniqueness, it is unlikely that acutely pleasurable experiences can easily feed nostalgia later on. If such experiences become the object of nostalgic recollection, they are likely to be heavily weighted by melancholy feeling. Discontinuity in these cases weighs as loss; instead of adding to the psychic value of the memories, transforming them into personal treasures, it poisons and destroys them. The loss of an admired chairman or a cherished character, as we saw earlier, may inspire nostalgia. The loss of a loved friend or a treasured child does not. Nostalgia is not a way of coming to terms with the past (as mourning or grief are), but an attempt to come to terms with the present. Unless the loss has been psychologically conquered, and this requires strength, nostalgia cannot adopt it as its material.

On the other hand, more mildly pleasurable experiences and less dramatic discontinuities can more easily act as generators of nostalgic feelings and reconstructions.[11] Such experiences may act like faded holiday photographs, old theatre programmes, or family heirlooms, no longer triggering specific reminiscences, but rather representing icons of a unique symbolic and emotional cosmos. Overwhelming experiences leave powerful memories, traumata, repressions; moderately pleasurable ones, on the other hand, can evade the rigours of memory and feed the plastic medium of fantasy. It is, therefore, not as memories, but as fantasies about the past through which we seek to come to terms with the present, that nostalgia works its spell. Nostalgic stories may contain epic, comic, tragic, or romantic ingredients. They may centre on the achievements of a heroic age, a trickster's merry pranks, a character's unique eccentricities, or even hardships endured and survived.[12] Yet, in the stories I collected the romantic mode predominates: the past is presented as a terrain of cherished objects and memories, in which love, generosity, forgiveness, and caring reigned supreme.

ORGANIZATIONS AS TERRAINS OF NOSTALGIA

While the neglect of emotional life in organizations has been rightly criticized (Fineman 1993, 1996; Flam 1990a, b; Hochschild 1983), it is easy to make the opposite error and exaggerate the freedom and strength of emotions in organizations. If emotions in organizations are managed, tempered, and defused, that only helps to make them fecund grounds for nostalgia. The modest satisfactions and successes of organizational life can, after some years, begin to feed nostalgic narratives, in a way that violent passions cannot. Equally, however, the very nature of *present* experiences in many organizations further enhances nostalgia. The discontents of today, in other words, find partial but effective consolation in gentle reverie of yesteryear.

[11] Winnicott (1964, 1980) referred to experiences that remain within certain manageable limits as 'contained experiences'; he viewed containment as an important condition for creativity and play. A similar argument can be made for experiences that can be turned into objects of nostalgia.

[12] The epic mode is indelibly linked to nostalgia, both by inviting us to celebrate a glorious past and by recounting a past still more glorious than the one in which the action takes place. Both the *Iliad* and the *Odyssey* are replete with nostalgic reminiscences of older men, such as Nestor, Priam, and Laertes.

To summarize: it is unlikely that nostalgia will feed on a past of extreme pleasure and extreme disappointments, preferring for its source material modest pleasures and enchantments; equally, nostalgia offers most effective consolation for modest disappointments and disenchantments, rather than for severe traumata and psychic injuries. Organizations, by their very nature bureaucratic, impersonal, emotionally cauterized if not emasculated, harbour the types of disillusionments and discontents for which nostalgia can supply effective consolation—namely, injuries to our narcissism.

Impersonality is a key ingredient of our experience of organizations ever since our first day at school, when we became one of many, a number on the register, a face among unknowns. Impersonality is a fundamental affront to our narcissism. From being unique members of a family, organizations from school onwards consign us to the status of cogs, important or critical perhaps, but dispensable and replaceable. I shall not develop this point here, but its relation to nostalgia must be clear. In its very insistence on community, family spirit, characters, warmth, personal care, and protecting leaders, nostalgia seeks to undo the painful effect of entering a world of impersonal organizations, *as if the organization of old was nothing but an extension of our loving, caring family.* And, in so doing, nostalgia seeks to reinvigorate our ailing narcissism.

Nostalgia is not the only or even the most powerful mode of consolation available. As we saw in earlier chapters, all forms of storytelling, in their different ways, accomplish not dissimilar ends—namely, providing temporary relief from the rigours of organizational controls, a symbolic means for turning powerlessness into control, and a source of meaning in relatively meaningless situations. Nevertheless, the role of nostalgia as a palliative should not be underestimated, most especially for older members. Nostalgia essentially resurrects the selfsame narcissism, towards which the modern corporation is so injurious, the narcissism of the time when we could convince ourselves that we were both unique and the centre of a loving world.[13]

---

[13] This is not the New Narcissism vividly portrayed and criticized by Lasch. The New Narcissist is self-consciously and militantly anti-nostalgic, living only for the present and having little time for sentimental diversions from the past. Far from being psychologically hurt by bureaucracy, he often thrives and prospers in it, just as the bureaucracy prospers on his services (Gabriel 1982; Lasch 1980, 1984). The very impersonality of bureaucracy sustains him and protects him. Unlike the New Narcissism, which derives from secondary narcissism (trying to cancel out the disappointment of rejected object love), nostalgia resurrects primary narcissism, seeking to restore the original state of oneness with the world. The golden age of the organization may then be seen as an attempt to recreate the blissful unity of mother and child.

NOSTALGIA AND INJURED NARCISSISM

Nostalgia is but one attempt to re-create the blissful unity of primary narcissism. In the celebrated essay that introduced the concept of narcissism, Freud singled out as a central feature of narcissistic processes, the raising of an ideal ego. 'To this ideal ego is now directed the self-love which the real ego enjoyed in childhood. The narcissism seems to be now displaced on to this new ideal ego, which, like the infantile ego, deems itself the possessor of all perfections' (S. Freud 1914: 74). In the conclusion of that essay, Sigmund Freud (1914: 81) noted that the ego-ideal is 'of great importance for the understanding of group psychology. Besides its individual side, this ideal has a social side; it is also the common ideal of a family, a class or a nation.' Schwartz (1987a) has developed this argument, by viewing organizations as capable of supplying an ideal, at least as far as highly 'committed' organizational members are concerned. These participants are willing to sacrifice personal and family lives and are prepared to commit grossly unethical and criminal acts in the interest of the organization. In exchange, the organization offers them an 'organizational ideal', an idealized image of themselves quite untainted by the failings of incompetent officials or the envy of outsiders, pledged to a noble, immortal, and anxiety-free future. This organizational image of perfection then becomes the shared ideal of each member, sustaining their identities. They too are perfect, in as much as they are part of a perfect organization. They too are immortal, as members of an immortal organization. As a member of an organization whose death is inconceivable, the individual too becomes immortal. Threats to organizational survival are seen as personal threats against one's self. Consider, for example, the uproar generated when government action threatens to put an end to a long-standing organization, like the British Broadcasting Corporation. The end of the BBC, following the review of its charter, would be experienced by its constituency (and especially by its own members) as death. Part of themselves would die the day the initials BBC were replaced by CCB, CBB, or some other neologism (Sievers 1990, 1994).

Schwartz's organizational ideal possesses a utopian, almost millenarian, hue, a true heir to the religious promise of salvation in a future paradise. The use of overtly religious rhetoric—such as organizational 'mission', 'visions' of the future, 'charismatic' leadership—indicates that some organizations seek to fashion their mythological ideals after the messianic prototypes of Judaism and Christianity. This may apply to revolutionary parties (hoping to save the world through political action), but in the case of modern corporations it stretches one's credulity, though not perhaps the faith of the most blinkered organizational participants. I argued in Chapter 4 that, for a larger number of organizational members, an alternative solution to the same problem—that is, the injurious effect of organizations on narcissism—is the erection of an organizational malignant, a grotesque caricature of all the undesirable qualities, summed up in metaphors like 'This place is a madhouse/nightmare'. The individuals or group may then derive considerable narcissistic satisfaction from demeaning the organization, celebrating its failures and deriding its absurdities, and placing themselves morally and intellectually above it. Identity is here constructed through its opposition to the organizational malignant; in a nightmarish world, where everything is evil, anything that stands for opposition, resistance, and defiance easily becomes the object of idealization (as do, for instance, those who resist an occupying force). In many organizations, narcissism is restored by such a demonizing of the present, evident in large areas of organizational folklore.

What I am suggesting here is that nostalgic idealization of the past represents a parallel solution, which in the case of some, but not all, organizational members can go hand in hand with the demonization of the present. Individuals who are too disillusioned, too inquisitive, too rational, or simply too old to 'buy' the organization's own ideal, to internalize it, and to make it their own (like Schwartz's 'committed participants') may create an alternative ideal, one built not around galvanizing utopias for the future, but around the warm and loving reconstructions of the past. The use of the family metaphor and constant allusions to togetherness, solidarity, caring, and purpose are linked not to a future paradise but to a lost one, a time and a place when all biological and psychological needs were met. This was a time when individuals were characters rather than impersonal agents, when they worked together under strong but just leaders, when they prevailed against adversity by pulling together, when relations between them were sincere and authentic, when life was exciting, unpredictable, and yet secure. In proclaiming this idyllic past, nostalgia marks the triumphant idealism of the spirit over the discontents of the present. 'Man needs to supplement reality by an ideal world', wrote F. A. Lange (quoted in Bettelheim 1990: 107). Like great art then, nostalgia can ennoble human experiences, lift them above the mundane realities of everyday life, and give them a higher and finer quality.

Perhaps, an alternative solution should be added here if only because it stands in such sharp contrast to nostalgia. In addition to individuals idealizing the future (Schwartz's 'organizational ideal'), demonizing the present (organizational malignant), or idealizing the past (nostalgia), on occasion one meets individuals who demonize the organizational past. The term 'nostophobia', coined by Davis (1979), comes to mind here. I can provide only one brief but vivid illustration, from a supervisor in the chemical organization, at the end of a twenty-five-year career in the same department that spawned numerous nostalgic texts, including some quoted earlier. The contrast of this account with the earlier ones is astonishing, yet it only underlines the malleable nature of fantasy.

When I joined the organization, it was more like a school and the supervisors' word was law; it was really quite terrible, all the ladies were called by their surnames, it was just horrid . . . Very stern and regimented. When I joined, of course, I had a slight Northern accent. I was told I would be given a month's trial and in that month I had to lose my Northern accent. But I needed the job, so I lost the accent . . . Supervisors in those days were a different breed of people. Tartars!

Although demonization of such power was far outweighed by nostalgic recollection in the organization in question, I would suggest that demonization and idealization are processes that frequently operate in tandem as solutions to the problem of narcissism created by organizations; even Schwartz's idealization of the organization is implicitly complemented by xenophobia, the demonization of what lies outside the organization—interfering state agents, competitors, unappreciative public, as well as their representatives within the organization—the fifth column.

It will by now have become apparent that organizational nostalgia tells us more about the discontents of today than about the contents of the past. Like humour, but in a radically different way, it seeks to provide a symbolic way out of the rigors of bureaucracy, seeking to re-enchant a long disenchanted world. Having lost faith in the future, it idealizes the past, constructing an idealized image of the self out of what has been rather than about what should become. The stories spawned by nostalgia, like all stories, are wish-fulfilling poetic constructions, partial satisfactions in the realm of fantasy of real desires. And, like most fantasies, nostalgic fantasies rarely tempt falsification by engaging reality. Within organizations their illusory nature can be safely preserved; nostalgic fantasies and stories serve today's organizations well enough.

In particular, we examined how nostalgia seeks to offer partial consolation for the injuries sustained by our narcissism in organizations, though as a general cultural phenomenon it is no doubt related to the wider disenchantment with the present, and the loss of enthusiasm for the future, whether this should be seen in technological, political, or moral terms. Within organizations, nostalgia acts as a cause of an emotional gulf between those with first hand experiences of the golden past, and those without. This reinforces many other divisions.

In closing this chapter we may offer a tentative evaluation of nostalgia. Is nostalgia good or bad? Rationalists have traditionally disparaged it (*a*) for its clouding of critical faculties, its proclamation of a set of often infantile illusions and its enmity to true historical enquiry, or, more commonly, (*b*) for the ease with which it becomes appropriated, trivialized, and exploited by capital's 'merchandisers of meaning'. Some commentators have observed that, under certain circumstances, nostalgia for a heroic past, a racially pure or culturally uniform past, can feed some of the ugliest and most reactionary ideologies. I feel that a more equivocal evaluation is in order, for nostalgia is a deeply equivocal phenomenon. In as much as it provides a groundrock of loving memories, a life worth having lived, a source of meaning and sensemaking, ennobling us and enabling us to endure present malaise, nostalgia is good. Its implications should not be pre-judged as conservative and regressive. Many radical movements and many noble causes have been sustained by myth or fantasy of golden age in the distant past (Lasch 1980: p. xvii). As a consumer, the individual may be vulnerable to attempts to control his or her nostalgia, to be manipulated or exploited. But, within the confines of organizations, nostalgia is harder to control, as the earlier quotes indicate. In this sense, nostalgia can be part of the unmanaged organization, those aspects of organizational life, emotion, and symbolism that resist attempts to control them through impersonal procedures by management (see Chapter 5).

Finally, when compared with some other psychological mechanisms addressing the same needs—namely, blind nationalism, hate-filled xenophobia, cynical withdrawal, or slavish conformity to the organization—nostalgia strikes me both as benign and honourable. If only through the means of inappropriate symbols and fictitious images of the past, it seeks to reintroduce idealism in organizations, to maintain a much-needed plurality of voices and views, and to vindicate a set of alternative values in organizations, from those of profit, rationality, efficiency, and domination.

9

Facing God

To many people in the lower echelons of organizations, top leaders do not appear altogether human, at least not in the sense that colleagues or immediate superiors are. The 'Big Boss' is the object of acute curiosity, fascination, and gossip, the more so when followers rarely catch sight of him or her, and then only on ceremonial occasions. A physical and psychological gulf seems to separate top leaders from ordinary organizational members, a gulf that is filled up by fantasy. Followers fantasize about their leaders. In these fantasies, leaders can feature in different ways—as benevolent, father-like figures, as demonic schemers engaged in plotting and machination, as cunning wheeler-dealers who strike clever deals for the organization, as impostors who attained their position by deception, and so forth. Leaders too fantasize about their followers—about their loyalty or heroism, about their scheming and disaffection.

This chapter charts the dominant fantasies that subordinates have about their leaders, by focusing on a particular scene, which features regularly in organizational stories, a scene in which an 'ordinary' member of an organization comes face to face with the organization's top leader. This echoes not only the archetypal Christian scene of meeting God as supreme ruler on the Day of Judgement, but also a fairly regular episode in some works of literature and the stage, such as Tolstoy's *War and Peace* or Mussorgsky's *Boris Godunov*.[1] In their

---

[1] In Tolstoy's *War and Peace*, for instance, we meet young Nikolai Rostov, who, having fantasized countless times the moment when he might meet his Emperor, finally gets his chance on the morrow of a military defeat: 'But as a youth in love trembles and turns faint and dares not utter what he has spent nights in dreaming of, and looks around in terror, seeking aid or a chance of delay and flight, when the longed-for moment arrives and he is alone with her, so Rostov, now that he had attained what he had longed for beyond everything in the world, did not know how to approach the Emperor, and a thousand reasons occurred to him why it would be untimely, improper and impossible to do so' (Tolstoy 1869/1982: 334). Tolstoy develops at length Nikolai's fantasies regarding his leader as indeed he does Pierre's plan to assassinate Napoleon. Both subplots converge on the moment when a follower meets the leader.

personal histories, individuals may experience their first meeting with a great leader or a charismatic individual as a 'liminal moment', pre-saging an important turn in their lives. Commenting on writings by sixty prominent Nazis, Dicks (1972: 79) writes: 'A good proportion of the writers stress the "unforgettable" magic moment when Hitler looked (or they felt he looked) into their eyes or squeezed their hand.'

In organizations, the theme of meeting the leader has been noted both in apocryphal stories, such as those reported by Peters and Waterman (1982) and Deal and Kennedy (1982), and also in literature dealing systematically with organizational myths and stories (Maccoby 1976; Martin *et al.* 1983; Mitroff and Kilman 1976; Rosen 1985*a*; Wilkins 1983; Wilkins and Ouchi 1983). As we saw in Chapter 8, stories of meetings with past leaders can feed nostalgia for the past. Meeting the leader may be the subject of a conscious fantasy or day-dreaming, when, as members of organizations, we imagine what would happen if we had such an encounter. We may then muse, for example, on the favours we might ask for, the grievances we might express, the enlightenment we might seek, the advice we might give, or the violence we might perpetrate. Alternatively, the theme may assume the form of a story—a wish-fulfilling embellishment of a meeting that actually took place. Such meetings have a memorable quality, often becoming landmarks in our personal history or even features of organizational folklore, recurring in different variants. Like all organizational stories, stories of such meetings open a win-dow onto the emotional life of organizational participants. In partic-ular, they lead us to some of the unconscious fantasies that subordinates spin around the figure of the organization's top leaders. These fantasies, in turn, reveal a great deal about the nature and dynamics of leader–follower relations, as well as the emotional needs of subordinates fulfilled or frustrated by leaders. In this chapter I shall argue that, because of the nature of these needs, subordinates often make superhuman demands on their leaders, elevating them (often with the leaders' own collusion) to heights from which they can rarely fail to disappoint. This chapter is intended as a contribu-tion not so much to the already bulging theory of leadership (Baum 1987, 1989; Bennis 1989; Bennis and Nanus 1985; Hirschhorn 1997; Kets de Vries 1988, 1990; Kets de Vries and Miller 1984; Krantz 1989, 1990) but to the less developed theory of followership. It is also intended as a further essay in story interpretation. Lately, organizational studies have started to take a keener interest in the psychology of followers, an issue that has been central to political science in general and political psychology in particular.[2]

[2] Since the publication of Sigmund Freud's *Group Psychology and the Analysis of the Ego* (1921), psychoanalysis has taken an interest in the psychology of the leader–

FACING GOD

This chapter is built around three personal accounts of meetings with the leader. The source of these accounts is different from the source of stories in the earlier parts of this book. Each one was written by an undergraduate student returning to the university after six months of industrial placement (internship). As part of their debriefing, students were asked to describe in detail an incident that they witnessed during their placement that captures the nature of their experience with the company. They were then invited to analyse the incident and discuss the emotions that it evoked at the time it happened, as well as the emotions it generated as they wrote about it. Between 1990 and 1995, 374 such reports were collected, analysed, and filed.[3] Several students chose to focus their reports on a crucial meeting with the organization's top leader(s), and several more reported such stories second-hand. The reports were submitted by students who had studied at the university only for a single year. The innocent eyes of these trainees can capture admirably some of the qualities, good and bad, that are projected onto leaders. Most older, seasoned members of organizations might find it embarrassing to discuss such fantasies with others. Student trainees, on the other hand, can write especially lucidly about their own feelings when they finally get to meet these distant figures upon whom so much is seen to depend. Another reason why these reports have a special interest lies in the widely recognized fact that late adolescents are particularly given to irrational attachments to leader figures, ranging from media stars and sports heroes to messianic religious and military leaders. These figures are called on to quell some of the anxieties

follower relationship, making some notable contributions (Adorno *et al.* 1950; Erikson 1968; Fromm 1941/1966; Reich 1970); it has also, sometimes rightly, been charged with psychological reductionism and unprovability. In this chapter I do not wish to enter the debates on the rights and wrongs of psychoanalysis (Crews 1995; Forrester 1997; Gabriel 1999; Grünbaum 1984), but I do wish to demonstrate some of the possibilities opened by a psychoanalytic perspective. These occur at three levels. First, at the level of interpretation, psychoanalysis enhances our comprehension of organizational symbolism and our ability to make sense of the seeming trivia of organizational life; it enables us to understand why, in organizational narratives, factual accuracy is sacrificed for poetic effect. Secondly, it provides some of the most powerful keys into human motivation, emphasizing the complexity, plasticity, and mobility of human desire and its manifestations. Thirdly, it offers a model of as well as a vocabulary for the mental personality, fragmented, at odds with itself and with the world at large, wicked and yet profoundly moral, savage and yet irreversibly civilized, which is uniquely attuned to the paradoxes of organizational life and especially the contradictions of leader–follower relations.

  [3] The reports were analysed, like the main database, with the help of Cardbox-Plus. Each report was entered on a separate record and the following information was recorded in distinct fields on each record: the names of the trainee and the organization, the type of incident described, the emotions it generated, the moral of the incident, the theory locations addressed by the report, and the overall narrative quality of the report.

resulting from transitional identity stages, resulting from leaving their parents' home and dealing with their burgeoning sexuality (Erikson 1968). As Lindholm (1988: 22) has observed, 'adolescents, of course, are great followers, and often form a central cadre of movements and cults, which tap their desire for identification by providing an appropriate object in the form of a charismatic figure. For teenagers, then, hero-worship is a predictable phenomenon.'

Leader-centred fantasies and stories may be more prominent among this age group than among older, more seasoned participants, but they are all the same a core feature in most organizations. No fewer than five of the seven major types of organizational story identified by Martin and colleagues (Martin *et al.* 1983) revolve around the leader.[4] In my own database, thirty out of 404 stories concerned the organization's top leader, and a further twenty-eight concerned a senior manager. The proportion of leader-centred stories varied across the organizations but they were a significant feature in most of them. Some of these stories will be presented to amplify arguments raised by the students' accounts, to illustrate the extent to which older organizational participants have fantasies about their leaders, and the nature of these fantasies.

THE LEADER AS REINCARNATION OF THE PRIMAL MOTHER

In the first report, Anna, a Greek student, recounts her meeting with the director of a publishing company.

Anna's story: The most precious experience of my placement

Is it really possible to capture the essence of an organization through a single event? This sounds quite scary, though it is a pretty attractive idea. For three or four days now, my mind has been travelling back to Athens, where I had my placement, trying to revive my working life and experiences. I remember people being stressed, running up and down in their offices, preparing themselves for meetings, people being happy or sad, people chatting or working non-stop.

I can remember my first day at work. My brother accompanied me to the office. I was literally shaking! I also remember the last day at work. I think that

---

[4] Nor should it be thought that such stories and fantasies are unique to business organizations. Portelli (1990) reports old Communists fantasizing about conversations that they might have had with the party leader, which might have changed the course of history and led to the elusive revolution.

this is going to remain in my memory as vivid as ever. I was sad. All the people in the department were sad also. I wanted this day to last longer than usual. People were coming to wish me goodbye and kept asking me when I will be back.

There is indeed so much to write about and thus it is very confusing to try and select just one thing to refer to. Yet, after a lot of thinking, I have decided on something that truly deserves to be written down. It is probably the most precious experience that I had during my placement.

Working was something new for me as this was the first time I had worked for a firm other than my Dad's. This was 'proper' work for the first time. As most people do when they find themselves in a new environment, I kept on observing and thinking. I was analysing people's actions and reactions, attitudes and overall behaviour. Everybody seemed to have his or her own role, every department its own aims and its own functions. The theories we had learned at the university, about roles, hierarchy, working groups etc., seemed to come alive right in front of my eyes, leaving me satisfied and even more interested in the subject of my studies. But what about this 'myth' of management? What is the top person's role in all that? What is it to lead people? These were the questions that I needed the answers for. After much wondering, I decided to try and have a discussion with my top manager, a conversation which would, hopefully, help me to solve the 'mystery'.

As the manager was extremely busy for days and days, I was becoming even more obsessed with the idea that I had to talk with her and ask her to reveal to me all the secrets that had guided her to success. Finally one afternoon she was free and pleased to talk to me. I then realized for a moment that my request was difficult. I wanted to find out about everything. *Was this feasible? I explained most of my thoughts to her, she understood all the worries that had been in my mind all this time. We discussed a lot of things involving managerial concepts and attitudes.*

The first issue was that of managerial style, in particular the ways in which a manager imposes him or herself on his or her subordinates. Can one win the trust of others by fear or by personal respect? The answer was respect. If you have knowledge of the work subject, and if what you want is the involvement and cooperation of your subordinates, then you have found a sure way to get what you want from your department. A successful manager must first of all have passion for his or her work. This is the basis for transmitting your personal enthusiasm to the people you are working with and to inspire them to work with you to reach the organizational targets.

A manager should try to analyse each one of his or her subordinates and aim for a better understanding, better cooperation, and finally positive results. By making a correct use of the abilities and the talents of each one, we help them set feasible goals that benefit the whole department, and enable them to succeed at a personal level as well.

A good manager must also be accessible *to his or her subordinates in both business and personal terms. People are indeed the most important issue within the organization and the art of handling them should be one of the major abilities a manager should be endowed with. Nobody starts his or her career as a manager. And if this is the case, they are bound to fail. Only by*

understanding and considering the position of a subordinate—this is by tak-
ing his or her place at least once—then the management of the people and the
department can be fair and effective.

The discussion continued for a long time and all the issues were mainly
connected with the human aspect of the organization. My satisfaction from
listening to my manager talk about these issues was indescribable. All these
theories I had seen applied in our department with great success were now
reconfirmed to me by my manager, a person whom I respect and admire
enormously. I consider myself very lucky to have worked as a subordinate for
this particular manager. I hope that one day I will have the chance to practise
all that I have learned and I am still learning, becoming a successful manager.

Anna recounts her meeting with the director in almost religious
terms. If the incident cannot be described as a 'Road-to-Damascus'
experience, it is because the encounter helped anchor and confirm a
faith rather than replace one set of beliefs with another. It does, however, have some of the marks of a liminal moment, which may
remain with her as a critical turn in her personal history (Kunda 1992;
V. Turner 1974, 1980). At that moment, without knowing it, she made
important decisions about her future and distilled a new set of
meanings regarding her university studies, authority relations, and
possibly life as a whole. Things that had been bookish theories, or,
more tellingly, 'mysteries' and 'myths' before the meeting, became
clear and full of meaning afterwards.

Idealization and identification

Anna's professed 'indescribable' satisfaction appears out of proportion to the views on management that she describes, views that
would strike some cynical commentators as pious platitudes. Yet the
very fervour with which she reports these views provides evidence
that banalities can sound extraordinary and clichés can appear like
wisdom when uttered by 'great' leaders, whose endorsement turns
mere ideas into 'gospel'. In fact, everything touched by the leader
acquires a glowing aura. This is a characteristic of the psychological
process of *idealization*, which imbues the whole narrative. Not a
single negative word or critical comment is allowed to spoil an image
of sheer perfection and bliss. This transformation of the commonplace into perfection has been singled out as a crucial feature, common to relations with both leaders and love objects (S. Freud 1921;
Lindholm 1988; Schwartz 1985, 1987*a*, 1990). Leaders as well as objects
of infatuation become endowed with 'all' the perfections, forming
part of an individual's ego-ideal, the set of idealized images against
which the individual measures him or herself. Anna's vivid descrip-

tion of her nervousness before the eagerly anticipated meeting as well as her feeling of relief that her manager had understood 'all her worries' in a flash have a romantic quality, reminiscent of the lover's inhibitions before meeting his or her beloved. Having the manager's undivided attention for 'a long time', in which 'all the issues', 'all the secrets', and 'all the worries' are gone through evokes a managerial *folie à deux*, a moment of initiation, meriting indeed the 'indescribable satisfaction' noted. Krantz (1989) has admirably captured this quality in the idea of the 'managerial couple'. The earlier quote from Tolstoy (see note 1) displays the feverish quality surrounding meetings with leaders or loved objects.

In addition to idealization of the leader, Anna's brief but poignant description of her last day at work suggests an identification with her colleagues, who shared her sadness. Even more vivid, however, is the description of Anna's identification with the leader herself, someone she not only 'respected and admired enormously', but also someone with whom she identified as a role model, someone she wanted to emulate as a successful woman in a business culture dominated by men. The fact that this outstanding woman took the time to talk to Anna in person, to address her worries and answer her questions, was very important for Anna. 'Only by understanding and considering the position of a subordinate—this is by taking his or her place at least once—then the management of the people and the department can be fair and effective.' In this revealing sentence, she indicates both the extent of her identification with her leader and also the way in which this identification serves as the basis of a promise, that she too will become a leader one day, just as her manager, who was herself once a subordinate, did. It is noteworthy how Anna stresses accessibility as an important leadership attribute, and sees her leader as an accessible one, notwithstanding the difficulties she had in meeting her. The leader is accessible, but, as a very 'busy' person, her time is priceless—a single meeting establishes the accessibility of the leader, without at the same time suggesting any undue familiarity. The leader is at once accessible and distant, her gifts of time, wisdom, and care to be accepted with gratitude rather than taken for granted.

Anna's description, saturated with narrative elements of both religion and romantic love, contains in a nutshell several features of the leader–follower relationship—idealization, identification with the leader, identification with other followers, suspension of most critical faculties, and an uplifting quality. A less sentimental but also idealized account of a meeting with the organization's top leader is offered by Bob, the librarian of the chemical corporation, several of whose stories have already been discussed. Like Anna, this account highlights the caring qualities of the leader and his accessibility, the fact that he is willing to give his precious time to a subordinate:

I suppose in a way, I had actually forgotten the date of my twentieth anniversary [with the company] and about a week before, I had a telephone from the chairman's office, and they said, 'Are you free at 3 o'clock next Friday?' and I said, 'Yes I am.' 'Oh, the chairman would like to see you,' so I thought, 'Uh, uh, this is it!' [Laughter]. You know . . . then I thought, 'Oh he wouldn't worry about that, he's got other people to kick me out.' Anyway, I thought about this for the rest of the week.

Now with Sir Roy [the previous chairman] I often saw him, and he used to ring me up or collar me about something or other, I could tell you a story about that later, anyway, the Friday came, and Sir Michael's secretary, said, 'Hello Bob, he's got somebody with him at the moment, hang on.' It was only a few minutes and then I went in. 'Oh hello, come and sit down, tea or coffee? Have some biscuits etc. I've had a little check and it's your twentieth anniversary and I've got a certificate for you.' I hadn't really thought that this is what it was all about. We chatted for about an hour. You know, talking about what I thought about the company. I was quite surprised really with what he knew, to be honest; I mean, I know that they've got files and they can check things out, but even so. About three months ago I saw him in the corridor, and I had had a kidney stone removed some time earlier, and he asked me how I was feeling.

Bob's description may lack the religious and romantic elements present in Anna's narrative but contains both the nervousness before the meeting with the great man (here accentuated by the auxiliary fantasy of being sacked) and the gratitude for being treated with consideration, care, and respect. What neither of these narratives contain is any echo of the leader as the harsh and omnipotent father, dominating his followers and enforcing social values. Instead, they are redolent with a quality of satisfaction and self-satisfaction that are characteristic of narcissistic gratification. The leader neither punishes nor judges, but gives—time, wisdom, affection, and faith. In all of these respects, the leader occupies the symbolic and emotional space occupied by mother in early childhood, the primal mother of later fantasy life (Chasseguet-Smirgel 1976). Instead of the *aloof* paternal leader, who rewards and punishes, leaving his followers with weakened egos, this accessible, primal mother-leader restores her followers' narcissism and provides a considerable boost to their self-esteem, by achieving a fusion between each individual follower and the wider group. Kohut (1985) has argued that leadership based on a primal mother fantasy is charismatic while that based on a primal father fantasy is messianic. Unlike the followers of charismatic leaders, who are prone to ecstatic phenomena and overflow with both self-regard and energy, the followers of messianic leaders are depleted of self-regard, stand in awe of their leader, and are ever-willing to sacrifice themselves in the interests of a superior cause. If meeting a messianic leader, like meeting God on the Day of Judgement, is a terrifying experience, meeting a charismatic leader is more likely to prove an invigorating and inspiring one, as in the earlier accounts.

UNCARING LEADERS

Meeting the leader, of course, need be neither terrifying nor inspiring. Such meetings, whether planned or accidental, can equally well end in an anticlimax or in disappointment, leaving a bitter aftertaste, as is shown by the account that follows.

Kim's story: Time need not be wasted on lesser mortals

Six months in a national retail organization. OK, so it's not a City firm and it's not everyone's idea of a high-flying business, but it seemed to offer what I thought I was after, at a wage that couldn't be laughed at.

I went to work with few preconceived ideas and no experience. Although, the organization turned out to be run like a military camp and was a complete shock to me socially and culturally, I just about managed to keep my head above water. As far as I was concerned, my placement had been a success, that is until I had a parting chat with the Managing Director of the branch. Much of my confidence in management and the organization collapsed when I went to see the 'Boss'. The event that discoloured my opinion appears to sum up a classic syndrome afflicting many senior managers: 'Time need not be wasted on lesser mortals.' Scathing generalization I know, yet in this case very relevant.

My conversation with the boss took the following course:

'Right, you've been here long?'
'Five months to date.'
'And you've come from a Poly?'
'No, from a university, Bath University.'
'And this is part of your degree?'
'Yes, I am studying for a degree in Business Administration.'
'And what has your placement with us consisted of?'
'Basically I have had a fairly comprehensive insight into the company, spending time in several different departments. I have covered both the administrative and shop floor departments.'
'Right, and have we been paying you for this?'
'Yes.'
'And how much is that?'

'£9,500 per year.'
'And when are you leaving?'
'This Saturday.'
'And do you return here on your next placement?'
'It's not compulsory so I will probably try and be placed in a City firm.'

It was in this style that the conversation went on. He had obviously not bothered to spend even five minutes going over my file, and hence spent the whole time asking what he should have already known. Although I was only a small cog in the machine, the impression he made upon me in those ten minutes was to be damaging to both him and organization that he represented. His inability to review my situation and relate to me reflected badly not only upon himself, but upon the company.

Having been so scathing about the MD, I do realize that he had very limited time, and probably more pressing engagements. And although this incident should not reflect on the corporation as a whole, my instinctive inclination and to a certain extent my naïvety meant that my opinion of the branch and its management had collapsed. In my view, it does not say much that a senior manager could not be bothered to find out about the subject in hand, and appear so unprepared.

My main thought on this incident is that certain managers within the company and probably in other organizations do not respect their subordinates, nor do they realize that it is the lesser mortals that account for the running of such businesses.

If Anna's meeting helped strengthen her faith, confidence, and self-respect, Kim's faith in the leader as well as in the organization 'collapsed' following the meeting. Kim attributes this collapse to her own naïvety; yet, the strength of feeling of injured pride made this the most telling incident of her placement. Kim does not claim that the director intended to insult her, yet the discussion of her feelings indicates that an unintentional slight is as hurtful as an intended one. The incident reveals the emotional vulnerability of the subordinate when meeting the organization's leader. It also shows how loss of faith in the leader often brings with it loss of faith in the organization as a whole.

Are Kim's negative references to the organization ('military', not a 'high-flying business') evidence that she never really identified with it? It seems more likely to be a retrospective emotional distancing from the organization, which, following the insulting behaviour of its leader, comes to be seen as the embodiment of 'all' negative qualities, an 'organization malignant', as discussed in earlier chapters. Following the meeting, her pride and self-esteem could be restored by severing her identification with the organization, by demonizing it, and by distancing herself from it. Had Kim never identified with the organization or its leader at all, if she had regarded it merely as a job, she would probably not have taken serious offence at the director's patronizing behaviour. Nor would his arrogance have affected her view of the entire organization, as it pointedly does. It would then seem that even in such an organization (impersonal, unglamorous, disciplinarian) a bond of identification linked a temporary member like Kim to the invisible leader and to her colleagues, until the ill-fated meeting.

Why did the meeting shatter this bond and destroy Kim's total image of the organization? Kim's use of the words 'lesser mortals', 'time wasted', and 'not bothered' indicate that she was hurt by his lack of care. In diametrical opposition to Anna's and Bob's narratives (well-briefed leader, long meetings), Kim's leader had no 'real' time for her (ill-briefed leader, perfunctory meeting). *Care* (or the absence of it) is a common feature of many followers' fantasies regarding their leader. Followers are prepared to endure the leader's harshness and, to a degree, arbitrariness in return for fulfilment of a need for protection, rooted in infantile helplessness and dependency. An uncaring leader does not merely deny his or her followers the satisfaction of a vital need, but forces them to confront their dependency and casts a serious blow to their pride (Bennis 1989; Hirschhorn 1988, 1997).[5] Kim was not merely hurt, she was angry. Anger is a response not so much to neglect, as to rejection. Had the leader not bothered to meet her at all, Kim might have felt hurt, but she is unlikely to have felt angry. Her anger is the product of injured pride and self-respect. What insulted her was the leader's double presumption; first, that she should feel grateful about being allowed to meet him at all, and, secondly, that no briefing was necessary for such a meeting. Not only did the leader not care about her, but he did so while pretending to care—that is, he took her for stupid.[6] As in Anna's account, the leader in Kim's narrative is accessible, but his accessibility is spurious, just as his pretence of caring conceals indifference.

---

[5] An uncaring leader is not the same as an 'aloof' or distant leader (Kohut 1985; Lindholm 1988). Such a leader may be endowed with caring qualities even in the light of overwhelming evidence to the contrary. Solzhenitsyn, for instance, reports how many Soviet people remained attached to the image of Stalin as a benign father, who would set everything right if only he knew the crimes perpetrated by his patsies. Aloof leaders keep their followers on tenterhooks as to whether they truly care or not. The mere suspicion that perhaps they do not care can be seen as betrayal of the leader and bring about feelings of guilt.

[6] A patronized follower shares several qualities of the spurned lover, just as the fulfilled follower (Anna) shares qualities with the lover whose feelings have been reciprocated.

THE ASYMMETRY IN LEADER–FOLLOWER RELATIONS

Anna's and Kim's stories highlight the fundamental asymmetry in most leader–follower relationships. Leaders meet many of their members in the course of their work. Shaking hands with the boss may be a unique experience for an employee; a leader, however, will shake numerous hands every day and it can be hard to make every handshake meaningful and warm, in the knowledge that it may be the other person's only handshake with the leader. The follower will usually know the name of the organization's leader, will be able to recognize his or her face from photographs, may know his or her likes and dislikes from press reports, interviews, and gossip. The leader, on the other hand, will probably not know the names of the majority of his or her followers, their faces will be virtually indistinguishable from those of members of any other organization, and their likes and dislikes are virtually immaterial. The essential difference between Anna's and Kim's stories is that, whereas Anna's boss bridged the gulf, making her feel valued and respected, Kim's boss (probably unknowingly) used the parting ritual to underline the status and power distance that separated them, treating her as 'just another trainee'. In doing so, he inflicted a blow on her narcissism, which was already tarnished by the inferior reputation of the company, compared to the prestigious 'City firms' in which some of Kim's friends did their placements.

Bridging the gulf

One variant of the fantasy of meeting God has the leader visiting the troops, meeting them *en masse* (rather than individually as in the earlier narratives), administering praise, largesse, or rebuke, or simply 'socializing' with them. Some leaders are especially adept at bridging the gap in this manner. In the case of Sir Roy, who featured in many of the nostalgic stories discussed in Chapter 8, a real folklore had developed around his impromptu meetings with subordinates. Here are some accounts in which he featured, several years after his retirement:

Sir Roy, the legend lives on. Generally speaking, he was very popular, people liked him, especially here at HQ but also throughout the company, he had the reputation that the troops appreciate. Here is a bloke . . . you'd be sitting down eating your lunch and he'd come and he'd sit next to you and say, 'How is it going, I am Roy Plum,' and he would chat to you. That gave him a better grasp of what people at the grass-root level were thinking, are they looking for jobs elsewhere, this sort of thing.

Several unsolicited accounts centre on impromptu meetings with Sir Roy either in lifts or in the bar.

If you got in the lift with Sir Roy, he talked endlessly with everybody; he always had something very pleasant, very amusing to say. He enhanced your day if you came across him. It wasn't that he knew you personally, but he always said hello to everybody; he was gifted at remembering names, but you wouldn't expect him to remember the names, I was at a very low level really, for him, you know, but he did remember people's names. He was a very outwardly pleasant easy-going chap, just like he comes across on TV.

Familiarity with Sir Roy only rarely bred contempt. In the majority of narratives he features as a character, either through his ability to support and encourage or through his penchant for the unexpected and the unpredictable. In fact, his frequent appearances on radio and television as a national celebrity made him an even more godlike leader, in spite of descriptions of him as 'human', 'humane', or even as 'one of the boys'. While he bridged the gulf between himself and his followers, there was never any question of the existence of the gulf. In the following narrative, expressions like 'go up to' and 'come down' offer an insight into the gulf and its bridging.

I am sure that if I went up to Sir Roy we wouldn't have too much to say to each other . . . [Why not?] Well, it depends. . . what I'd go up to talk to him about, whether or not it was all superficial, just to look good and human, yet to me it was all pretty good. Some people gave him a lot of flak for coming down, but the way that I saw it was that it was nice that he came round and spent time in the areas that we did. At least he could see that, if the bar was dirty, for instance, it wouldn't be all cleaned up for him to come down; he'd just drop down like everybody else.

Unlike Sir Roy, many leaders find mixing with the troops difficult or embarrassing. The result then may be traumatic (as it was for Kim) or merely disappointing, as is the case with more seasoned organizational participants. The following brief story, told by Norman, a senior researcher in the research and publishing organization, illustrates the consequences of a leader's inability to bridge the social and emotional gap that separates him or her from subordinates:

I've only met him [the director] once, after last XMAS when we all went to meet him in groups, a particularly stilted affair. It was wine and something to eat for each group at a time, but hardly anyone talked to him directly. [Do you talk a lot about him?] Yes. Usually disparagingly.

Norman, as an older and more cynical organizational participant than Kim, did not allow his disappointment with the director to make him angry; instead, it was absorbed in a litany of criticisms of the director, told in a knowing, dismissive manner. The director's inability or unwillingness to bridge the gap between himself and the ordinary organizational members became emblematic of his general isolation and unconcern.

Meeting the leader: Where fantasy confronts reality

Why is meeting the organization's leader such an important event in people's emotional life? Why does it feature in so many organizational stories? As we argued earlier, fantasizing about leaders is common in organizations. Meeting the boss tests these fantasies, reinforcing some, and turning others into their opposite. All the narratives discussed so far revolve, whether positively or negatively, around the fantasy of a *caring* and *accessible* leader who acknowledges and recognizes his or her followers and addresses them as worthy members of the organization.[7] As we saw in Chapter 2, one dominant characteristic of our fantasy life is its disregard for the endless complexities and nuances of the real world, which come to be replaced by certain binary oppositions, like good/bad, true/false, real/unreal. These oppositions have been noted in many fairy tales (Bettelheim 1976), myths (Lévi-Strauss, 1963*a*, 1966, 1978), as well as organizational stories and folklore. Such fundamental oppositions are also a feature of many follower fantasies about their leaders.

THE LEADER AS REINCARNATION OF THE OMNIPOTENT PRIMAL FATHER

The following report introduces a new dimension in the fantasies held by subordinates apropos of their leaders—omnipotence. It is

[7] The image of the leader singling one out from a crowd of followers and according one special recognition is a common fantasy of followers aspiring to the role of favoured disciple or child and possible successor. It is also a fantasy regularly acted out—for example, when students want to be 'noticed' by their teacher or conscripts by their commanding officer. Kapuscinski (1983: 113) provides the following vivid account: 'A crowd awaited the Emperor . . . We all gathered early so as not to miss the Emperor's arrival, because that moment had special significance for us. Everyone wanted very badly to be noticed by the Emperor. No, one didn't dream of special notice, with the Revered Emperor catching sight of you, coming up, starting a conversation. No, nothing like that, I assure you. One wanted the smallest, second-rate sort of attention, nothing that burdened the Emperor with any obligations. A passing notice, a fraction of a second, yet the sort of notice that later would make one tremble inside and overwhelm one with the triumphal though "I have been noticed." What strength it gave afterward! What unlimited possibilities it created!'

perhaps not accidental that this account was provided by a male trainee, since it treats the leader less as a primal mother figure, caring, supporting, and recognizing, and more as a figure of authority, reverence, and fear. The fantasy of the leader's omnipotence (and the associated fantasy of the leader's omniscience) is one of the commonest, if not the commonest, fantasy about leaders. It is often consciously furthered by leaders themselves, whose own narcissism is enhanced in this way, though followers tend to project truly superhuman powers onto them. One of the most potent organizational experiences, spawning numerous stories and myths, centres on the discovery that leaders themselves are only human and fallible, that they too are afraid, and that they too may be driven by someone standing above them. In the story that follows, Steve vividly describes how his faith in his own leader, in a large transnational corporation, was shattered when he realized that he was but a puppet on someone else's string.

Steve's Story: The day I lost faith in Mike McKie

Before discussing the incident in question, it is helpful to give a few details of the company. Although DACRO UK is an affiliate of DACRO International based in the US, it is officially a separate entity with its own management, culture, and vision. DACRO UK is split into seven major product divisions—each of which functions independently of the others. The division to which I was assigned is called the Consumer Appliances Division (CAD) and deals in the traditional appliances. CAD is headed up by an executive named Mike McKie.

When I joined DACRO the demands on McKie appeared to come from two sources. I have already mentioned the US connection, but DACRO UK prided itself on its independence, its distinct culture, and its ability to outperform its US parent company. If the British subsidiary's independence was genuine, McKie should be answerable to the demi-gods of DACRO UK (i.e. the Board of Directors). Perched on the seventeenth floor of DACRO House these mythical creatures are reputed to rule from sumptuous quarters of mahogany and leather. Nobody you meet within the company has actually entered the seventeenth floor and nobody is quite sure what goes on there. However, most people have their own story of a personal encounter with Zeus himself—Erroll Bates, CEO of DACRO UK.

This report describes the events surrounding 9 December, the day I lost faith in McKie. McKie had stressed on frequent occasions that CAD needed a radical change in structure in order to become more 'customer focused'—a condition he believed to be essential if DACRO were to remain successful in the 90s. He had developed his own plans to this effect and had begun to implement some of them with considerable ceremony. However, all these plans were laid to rest on 9 December, when Peter Kellner, Head of CAD world-wide in corporate

Headquarters in Boston, announced his global strategy for change. DACRO UK senior management were told of the announcement a fortnight before the event. They spent two weeks anticipating what Kellner would announce and how his 'decree' would affect CAD UK. Indeed they were so anxious, that they arranged a satellite link-up with the US so that they could listen to Kellner 'live'. However, there was little or no communication between senior management and the rest of the workforce during this period. The workforce sensed how significant the announcement was to senior management and began to speculate on what it would mean for the future of DACRO UK—negative rumour was rife. Incredibly, management did absolutely nothing to dispel these rumours: they must have known what scenarios were being discussed and yet they stuck their heads in the sand and pretended that it was business as usual.

9 December came to pass and Kellner made his speech. His 'grand design' was swallowed hook, line, and sinker—and McKie has made changes in line with the 'edict' ever since. No consideration has been given to the possible culture differences and market disparities between the US and the UK, or any attempt to 'interpret' the edict in line with the strategy of DACRO UK. In fact, McKie completely disregarded his own strategy for the future of the division and appears to have adopted enthusiastically Kellner's plans in their entirety.

Initially, I had a lot of time and respect for McKie. He was (in my mind) an unsuccessful [sic] executive who would in time turn CAD around by adhering to his principles and 'sticking it out'. He was very much a 'people' manager with a high profile—always encouraging, and seeing the silver lining in every cloud. All my preconceptions were shattered by the events of and around 9 December. The way McKie and his management team acquiesced to Kellner's announcement was spineless. Why didn't McKie have the guts to continue with his strategy for the UK? The sudden change in vision and direction was detrimental to the division's morale and devastating on McKie's authority. Kellner had made the call and McKie had jumped. During the weeks preceding 9 December, McKie frequently scurried off to Boston, presumably to ingratiate himself with US senior management (this only served to alienate him further from his UK workforce). I completely lost faith in his authority because it became so second-hand in my eyes. I also experienced a feeling of vulnerability as an employee. The security that a strong management provides had been removed—the UK management team appeared to lack the guts to lead—it was as if they would stick their heads in a fire at the whim of the US.

Perhaps more important was the impact on morale. Management did not effectively communicate with the rest of the workforce in any shape or form. We were sent one communiqué outlining what was happening on 9 December, 'a critical announcement which may result in radical changes within CAD'. That was all the information which we were given and so we were left to speculate what these changes might involve. Many scenarios evolved, and, human nature being what it is, these inevitably included much doom and gloom: massive job cuts and reshuffling were the favourite elements in most prophecies. Consequently for a week leading up to the announcement morale at work plummeted. The atmosphere became polluted by fear and suspicion. CAD has been going through difficult times recently but until this inci-

dent the management still enjoyed the support of those under them. However, their complete disregard for anybody other than themselves over this affair really lowered the esteem in which they were held.

It would be worth mentioning that this incident was of much more signifi-cance to me than to others within the division. Those employees who had been with the company for a while had perhaps come to terms with the fact that their senior management were little more than puppets of Boston. However, because I was new to the company, I felt 'let down'. Initially, I had almost idol-ized the executives at DACRO UK, and when my image of them was shattered I became bitter and resentful. To cope with my feelings, I found myself turning my attention away from the UK senior management team towards the US for signs of where the company was heading. Directives that were endorsed by Boston became highly significant, while those of UK origin I dismissed as petty.

Finally, it is worth pointing out how the whole affair destroyed the 'magic' of the seventeenth-floor myth. I had adopted the fantasy that surrounded Bates and the directors and it had become a form of motivation to think of these overseers controlling operations. However, the implication of the Kellner affair is that Bates and his Board are little more than figureheads, with no real power or purpose. This realization filled me with disillusion and the seven-teenth floor became quite a pathetic spectacle.

Certain elements in Steve's narrative echo the earlier ones. Like them, it touches on the leader's caring, accessible qualities, embod-ied by McKie before his fall from grace ('a "people" manager'). Yet, the image of leader as protector ('I also experienced a feeling of vul-nerability . . .'), goes beyond them. Unlike Anna and Kim, who saw a caring leader as one who offers recognition and guidance, Steve looks at the caring leader as someone who should protect him in a hostile environment. Several other features set this narrative apart from the earlier two. In the first place, the theme of meeting the organization's top leader features only indirectly ('Most people have their own story of a personal encounter with Zeus himself'). It is alto-gether on a grander scale ('global strategy for change', 'Head of CAD world-wide'), revolving crucially around the power of leaders, who are invisible, mysterious and terrifying. Its language (demi-gods, mythical creatures, spineless, guts, ingratiate, etc.) is overwhelmingly a language of masculine qualities, a language of rude power and raw fear. Leadership features in this narrative not as a unitary entity (a single leader) but as a fairly elaborate authority structure (McKie, the UK directors, the Head of world-wide CAD and, finally, 'Boston'). Moreover, unlike the earlier narratives, Steve is fully conscious of the fantasy of omnipotence he was projecting on Bates and the directors ('I had adopted the fantasy . . .'). His loss of faith in the company's British leadership coincides with what he sees as the shattering of this fantasy. He therefore presents himself as one wiser and less gullible, like the longer-standing members of the organization ('Those employees who had been with the company . . .'), in contrast to his younger, more impressionable self.[8]

If accessibility and caring form the two axes around which Kim's and Anna's fantasies revolve, Steve's self-professed leadership fantasy revolves around a complex of ideas that include aloofness, indifference, power, and mystery; these have been discussed extensively by authors such as Sennett (1980) and Baum (1987). Baum (1987: 66), for example, argues, that

the indifference of someone who is powerful simultaneously poses a riddle and increases that person's control. The riddle concerns the identity of someone who exercises such undeniable authority in virtual anonymity. How does this person do it? And what does he or she want from subordinates? Efforts to solve the riddle lead to greater attentiveness to and, consequently, dependence on the authority.

The mystery surrounding a leader's provenance and his or her personal circumstances doubtless reinforce his or her psychological hold over his or her followers.[9] Conversely, acquaintance with the mundane realities of a leader's everyday life (marriage to an 'ordinary' spouse, perfectly 'ordinary' bourgeois tastes, etc.) severely dents the leadership mystique.[10] Mystery features not only in Steve's story, but, in a different way, in Anna's too; it is not accidental that both of these narratives deal with *faith* in the leader.[11] Anna's meeting with the leader clarified the mysteries without destroying the mystique of the leader. Her meeting with the director was a unique and special occasion ('probably the most precious experience'), and in no way could it be seen as marking familiarity. In Steve's account, the mystery of the leader as well as the mystique of the unvisited seventeenth floor are sustained by his faith in the leader's omnipotence.

---

[8] We shall presently see that, far from losing his faith in the omnipotence of leaders, Steve has merely shifted his fantasy from the company's British to the US leadership.

[9] The Japanese people had not heard the voice of their revered Emperor until his famous radio broadcast in August 1945 ('The circumstances of the war have not developed necessarily to Japan's favour . . .'). It is almost self-evident that the loss of mystique of the British 'royal family' has cast the final blow on any claims it may have had to leadership.

[10] Goffman (1959) recounts several instances when Sir Frederick Ponsonby, late Equerry of the British Court, advised monarchs to keep their distance from their subjects. The view that familiarity breeds contempt seems uniquely apt to people's attitudes towards monarchs.

[11] Mystery is, of course, a central element of Christian faith, as indicated by the dictum 'Credo quia absurdum'.

False messiahs

Steve's loss of faith in the leader is accompanied by some of the distancing and disidentification noted in Kim's account. Unlike Kim's feelings of anger, however, Steve's feelings are closer to contempt, his scarcely concealed sarcasm in sharp contrast to Kim's injured pride. If Kim's response is similar to that of a spurned lover, Steve's response is that of someone who placed his or her faith in a false messiah. Unlike Kim, Steve's loss of faith and respect for the leader is precipitated by the experience not that 'the leader does not care' but that 'the leader is not strong enough'. Time and again in the narrative we read that McKie's authority became 'second-hand', that the idolized demi-gods of DACRO UK turned out to be mere puppets of Boston, and so on.

If Kim's and Anna's fantasies cast the leader in the role of the primal mother, recognizing, fusing, and restoring, Steve's fantasy is much closer to the view of the leader as a father surrogate, a person of formidable strength, at once judgemental and severe, caring and punishing. Could then his leadership fantasy be described as messianic (Kohut 1985), in contrast to Anna's and Kim's charismatic leadership fantasies? Instead of highlighting fusion and unity, his report vividly depicts the great powers with which leaders are endowed in some followers' eyes and also the devastating consequences of discovering that they are only fallible after all. Leaders who inspired faith, commitment, and awe are relegated to mere mortals and become targets for extraordinary hostility and contempt. Discovering that the leader is not omnipotent undermines his or her perceived capacity to protect the subordinates and to stand up for them. The leader's weakness makes the followers feel vulnerable and exposed, undermining his or her legitimacy. More importantly, it makes them feel betrayed, as if the messiah has turned out to be an impostor.

It is hard to overemphasize the importance of the impostor theme in our emotional lives, both inside and outside organizations. This theme may assume several forms, attaching itself both at an individual's self and at others. It may manifest itself as a crisis in self-confidence; we may fear, for instance, that a certain lack of knowledge or expertise, an inferior qualification, or an earlier failure will be uncovered, thus destroying our credibility.[12] The impostor

---

[12] Chasseguet-Smirgel (1976: 352) examines nightmares regarding examinations in the light of this theme. Even if an examination was passed in practice, the nightmare builds on the suspicion that the success was undeserved and might one day become discovered. There is a substantial literature on the impostor phenomenon as it applies to an individual's own self. What is novel about the presentation here is the projection of the impostor theme onto an organization's leader.

theme can also be found in the fantasy common in fairy tales known as 'the family romance'—a child imagines that his or her real parents are king and queen, and his actual parents mere impostors, who seized him or her at a young age.[13] The theme is also rehearsed in numerous organizational stories, in which the legitimacy of an individual and especially a leader is questioned, for a wide variety of reasons, such as that his or her claims and qualifications are fraudulent, or even that he or she has attained a position by usurping it from its rightful holder. Goffman (1959: 77) has noted that Western culture regards an individual's performances as *either* authentic *or* fraudulent, so a person can be either true or an impostor. He argues that this is logically far from true, though perhaps he underestimates the vital psychic needs fulfilled by this dichotomy. In our fantasy life, a claim is either true or false; this is especially so in the case of a leader's claim to be the messiah. One cannot be half a messiah or a different type of messiah; if the messiah is found to make fraudulent claims once, his entire credibility is destroyed.[14] From a poetic point of view, the idea contrast between messiah and impostor represents a clear case of attribution of uniform and fixed qualities to particular individuals.

The librarian in the research and publishing organization reported earlier in Norman's story admitted to some detective work to unravel the mystery of the director.

One couldn't find out much about him . . . I remember doing an on-line search, it was all about his handling of the Pilkington affair. He claimed to have written a lot of scientific papers, but I couldn't find any of them. He claimed to have written a book, but in fact he'd only edited it, in fact he'd hardly edited it, I think the second editor got it out actually. I certainly discovered that he had a reputation that he'd tried to ruin libraries, he'd done it at both institutions he'd led. I don't think he likes me and all the librarians. [Why?] I don't know, he thinks that libraries are expensive and a waste of time and money . . . He is very keen on computers.[15]

---

[13] It is also a theme dominating Mussorgsky's great opera *Boris Godunov*, in which, against a background of rebellion and a false Czar, the Pretender Dimitri, the simpleton, confronts Boris, accusing him of being a murderer and an impostor. The family romance, in its straight Freudian variant, is acted out in Mozart's *Figaro*, where the eponymous hero turns out to be the son of noble parents. It can be found in countless fairy tales and myths. One of the strongest and most elaborate versions of the impostor theme is in the Grimm brothers' tale *The Goose Girl*. This theme has been discussed in great depth by Bettelheim (1976).

[14] In *Group Psychology and the Analysis of the Ego*, Sigmund Freud (1921) speculates the effects on Christianity of a hypothetical discovery of a written confession by Joseph of Arimathea that debunks the claims of Christ's Resurrection.

[15] But if the director's claims to scholarship were suspected of being fraudulent, so too was his excellence in computers. He is the subject of the story discussed in Chapter 7, where he is meant to use computers only to enhance his image.

This story casts the director as an impostor (fraudulent claims) and as a persecuting figure. Similar elements featured in other narratives obtained in that organization, though none questioned the director's power and even omnipotence. By contrast, what in Steve's imagination turns McKie from messiah to impostor is not a major revelation about his mysterious past, but a relatively routine discovery, that he is not self-driven, but a cog in an organizational hierarchy. His fraudulence lies not in his qualifications or credentials but in his bravado, his closeness with his staff and his presumed power, all of which had encouraged Steve's faith in him in the first place. The standards by which Steve judged McKie may seem harsh and unrealistic. Yet they are not untypical of standards by which we often judge our organizational superiors. Why do subordinates use such harsh standards when judging leaders? Why do they deliberately forget that they too are members of hierarchies, with superiors of their own? Why can they not merely treat leaders as ordinary humans, just like themselves, confused, fallible, capable of great deeds but also of great errors? Doubtless many leaders connive in the power mystique that surrounds them, by isolating themselves on seventeenth floors and executive suites, awarding themselves awe-inspiring salaries, wearing masks of unshaken certainty and conviction, and eschewing all traces of humility, doubt, or hesitation. Other leaders, possibly like McKie, connive with the mystique by being defiant or disparaging towards the organization's top management in front of their subordinates, yet obsequious and subservient in front of their own superior. Yet, what Steve's account suggests is that leaders, like McKie, are often invested with powers that are totally out of proportion with their actual position or personal qualities.

THE FOLLOWERS' CORE FANTASIES ABOUT THEIR LEADERS

The stories explored in this chapter have revealed a number of fantasies that subordinates construct around their superiors. In these fantasies, leaders are attributed with certain fixed qualities, which revolve around four axes:

- First, the leader is imagined as someone who cares for his or her subordinates, offering either recognition and support or protection. The reverse of this is the leader who is indifferent to the plight of his or her subordinates and may even be an axeman, willing to sacrifice them in order to achieve his or her ambition.

- Secondly, the leader is imagined as someone who is accessible, who can be seen and heard, even if his or her appearances constitute special occasions. Conversely, the leader as someone who is mysterious and aloof, distant and inscrutable.
- Thirdly, the leader is imagined as someone who is omnipotent, unafraid, and capable of anything. Omnipotence sometimes extends to omniscience, especially an ability to read the minds of his or her subordinates and recognize true loyalty from flattery and sycophancy. Conversely, the leader as someone externally driven, afraid, and fallible.
- Fourthly, the leader is imagined as someone who has a legitimate claim to power. Conversely, the leader as a impostor, someone who usurped power and whose claims are fraudulent.

Fragments from different axes may combine or may turn into their opposites. Anna's and Kim's narratives revolved primarily around the first two axes, the leader envisioned as the agent through whom dreams may turn into reality. In this way, it was suggested that the leader was constructed as a reincarnation of the primal mother, restoring the members' narcissism and rewarding them for who they were rather than for what they had achieved. Steve's narrative, on the other hand, included elements from all four axes, though the last two had special prominence. Here, the leader was envisioned more as a father-substitute, who rewards and punishes, arousing at once fear, loyalty, jealousy, and suspicion. It was suggested that the former was close to Kohut's (1985) account of charismatic leadership fantasy, while the latter was closer to his account of messianic leadership fantasy.

If we are reluctant to draw a firm distinction between the messianic and the charismatic, it is because identification and idealization do not follow the clearly separate paths suggested by Kohut and elaborated by Lindholm (1988). Instead, all accounts presented here display some common properties, like idealization (or its obverse, demonization) *and* identification (or its obverse, disidentification) as well as an underlying narcissistic quality. We could, therefore, view all of them as creative amalgams of leadership fantasies. If most of us project onto leaders qualities of omnipotence, omniscience, and wisdom we once attributed to our father, we also project onto them the fusion and unity that once tied us to our mother.

Instead of looking at the distinction between charismatic and messianic leaders as determined by the qualities of the leaders themselves, we would therefore be inclined to see it as the product of follower fantasies. A leader may be perceived as messianic by some followers, charismatic by others, and as a mixture by yet others. He or she may be seen as an impostor, as caring, or as aloof by different followers. Organizational participants rehearse and trade different fantasies regarding their leaders through stories, jokes, rumours, and gossip; eventually certain core fantasies may predominate, expressed in shared folklore, as in the narratives concerning Sir Roy.

What all the narratives in this chapter highlight is the idea that followers' relationships with leaders are strongly affected by early relationships with mother and father; these early relationships provide a core of primal political experiences that forever colour subsequent relationships with authority (Oglensky 1995). Different individuals will relate to authority in different ways, develop distinct fantasies, and spin different stories about their leaders. For some individuals, the legitimate–impostor axis may dominate their political fantasy life, for others the caring–persecuting axis may predominate. In Steve's story the impotence–omnipotence axis overshadows the legitimate–impostor dimension. Even though his faith in McKie was shattered when faced with McKie's weakness, he quickly substituted Boston for McKie, and preserved his fantasy of leadership omnipotence. The loss of faith in one leader did not undermine his faith in all leaders, but rather brought about the substitution of a false messiah by a supposedly true one.

In this Steve is neither naïve nor untypical. His reaction reveals that most people find it difficult to accept working for an organization led by ordinary functionaries, appointed in bureaucratic ways, and subject to both regulations and hierarchies. Weber's essential insight that impersonal hierarchies kill leadership (or at least what he saw as leadership based on emotion) cannot be reversed merely by elevating leaders to superstar status and according them the public-relations treatment. At the same time, the Weberian insight cannot banish people's continuing psychic needs for leaders on whom to transfer emotion by turning them into objects of fantasy. Leaders must be endowed with superhuman qualities because only then can they really be perceived as real leaders, accepted and respected. Yet, the entire apparatus of bureaucracy conspires against this illusion. Ordinary power-brokers cannot turn into messiah figures through the force of fantasy alone.[16] Meeting an organization's top leaders is

[16] The realization that the leader is merely human, the experience of seeing an idol cut down to size, can be highly unsettling to a young man like Steve. The discovery of the father's weakness is one of every boy's great traumatic discoveries. It is discussed in supremely insightful terms in Dostoevsky's *Brothers Karamazov* (see Chapter 10). Yet the realization that the leader is 'merely human' can be quite liberating, as if accepting the fact that leaders are fallible, confused, and human helps one overcome one's own fear of them; feared supervisors, managers, or teachers can lose some of their terrifying qualities if they can be seen as fearful of their own superiors.

usually a memorable experience, either because they temporarily manage to live up to the extraordinary fantasies subordinates spin around them, thus reinforcing these fantasies, or, more frequently, because their human limitations cannot but lead to the dislocation of the fantasies across the axes noted earlier.

In developing the theory of followership, the arguments put forward in this chapter do not imply that leaders themselves have no influence on the nature of fantasies generated by their subordinates or that theory of leadership is separate from the theory of followership. Certainly, fantasy, as expressed in jokes, gossip, nicknames, graffiti, cartoons, and above all stories, enables us symbolically to refashion organizational practices in the interest of pleasure. Fantasy may distort, reinterpret, or subvert any real action in accordance with unconscious wishes, creating charisma out of mediocrity or diminishing genius into ordinariness. Yet, the leader's own behaviour when meeting subordinates (as highlighted in the examples involving Sir Roy) has a crucial, though not determining, influence on the follower's fantasy. The length of time he or she spends with them, the quality of his or her briefing, the warmth of the handshake, the words used for the occasion, the strength and sincerity of his or her feelings for the followers, these are all matters over which leaders, through their own behaviour, may influence their followers' fantasies.

This is the point where the theory of followership must engage with the theory of leadership, in at least two ways. First, if leaders feature in the fantasy life of their subordinates, so too do subordinates in the fantasies of leaders. Thus groups of subordinates may feature as recalcitrant malcontents, as potential rebels, as tireless workers, as pawns to be manipulated and exploited, or as potential heroes open to 'mutual stimulation and elevation' (Burns 1978: 4).[17] Secondly, if leaders, taking a cue from Burns, manage to read the deeper wishes, emotions, and needs of their subordinates, they may then engage with them, stimulate them, frustrate them, deflect them, or satisfy them. In doing so, they may use power not merely to meet targets or gratify personal ambition but to achieve what Burns (1978: 251) sees as the ultimate test of true leadership—realization of collective purpose in unleashing real and intended social change.

---

[17] It is possible to explore the leaders' fantasies as they 'go down' to meet the troops, just as this chapter has investigated the followers' fantasies.

10

Insults in Storytelling

'There are three forms of belittlement: contempt, spite and insult
. . . Insult is belittlement. For an insult consists of doing or saying
such things as involve shame for the victim, not for some advantage to oneself other than these have been done, but for the fun of
it.'

Aristotle, *Rhetoric*

'Vronsky's life was particularly happy in that he had a code of
principles, which defined with unfailing certitude what should
and what should not be done. This code of principles covered
only a small circle of contingencies, but in return the principles
were never obscure, and Vronsky, as he never went outside that
circle, had never had a moment's hesitation about doing what he
ought to do. This code categorically ordained that . . . *one must
never pardon an insult but may insult others oneself.*'

Tolstoy, *Anna Karenina*

Insults are as regular a feature of storytelling as they are of epic
poetry, myths, fairy tales, and drama. They are also a major element
of everyday life, capable of generating enormous anger, shaping our
outlooks on ourselves and others. Yet academic theory has little to
say about them. This chapter seeks to provide an introduction to the
social psychology of insults, through the medium of organizational
stories. It charts different forms of insulting behaviour such as exclusion, stereotyping, obliteration of significant identity details, ingratitude, scapegoating, rudeness, broken promises, or ignoring; even
more potent insults may involve the defamation or despoiling of
idealized objects, persons, and ideas. The chapter then examines different interpersonal dynamics and different outcomes of insults,
including a resigned tolerance, the request of an apology, and a
retaliation. While the chapter explores the social psychological
dimensions of insults, it also places them within political discourses

of organizations, suggesting ways in which they reflect, sustain, and challenge underlying power relations.

Insults include behaviour or discourse, oral or written, which is perceived, experienced, constructed, and at times intended as slighting, humiliating, or offensive. This chapter does not examine the slurring or scapegoating of third parties in absentia (Baum 1987; Fineman and Gabriel 1996; Hirschhorn 1988), concentrating instead on insults addressed directly at an individual or at a group of which an individual is a member, often in the presence of an audience. Nor does it examine insults that are traded in horseplay in what are known as joking relations (Collinson 1988, 1994; Sims *et al.* 1993) where no offence is meant and none is taken. Finally, the chapter draws a distinction between bullying or harassment and insult. Cumulatively or individually, insults may, of course, amount to harassment (including sexual or racist harassment). It will be argued, however, that not all types of insulting behaviour are equivalent to harassment. For example, failure to invite someone to a function or a party can hardly be conceived of as harassment, but it can certainly be an insult. Yet, like harassment, insulting behaviour is part of the nexus of political relations in an organization and must be studied as such.

Within these narrower parameters, insults are a topic that has been neglected by research in organizations and the social sciences in general.[1] There are very few references to insults in the academic literature, and, surprisingly, neither of the currently burgeoning literatures on emotions and narrative and discourse has addressed them. This neglect seems unjustified, as insults would appear to be an important feature of human behaviour and human experience. As a cardinal feature of many people's personal histories, they are often remembered long after they happened or, alternatively, they are denied through elaborate rationalizations and constructions.

Insults, this chapter will argue, are also a fairly regular phenomenon of organizational life, featuring in organizational narratives whenever expressions like 'rubbing salt in the wounds' or 'adding insult to injury' are invoked and leaving long-lasting marks on histories, both personal and collective. They are a common theme of tragic narratives, where they generate strong feelings of resentment and anger. Indeed, as Kapuscinski (1983: 83) has suggested, rebellion

[1] There is one group of researchers who have discussed insults as a feature of the workplace, offering some examples, especially in connection with jokes, stereotypes, and harassment. This could be loosely referred to as research into psychic injuries and psychological survival at the workplace (Fineman and Gabriel 1996; Sennett and Cobb 1973; Terkel 1985; Wallraff 1985). This chapter goes beyond this work by placing insults and the emotions most closely associated with them—anger, shame and embarrassment—squarely at the centre of its investigation.

and resistance may more commonly spring from insulted dignity than from the routine discontents of oppression or exploitation. Machiavelli himself advised the prince to keep his subjects in terror if necessary, but never to insult them. For these reasons, insults are a promising area of social investigation in organizations.

Insults can be verbal, consisting of mocking invective, cutting remarks, negative stereotypes, rudeness, or straight swearing. They can also be performed in deed, as when valued objects are defamed, symbols desecrated, gifts returned, or invitations refused. They can be subtle, residing in verbal innuendo or the facial expression of the aggressor, leaving room for a face-saving retreat or an affected disregard by the aggrieved party. Alternatively, they can be brutal, unambiguous, and direct, as in cases of indecent gestures or racist and sexual harassment.

Insults involve two parties, a perpetrator and a target, and possibly an audience. There can be no insult without a perpetrator or an insulted party. A remark or action intended as an insult but not registered or experienced as one by its target can hardly be said to constitute an insult, even if an audience recognized the intention. It may instead be regarded as ridiculing, vilification, scapegoating, or oppression.[2] Yet, the *intention* to insult is not a necessary ingredient of an insult. Some insults, notably in cases of blasphemy, may occur without any intention on the part of the perpetrator, who finds that he or she may unwittingly have broken a taboo or violated a deep sensitivity. If insult can occur where none was intended, it can, more paradoxically, also occur where none was properly experienced. This is evident in 'constructed' or manufactured insults, as when an offer or a gift is dismissed as derisory or offensive, even if no offence was intended and no taboo was broken.[3] Insults can then be part of a scapegoating process, the insult but an engineered pretext or provocation for disproportionate retaliation. It is also important to recognize 'second-order' insults—that is, insults that are built on top of an initial one. For instance, when an individual is genuinely and deeply insulted, the perpetrator may offer the excuse that no insult was intended or that the target has misinterpreted the incident. In this way, the perpetrator may actually compound the insult by insinuating that the insulted party is oversensitive, paranoid, or lacking a sense of humour. In some instances, the perpetrator may then

---

[2] Throughout this chapter it will become apparent that individuals very rarely admit an intention to insult someone else. Yet insulted parties almost always impute the intention to insult to their assailant. The intention of the assailant is a highly complex motivational matter, far more so than the experience of the victim, which includes an unambiguous attribution of motive. For this reason I prefer to define insults in terms of the latter rather than in terms of the former.

[3] Iago in Shakespeare's *Othello* is master of the affected or manufactured insult.

present him or herself as the target of a constructed insult. From a poetic point of view, it can be seen that insults rely on two types of attribution on the part of the target: attribution of motive—namely, the assailant's motive to harm—and, secondly, attribution of emotion, the pleasure in causing harm to the other.

THE RESEARCH MATERIAL

The research material on which this chapter is based is the same as that used in Chapter 9—namely, some of the 374 reports provided by university undergraduates about significant moments they experienced during six-month industrial internships. These reports cover a range of organizational incidents and experiences, encompassing a great variety of emotions, including amusement, frustration, pride, anxiety, boredom, shame, guilt, fear, excitement, and despair. The material was collected in the first place as part of the students' learning process and its use as research material must be qualified. In no way do the students or the organizations where they spent their internships represent a sample. Nor is the material untainted by the students' attempts to impress their lecturer and to show how much they learned.[4] Yet the material possesses several positive qualities. Students observe their organizations with fresh, sharp eyes. They can 'see' what more seasoned employees no longer notice or care about. An articulate, critical, but naïve worker can offer poignant insights on the rights and wrongs of organizational life, its twists and turns. As short-term employees, trainees have access to information unavailable to other employees, many of them readily taken into the confidence of managers and peers, whose positions they could appreciate without threatening. Furthermore, as short-term employees, they have no obvious axe to grind—their stories are not moulded by vested organizational interests and long-standing agendas.[5]

This kind of relatively unstructured and unmotivated material serves well the purposes of an exploratory enquiry like the present one. Clearly, no exhaustive survey or taxonomy of all types of insult can be based on those data, nor is there here any evidence regarding

[4] Interpretations of this type of material can never be unproblematic—in some instances the students may have been expressing themselves within a strong relationship with their lecturer, seeking to elicit his or her sympathy, support, or admiration. However, my knowledge of those who provided the material enhances my confidence in the interpretations that follow. This will become clearer in the interpretation provided for Narrative 6.

[5] Some of this material has been systematically analysed by Fineman and Gabriel (1996).

the extent or severity of insulting behaviour in different organizations. The data do, however, contain a number of characteristic incidents in considerable detail, which allows an insight into the psychological as well as the political consequences of insulting behaviour. The research material was narrowed, in the first place, to ninety-four reports, by selecting only those reports whose key emotional qualities included the emotions traditionally associated with insults: anger, shame, embarrassment, and guilt. These were subsequently narrowed down to twenty-one reports, involving stories centring on insults and associated emotions. These stories have provided the basis of most arguments in this chapter; seven of them will be quoted at length.

INSULTS AND JOKES

Jokes are a good place to begin an investigation of insults. Like jokes, insults depend on timing and must touch a vital nerve. Like jokes, insults play on hidden desires and vulnerabilities. Like jokes, they can be highly imaginative and ingenious. Ingenuity is one of the features that distinguishes insults from mere abuse. Like jokes, insults can release a lot of emotional energy with relatively small effort. This economy of effort gives insults both a magical and an aesthetic quality. Like magical words, a few well-chosen insulting words can produce disproportionate results, such as the crumbling of a self-confident exterior or the unleashing of immense amounts of anger (La Barre 1979). The aesthetic quality of insults resides in the appositeness of the stimulus; like an elegant mathematical proof, an inventive, well-aimed insult proves the vulnerability of the subject, cutting him or her down to size.

The main difference between insults and jokes would seem to lie in their emotional content. Jokes release mirth, whereas insults unleash anger. Yet, as was discussed in Chapters 2 and 3, many jokes contain an aggressive intent. Thus setbacks and misfortunes of others may afford us comic pleasure if they can be presented as 'deserved'. Observing or recounting the afflictions of a pompous or ill-tempered person is funny, in so far as these afflictions have the quality of comeuppance or just deserts. A joke, then, just like an insult, can express aggression and hostility. Some insults indeed *are* jokes; ridicule is an insult under the guise of joking. We shall not be surprised then if we discover that many of the theories and concepts that have enhanced our understanding of jokes prove helpful in this discussion of insults.

AN EXAMPLE

Here is an insult described by the target, Jon, a trainee in a hospital department:

The incident occurred towards the end of my placement. I had returned from lunch and was settling into my afternoon routine when Dick, my 'boss', asked Val, the accountant, whether she was ready to go. She replied that she was and the two of them, together with Val's assistant Carol, promptly donned their coats and filed out of the room. A little later, I noticed through the window that the original three had joined four more members of my department: the totality except for me.

Not only had I been excluded from a departmental matter of some import-ance, I hadn't even been informed of its existence. So I went over to a trainee from another department (our office is shared by four departments) and asked about the event. Just then, the others returned to the room as the meeting was rearranged for later that afternoon.

Then, Lyn, in an intentionally loud and sarcastic voice, said:

'Dick, you should really inform "your boss" (meaning me) when you leave the room.'

I felt I had to defend myself to the now confused crowd (everyone in the room was listening):

'It's just that it looked like I wasn't allowed to come along.' (The words didn't come out right.)

Dick retorted, uncharacteristically: 'Well, you weren't!'

Everyone laughed.

I expressed my point of view more clearly:

'OK, Dick, I take your point, but it doesn't make me feel very good, I'm sup-posed to be part of this department and I wasn't even told there was a meet-ing, let alone asked if I wanted to come along.'

Later Dick apologized, and he meant it.

This incident summarized my placement experience and especially the attitudes of key employees I had to work with. What did the incident mean to me? Firstly and most importantly, the fact that I wasn't informed of the meeting demonstrated my fellow employees' view of me as short term and unimportant. A simple 'I've got to go to this meeting now, Jon, OK?' would have been the minimum etiquette I deserved, and would have allowed me to ask whether I could come along. Even if there was no other reason, it would have given a more extensive look into the workings of a real organization, and would therefore have helped me when I was to come back to study. It was as if they didn't realize these things were valu-able to my experience and therefore I should experience them: it was all one-sided.

Dick's lack of attention towards me was constant throughout the place-ment. I don't believe it was intentional in my opinion; he simply didn't know how to handle a subordinate. I also don't think he realized how capable and aspiring a trainee can be. I probed him on the matter: he was a 'you should be grateful for getting any job in a recession' and 'I had to work my way up through the ranks' sort of person.

And what of Lyn's outburst? She had overheard my conversation but could not see my point of view at all. She epitomized the others' feelings but actually spoke them, saying that Dick was my boss, not the other way around [sic] *(as if being my boss gave Dick a right to not treat me decently). I was laughed at. OK, it probably always happens, people not realizing someone is upset about something, but it showed that no one felt I had a right to be at that meeting.*

At the time, I felt neglected and alienated—also ANGRY *that no one understood that I wanted to be an integral part of the team. The incident reinforced the view that I never quite fitted in.   (Narrative 1)*

The insult in this story comes in three instalments: first, exclusion from a seemingly important meeting; secondly, a sarcastic jibe ('Dick, you should really inform "your boss"'), which ironically reverses the subordinate–inferior relationship; and, thirdly, the refusal to offer a face-saving excuse ('Sorry, we didn't think the meeting would be of interest to you' or 'Sorry, we forgot').

Exclusion

Refusal or failure to invite a person to an important function or party is a cause of innumerable family feuds and conflicts. It is also encountered in countless stories and myths, such as the incident that set in motion the Trojan War. Eris, the goddess of discord, who has not been invited to the nuptial reception of Thetis and Peleus, takes her revenge by sending her visiting card, the apple of discord. This will precipitate the dispute among the goddesses, which, in turn, will spark off the ten-year war between Greeks and Trojans. In the Grimm brothers' story *Little Briar-Rose* (the source text of *Sleeping Beauty*), one of the thirteen 'wise women' was not invited to the feast in honour of the newborn princess, because the king 'only had twelve plates'. She pronounced her curse that the princess would prick herself with a spindle and die on her fifteenth birthday.

Exclusion lies at the heart of many insulting experiences, and invitations are occasions *par excellence* when sharp lines between those in the guest lists and those out of them are drawn. Even if no slight is intended, it is easy for a person left out to feel offended. But, as the trainee's story suggests, the offence is compounded by three factors. First, exclusion derives from status and power differences, between Jon, the temporary, casual trainee and the others. The sarcasm 'Dick, you should really inform "your boss"' serves to 'put Jon in his place', not only reminding him who is boss but further reinforcing his marginal position in the organization. Secondly, the humiliation is public, so that the shamed victim finds himself further isolated. None of the audience hastens to take his side or offer him a face-saving lifeline. Thirdly, the insult, as though it were a physical blow, throws the victim off balance, so that his retort is feeble and ineffectual by his own admission. This allows for a clumsy but weighty rejoinder ('Well, you weren't!') to complete the insult. Jon ends up feeling ashamed not only for the insult but, as importantly, for his own ineffectual response.

Several of the incidents in the data derive from the perceived inferior status of trainees as compared to full-time staff. In some instances student trainees feel insulted not for being trainees but for being students. The following telling example was provided by Claire, a trainee at a provincial accountants' firm:

> Mr North has worked at Porters for thirty years and this has earned him the unofficial title of 'Office Manager'. Our conversation moved onto what and where I was studying. Once he had grasped that I was at university, that was it! Mr North went off the rails about how being a graduate meant nothing in accountancy. He hoped I realized that even though I might have a degree one day, he would still be far superior to me and not the other way around. I stood in his office nodding my head in agreement but absolutely seething at his unprovoked attack. He seemed to think that all university graduates viewed themselves as more knowledgeable than him. Mr North certainly made sure that I would not be under the same impression.
>
> The close of our conversation only added insult to injury. Having made me feel thoroughly ashamed to be in Higher Education, he added: 'When are you returning to BRISTOL to resume your holiday!' Politely, I answered his question without correcting him on the location of my studies and left the room, closing the door quietly behind me.   (Narrative 2)

The insult here takes the form of a tirade that the trainee finds hard to fend off. Her inability to confront her tormentor and reject his allegations leaves her feeling both angry and ashamed. Mr North's final comment illustrates two characteristics of insults that did not feature in the earlier example, *stereotyping* and *obliteration of significant details in the victim's identity* (see below)—a combination of an unsubtle stereotype (students on a permanent holiday) with what Claire evidently regards as a belittling remark about her university (which Claire sees as a superior institution to Bristol).

Stereotyping

Stereotyping is a common characteristic of insults; it is also an area of extensive theorizing. Paradoxically, however, most of the theory on stereotyping is unhelpful in elucidating the emotional experience of an insult's target. Much of the academic literature on stereotypes regards them as oversimplified views of reality or as errors of over-generalization. Martinko, for instance, approaches stereotypes as 'a subcategory of perception and attribution' (Martinko 1995: 533), offering an equivocal view of their advantages and shortcomings. This tradition of theorizing scrutinizes the cognitive and perceptual processes involved and identifies the deleterious group and organizational consequences of stereotyping, in phenomena such as 'groupthink' (Janis 1972) or authoritarianism (Dixon 1976).

In contrast to this cognitive approach to stereotyping, the political and the psychodynamic approaches seem to ground stereotypes in the political and psychological realities of organizations. The former views stereotypes as forms of discrimination and oppression, and, the second as wish-fulfilments, especially as manifestations of unconscious aggressive fantasies and desires. The political approach is adopted by Kanter (1977: 230 ff.) and feminist theorists (Auster 1993; Gutek 1985, 1989; Leidner 1991; Sheppard 1989), who regard them as instruments of sexual oppression in and out of the workplace. Far from being the result of ignorance, naïvety or cognitive blind spots, these theorists view stereotypes as barriers to equality that are systematically maintained and reproduced. Enlightenment alone is not enough to overcome them, since they support material interests. The psychodynamic view, that of stereotypes as wish-fulfilments, reinforces the feminist contention that sexist stereotypes support not only material male privilege but also male psychological needs. What these two approaches have in common is the view that stereotypes are not mere generalizations or even errors (attribution of fixed qualities), but are mental forms supporting and supported by psychological and political structures.

Stereotypes assume the character of insult precisely when the target finds him or herself literally trapped by the perpetrator's biased perception, where his or her every action can be skewed to reinforce the stereotype. Allowing the perpetrator to get away with an insulting stereotype enhances its social acceptability and may lead to escalating insults. Challenging or contesting the stereotype may often be accommodated within the stereotype, under the guise of 'temperamental', 'obstreperous', 'lacking in sense of humour', etc. Thus, stereotypes strike at the heart of the victim's self-esteem, placing him or her in a position that exacerbates feelings of powerlessness and shame.

In the following narrative, Kevin found himself scapegoated when his supervisor's new computer developed a fault. His anger ('awful feelings of . . . angriness') can hardly be contained, not so much because of the gravity of the accusation against him as because he finds himself trapped in the stereotype of 'irresponsible student messing up other people's computers'.

As they struggled to correct the problem, a mini 'investigation' started, to find who had altered the configuration of the new computer. As time elapsed, I began to realize that Mandy was quietly blaming me, after she was informed that I had used her machine the previous evening. She made some sarcastic remarks, in effect accusing me of making the mistake: 'This wouldn't have happened if someone hadn't messed around with my machine last night.'

I protested my innocence—stating that I hadn't used Lotus, but I was sub-consciously found guilty by the office, and henceforth I didn't use Mandy's machine again as a matter of principle. This caused a great deal of friction between Mandy and myself, because it was obviously she who had made the mistake, and it riled me to be a scapegoat for someone who didn't have the strength of character to admit her own mistakes.

In my opinion I gained a great deal of knowledge from this incident. Not only was Mandy exercising her formal power but also taking advantage of our relative positions within the hierarchy of our office to influence the opinions of the other office members; and the more I protested my innocence, the further I fell into a grave which had been dug for me . . . The image of British Plastics likes to, and does, communicate is that they are a very efficient and caring company. Not very true! This is especially so in Mandy's case, as she was con-tinually criticizing students, and in my opinion her attitudes got the better of her.

There is a system within the company which enables dissatisfied staff to air their grievances . . . I complained I had been unjustly accused. My complaint didn't succeed; it was met with quite a cold response. I left with awful feelings of frustration, angriness [sic], uselessness, *and* betrayal.   *(Narrative 3)*

Obliteration of significant identity details

If stereotyping is one characteristic of insults that strikes at a person's feelings of individuality and self-esteem, so too does the related characteristic noted earlier—failing to acknowledge or honour an important detail in a person's identity or ego. The use of the wrong form of address, such as Dr instead of Professor, though rarely intentional can be read as insulting. Several examples in the data suggest that students are insulted when a manager or an employer fails to register the prestige of their university, mistaking it for a lesser institution.[6] Even more insulting, however, is the mispronunciation or misspelling of a person's name. Still more insulting can be forgetting someone's name or getting it completely wrong. In the following example (for a full discussion, see Fineman and Gabriel 1996: 75–8), a long litany of maltreatment is crowned by the following observation:

[6] Kim's story in Chapter 9 is one such typical example.

INSULTS IN STORYTELLING

It is characteristic that, when speaking to me on the phone, Paul called me 'Geoffrey', as always, although I am known to all else as 'Geoff'. He likewise insists on calling his secretary Suzanne, although her name is Su and is printed as such on her birth certificate. (Fineman and Gabriel 1996: 76) *(Narrative 4)*

Mispronunciation or misspelling a person's name may be an eccentric affectation, a sign of familiarity and affection or, as in the case above, an insult. Given the enormous power difference between Geoff, a student trainee, and Paul, a brash £200,000-per-year merchant banker, it seems fair to hypothesize that mispronouncing Geoff's name is part of a ritual humiliation, as if to show that even Geoff's and other subordinates' names may be used and abused as Paul pleases.[7]

The importance of detail in insults

Narratives 2 and 3 underline the importance of small details in insults. This is further illustrated in the following narrative, where the assailant's reference to 'primroses' seems to touch a raw nerve; it is offered by Matt, a trainee with one of the Big Six accounting companies:

On my last audit, I worked for the firm's head partner. When he first turned up, I was formally introduced to him by one of my colleagues. In the first instance, he appeared to be a pleasant enough chap and I thought little of working for him. However, during his review of the work papers I had produced, he proceeded to vocalize any spelling errors which he could manage to find. These work papers are simply drafts for internal use only, so making spelling errors had seemed quite acceptable. Even so, he only managed to find three errors out of several thousand words. I thought him quite UNFAIR *when he finally turned around to me and asked what kind of schooling system I went through. When I told him that I went to a comprehensive school, he asked what A-level subjects I had taken. I had hardly got the word 'biology' out of my mouth when he laughed and interjected with, 'Well, what can one expect from a man who has spent his life dissecting primroses!'*

I was justifiably annoyed by this comment and had to leave the room before my mood became obvious. A few hours later, after he had left, I overheard a conversation in which one of my colleagues told another that it appeared David had decided to spend the day insulting the 'grunt' ('grunt' being the affectionate term applied to all new starters at the company). (Narrative 5)

---

[7] Alternatively, it may be that Paul is a stickler for formality. This could also be a reason for Geoff to be insulted, given that in his report he describes how Paul expected him to do him 'personal favours' and to be his 'personal chauffeur' and 'errand-boy'. See Fineman and Gabriel (1996: 75–8).

It is interesting that Matt seems prepared to accept a degree of being put down as acceptable (the 'grunt' label), while he views the spelling corrections and the primrose barb as gratuitous and insulting. Insults are experienced as surplus to functional requirements, as suggested by adjectives such as 'unwarranted' or 'uncalled for', which are often used to describe them. Aristotle was aware of this in commenting that insults are 'not for some advantage to oneself . . . but for the fun of it'.

What is even clearer, however, is that the insult, in this instance, seems to touch a sensitive spot in Matt. It is not certain whether this vulnerability derives from Matt's comprehensive education or from an unconscious guilt regarding the spelling mistakes. It is clear, however, that, as with the obliteration of significant personal details, the highlighting of significant personal defects is a common and successful target for insults. This is particularly so if the target of the insult is sensitive to these defects or has been repeatedly insulted on their account. This explains why a relatively small effort targeted at the appropriate point can produce disproportionate effects. It also explains why insults hurt even if not factually true, in that they touch an area of subconscious self-doubt. Two further reasons why untrue insults may be effective must be noted here. First, as Narrative 3 suggests, an audience may seem to believe the allegation, while the target's denials tend to reinforce the appearance of culpability. Secondly, an insult may be untrue, but the targets may blame themselves for being in a vulnerable position—for example, by trusting someone they should not have trusted. This may also account for the fact that many insults (including the ones reproduced here) retrospectively tend to appear quite innocuous and seem to produce emotion disproportionate to their offensiveness.

Allegations of shoddy work, such as the sarcastic pointing out of spelling mistakes, feature in several of the reports. In some cases, the trainees are candid about accepting their responsibility in 'honest mistakes'. These ranged from the production of expensive newsletters for a highly image-conscious company that included some embarrassing printing errors to an error of over £1 million in compiling trading debt statistics. When trainees are reminded of such mistakes in a sarcastic manner, they feel embarrassed rather than insulted. When, on the other hand, they are insulted on account of mistakes that they categorically deny being responsible for, then feelings are more likely to be anger and frustration.

Insults aimed at deeply held beliefs and revered objects

In most of the examples examined so far, insults have focused on relatively small, though psychologically significant, facets of the victims' personality or performance. In other instances (which cannot be discussed here for reasons of space), insults are directed at a person's intelligence or tastes and fashion-consciousness (Bourdieu 1984: 511; Gabriel and Lang 1995: 111). In some cases, they strike at some of an individual's most deeply held beliefs or indeed revered individuals. It is in cases like these that insults become akin to blasphemy. In one incident, Andrew, a deeply religious trainee, relates his feelings when a religious poster he had displayed was removed:

I decided to use the notice board above my desk to display a yellow A4 poster advertising a Mission to Gloucester being held at that time. This poster went up on Wednesday and, while nothing was said to me about it, it was turned back to front two evenings running—I reversed it the following morning on both occasions. That Friday, the thirteenth of September, while I was out of the office, the poster was torn down (it ended up in the bin) and a large Health and Safety poster was put up.

At lunchtime, Chris, my manager, had a quiet word with me in the rest room. The upshot of this was that she told me I had upset more than one person's feelings with the poster and that it was official policy for the office manager to approve posters before they were put up.

At the time of the incident my feelings were a mixture of pain and anger. It is one thing to have your beliefs challenged as to whether or not they are reasonable but quite another to have your beliefs opposed and not be given the chance to defend them. When Chris had a word with me it was like she was accusing me of being narrow-minded and trying to force my views down other people's throats. This I felt to be particularly unfair since, at the time, my two closest friends were Muslim and Bhuddist respectively. Looking back at the incident now I feel a little embarrassed that such an incident could be the cause of so much pain and worry for both myself and the others in the office. (Narrative 6)

This narrative may be interpreted in line with earlier ones; Andrew is insulted because he feels stereotyped on the basis of little evidence, as a religious zealot who seeks to force his views on others. Yet the tone of the incident and the use of the word 'pain' (which does not feature in any other narratives) may suggest a deeper type of insult than those of the earlier examples. Unlike the earlier examples, the insult here is seen as perpetrated in deed (the removal and binning of the poster) as well as in word. Furthermore, unlike the previous cases, the perpetrator of the insult is anonymous, unseen, and unwilling to take responsibility for his or her action. It is possible to conjecture the binning of the poster as a kind of profanation, compounded by the anonymity of the culprit and further exacerbated by Chris's condoning of his or her behaviour.[8] Such interpretation may seem speculative and cannot be corroborated on the evidence of the above text alone. Having observed this student respond in the same manner to perceived insults to his religious sensitivities on several occasions, I feel fairly confident about this interpretation. This suggests that different insults may strike at different parts of our psyche. In most of the earlier examples, insults were directed at the individuals' identity, pride in their work, intelligence, or institutional affiliation, in short at their ego or their social persona. This instance indicates a deeper type of injury, an injury predominantly to a person's ego-ideal, the part of the mental apparatus that contains idealized images (such as role models) and objects (such as religious or patriotic relics and family heirlooms), which we may seek to emulate or which inspire us. The sense of outrage when such idealized things are insulted may be even more acute than the anger and shame caused by insults to the ego.[9]

RESISTING INSULTS

In the examples thus far, insulted individuals feel upset, shamed, and angry but seem mostly unable to act on these feelings. In the next and final example, Tonya describes her outrage at what she views as a sexist slur, in one of the world's largest corporate finance providers. This report, which hinges on an overlap of three negative stereotypes 'woman', 'student', and 'back office', elaborates considerably the points raised earlier and raises two further issues, resistance to insulting behaviour and the trading of insults.

I worked in the foreign exchange (FX) back office, where deals done by our 150 dealers were checked, payment instructions were added, and queries

---

[8] A different interpretation of the incident is that Andrew simply has not understood the secular norms of the organization and that he is overreacting in a situation where no insult to him or his religious belief was intended. Thus a 'neutral' observer may adjudge that no real insult has taken place. Yet the fact remains that Andrew feels insulted in a profoundly moral way and he imputes the intention to insult him to the person who binned the poster. The position taken in this chapter is that the occurrence of the insult is coextensive with the experience of the victim rather than the intention of the perpetrator, which is very much harder to establish (see below).

[9] It is possible that some of the earlier examples also entail elements of ego-ideal insults. The student who has idealized her university is insulted when someone seems unable or unwilling to distinguish it from a supposedly lesser institution. Likewise, criticisms of a trainee's spelling strike both at his ego (his competence and performance) but also his ego-ideal (his idealized image of himself as a flawless professional).

addressed. My job was to resolve problems arising from deals. Much of the time, this meant going upstairs and talking to the dealers.

Now, you never told a dealer that he or she was wrong, even when handling those dealers who, throughout the whole of my placement, were never correct. You just briefly stated what the problem was and asked them kindly to look into it.

This particular incident involves Nick, one of the men who always 'cocked up'. This time he had mixed up the currencies on a deal. The payment was due in half an hour, so it was important to get him to amend the deal. I went up to see him, but Lee, also from the back office, was already talking to him about something else. Because my problem was urgent, I waited for Lee to finish. When Lee left, Nick glanced at me and then, to my surprise, left his desk and went over to another dealer, John, from whom we had heard juicy comments for quite a while. A group of dealers assembled and I could hear and see from their behaviour that they were not discussing business.

I went over and discovered that the reason for their behaviour was two pages from The Sun *newspaper filled with pictures of posing, naked women. Something inside me just snapped. I told Nick that my job was actually meant as a service to the dealers, to help make them aware of errors before they cost them money. I explained how much work I had to do and how much other dealers appreciated my corrections, so by ignoring me he was not only wasting my time, but his own colleagues' right to the service of the back-office officers. And with his error statistics, I would imagine he had better things to do than to stare at page-3 girls.*

I turned round, left my sheet of paper on his desk and departed.

My main emotion both then and now is anger. I felt I had been patient and taken much more stick and rude behaviour than was acceptable. The way Nick ignored me to go and look at page-3 girls was the straw that broke the camel's back. I also felt helpless and vulnerable. They were discussing naked women in detail in a room with almost only men, and I knew my views were in a minority. I was afraid any reaction from me would be ridiculed. Writing about it now, I also feel proud for having had the courage to tell him off.

The Foreign Exchange dealers, nearly all men, were the most arrogant group of people I have ever come across in my life. If it had not been for me gradually understanding some of the reasons for their behaviour, an outburst like the one I have just described would have come much earlier. You need to appreciate the fact that the FX department is, at the moment, one of the best departments result-wise in FinInter and this creates a feeling of invulnerability and extreme self-importance among those working there. I did not feel that this was a valid excuse for their behaviour; still, I learnt to accept it.

The back-office policy was to accept any amount of stick from the dealers, and then let it all come out afterwards when you were safely back at your desk. This policy was no good, as it only helped to increase the hostility between dealers and back-office. My telling the dealer off meant that I had broken the main taboo in the office. Over several weeks, I realized that this earned me much respect. I had done something many of my colleagues had wanted to do for years, but had not dared to. The risk was smaller for me, as I was only there for a short while. So, I achieved respect both from the back office and from

*some of the dealers. And perhaps, even more importantly, I respected myself
more for having done what I felt was right.   (Narrative 7)*

The essence of the insult in this report is contained in the sentence
'The way Nick ignored me to go and look at page-3 girls was the straw
that broke the camel's back.' Being ignored is a common enough
type of insult. In organizations, it takes the form of having one's
requests, memos, and reports disregarded, or, more commonly,
being kept waiting. No fewer than nine of the twenty-one incidents
of insult reported by trainees contain direct or indirect reference to
their time being wasted. However, it is clear that what is experienced
as insulting is not the actual wasting of time but the presumption
that their time has a low value compared to someone else's. This
confirms the Aristotelian idea of insults being gratuitous, something
aimed at consciously or unconsciously humiliating people's pride
rather than at exploiting them directly economically or even politically. The wasted time, however, is often but a token of deeper
humiliations. In Tonya's case, it is clear that the wasted time is symp-
tomatic of a status differential, an attitude of 'She can wait; she's only
back-office.' Yet, what turns an everyday indignity into a major insult
is the dealers' ostentatious leering, which makes Tonya feel insecure
and exposed. It is the dealers' sexism, no less odious for being
accepted as the prerogative of financial success, which Tonya finds
insulting.

Helplessness and vulnerability turn into anger when compounded
by insult. What sets this narrative apart from previous ones is that it
leads to an act of resistance, in which Tonya gives the assailant a
'piece of her mind', expressing her moral indignation at his behaviour. When she speaks out, she crosses the boundary between
acceptable behaviour ('disparage and belittle dealers behind their
backs') and unacceptable behaviour ('tell them to their faces'). What
Tonya told Nick is perhaps less important than the act of crossing of
this boundary, which turns the incident from an instance of psychic
injury into an episode of organizational politics.

Her rebuke to the dealer is not a head-on challenge of his sexism,
which may have laid her open to ridicule and disparagement.
Instead her rebuke is 'professional', giving him little leeway for retaliation, but its tail contains a sting. The meaning of 'and with his error-
statistics, I would imagine he had better things to do that to stare at
page-3 girls' is unlikely to have been lost on the dealer. It is, in fact,
an attempted insult, in its own right. We do not know whether the
dealer read it as an insult and how he may have reacted. It is certainly the case that, like the other insults we have examined thus far,
it could be painful even if not exactly true, provided that Nick had a

sensitive spot about being erratic. If, on the other hand, Nick was the kind of person who, rightly or wrongly, regards the making of superficial mistakes as a prerogative of his brilliance, then the insult might have gone unnoticed.

RETALIATION: FROM PSYCHIC INJURY TO POLITICAL CONFLICT

This example further highlights the political nature of insulting behaviour. While individual insults have a gratuitous character, cumulatively insults can be seen as a device for keeping subordinate parties in their place, by underlining their helplessness and vulnerability. An unanswered insult has a lowering effect on an individual's self-esteem. An unanswered insult in the presence of an audience has a still more devastating effect. What can be more devastating for a young boy than to see his own father insulted, yet be unable to retaliate? In Dostoevsky's *Brothers Karamazov*, Dmitry Karamazov insults an old army captain, whom he drags by the beard, in front of a group of children, while Ilyusha, the captain's son, in vain tries to help his father. Karamazov challenges the captain to a duel, knowing full well that such a challenge would ruin the latter. The father's humiliation (both his being dragged by the beard and his unwillingness to face his assailant in a duel) leads to vicious baiting of Ilyusha by his schoolmates. This incident drives one of the most moving subplots of the novel, which involves the younger Karamazov trying to expiate his brother's wrongdoing and culminates in the death and funeral of young Ilyusha at the very end of the novel.

An unanswered insult then marks a breach in justice which goes unpunished. It is highly effective at reaffirming power relations and laying bare relations of domination and subordination. The insulted party internalizes his or her anger into shame, an inability to restore justice by doing what is seen as the honourable thing, hence he/she is dishonoured in addition to being humiliated. The assailant, for his or her part, manifests his or her power and draws the audience into a coalition at the expense of the victim (Bacharach and Lawler 1980).

By contrast, an insult that is met with a counter-insult can restore the honour of the insulted party, even if it does not transform the balance of power. It may be accepted by the perpetrator of the initial insult as acceptable retaliation, repartee, or face-saving gesture. As with the trading of gifts, the trading of insults follows certain rules of commensurability. A poor relative may successfully reciprocate an expensive gift from a rich relative by offering a gift that requires a lot of time, care, and thought, even if it does not compare in price with the rich relative's gift (Gabriel and Lang 1995). Likewise an insulted party may be allowed to save face with a token retaliation. Provided that the magnitude of a counter-insult is not incommensurable with that of the initial one, it may restore order. Football crowds supporting opposing teams routinely engage in the trading of insults, seeking to outdo each other in wit, inventiveness, and targeting of sensitivities, though they rarely exceed the limits that would lead to physical violence.

There are times, however, when, under the partial amnesty afforded by an insult, a disproportionate retaliation leads to a state of continuous and possibly escalating strife. This is akin to a *vendetta*, where each insult or blow must compensate for and surpass its predecessor. Calasso (1983: 185) observes precisely this sort of escalation of insults in the ancient Greek myth of the brothers Atreus and Thyestes. 'The vendetta between the two brothers loses all touch of psychology, becomes pure virtuosity, traces out arabesques. Thyestes disappears again, a horrified fugitive. There's just one thing in his mind: how to invent a revenge that will outdo his brother's, who in turn had thought up his with the intention of making it unbeatable.' The plot of many Greek tragedies is built on a still more unequal dynamic of insult trading. A mortal's temporary lapse of arrogance, a hubris against a god, brings about disproportionate retaliation from the god, the hero's nemesis. As Dodds (1950/1968: 32) observed, 'to speak lightly of a god, to neglect his cult, to maltreat his priest, all these understandably make him angry; in a shame-culture gods, like men, are quick to resent a slight'. Alasdair MacIntyre has further emphasized the centrality of insults to the cultural *and political* life of ancient Greeks and other societies that are organized along the axis shame–honour. 'To dishonour someone is to fail to acknowledge what is thus due. Hence the concept of an insult becomes a socially crucial one and in many such societies a certain kind of insult merits death' (MacIntyre 1981: 116). MacIntyre goes on to suggest that in modern societies insults are no longer political events. 'Insults have been displaced to the margins of our cultural life where they are expressive of private emotion rather than public conflicts. And unsurprisingly this is the only place left for them in Goffman's writings' (MacIntyre 1981: 116).

Tonya's narrative casts a doubt on MacIntyre's hypothesis that, along with morality, insults have been restricted by contemporary societies to the cultural margins, reduced to personal chagrins and humiliations. Insults may be endured passively, generating feelings of shame, anger, and guilt for the victim. Alternatively, however, they may set in motion a dynamic whose nature is undoubtedly political.

This may lead to a resolution through an apology or an acceptance of a commensurable retaliatory insult. Furthermore, they may lead to a continuous state of insult-trading, which may be contained within certain parameters (as with football crowds) or may escalate into ever-increasing, offensive, and damaging actions. The trading of insults can observe highly elaborate rules of reciprocity and equivalence. At times, the trading of insults, like the trading of gifts, may become institutionalized into a ritual, as is the case in joking relations. The trading of gifts and the trading of insults can turn into each other. Insults can take the form of insolent gifts or may result from the spurning of supposedly unworthy ones. Likewise a truce in the exchange of insults may be marked by an exchange of gifts.

INSULTS AS TESTS ESTABLISHING ORGANIZATIONAL PECKING ORDERS

Narrative 7 is the only one of the twenty-one in which the narrator actively insults, albeit in self-defence, someone else ('with his error-statistics'). It is a curious thing about insults that they far more commonly feature in narratives as suffered rather than as perpetrated—that is, they are part of tragic narratives from the perspective of the victim, rather than of epic narratives from that of the perpetrator. Indeed, it is unlikely that most people would admit to insulting anyone without provocation. Yet, in most cases individuals who are insulted impute motive on their assailant. This is what makes the 'intention to insult' so difficult to establish and an unreliable criterion for defining insults.

We have noted that cumulatively insults are part of a trading process, itself part of an organization's political process. But what drives individual insults? Here we enter into more speculative terrain; the research material does not warrant anything more than some tentative conjectures. Clearly some insults are unintentional, therefore motiveless. Others, like Tonya's reprimand in Narrative 7, are retaliatory. But would Nick, the page-3-admiring broker, have recognized his own behaviour towards Tonya as insulting? This seems rather unlikely. He may have viewed the situation as an instance of overreaction by an over-sensitive trainee who has not yet learnt the organizational ropes. Yet, were his ostentatious reading of material intended to provoke the trainee and his deliberate shunning of her not precisely aimed at 'teaching this awkward young customer a little lesson'? The excuse that 'No insult was intended' may have been genuine yet one suspects that, even if not consciously, Nick's behaviour was driven by a desire to deflate, if not to humiliate, Tonya. If Tonya's reference to Nick as 'one of the men who always "cocked up"' is not a *post-facto* construction, could it be that Nick was himself the target of insults by other dealers or by his superiors? Unable to retaliate against them, he redirects his aggression at a soft target, a young female, back-office trainee, whose humiliation is meant not only to keep her in her place, but also to earn him the esteem of his peers. In this way some insults could be said to be *re-directed retaliations*—that is, retaliations against innocent but weaker surrogates. It is, of course, not possible to test this hypothesis on the material available, but what it suggests is that insults are not merely instruments for establishing inclusion and exclusion, domination and subordination, but also finer gradations of status and power. We may hypothesize then that insults help to establish coalitions and sustain a 'pecking order' among members of a collectivity while at the same time allowing for a degree of mobility by testing the resilience and morale of people up and down the order.[10]

In this way, some insults may be construed as *tests*. They can function as initiation rites, establishing inclusion and exclusion, or classification rites, establishing status and power hierarchies, or tests of loyalty, establishing coalitions and alliances. Assailants' motives then are to provide themselves and their targets with a challenge, an opportunity to prove themselves, from which they hope to improve their position in the pecking order or to mould a new coalition. Under such circumstances, insults provide a continuous mechanism for maintaining some mobility within a hierarchy of power and status. At times, an insult may thus prove a visible use of power, which, Pfeffer (1981, 1992) has forcibly argued, is a preamble to its own dissipation. Power is lost through the subordinate's successful retaliation or through the undermining of a coalition.[11]

Is there a class of insults that, unlike motiveless and retaliatory ones, is driven purely and simply by destructive desires, whether conscious or unconscious? Clearly the research material does not permit any systematic discussion of this possibility, since no accounts are provided by the assailants. We may speculate, all the

---

[10] Casual observations of children's behaviour in schoolyards and conscripts' behaviour in military camps suggests to me that insults may indeed be a primary type of social ritual for establishing social pecking orders. Insults allow sharp, quick-witted individuals to move up such pecking orders, unlike pecking orders based entirely on physical violence,

[11] David Sims has pointed out that human groups usually entail multiple pecking orders, and that actions that raise one in one pecking order simultaneously lower one in one of the concurrent ones. A mischievous child may be raising himself in the pecking order of his peer group, even as he lowers himself in the school's pecking order. This opens up some intriguing possibilities for the study of insults.

same, that some insults, notably those perpetrated by some of Dostoevsky's anti-heroes, like Dmitry Karamazov, assume an existential, life-affirming and life-denying quality, setting them apart from the ones discussed in this chapter. Not content to defeat opponents, such characters seek, in an irrational Nietzschean way, to humiliate and obliterate them, as if their own life and vitality derive from the unpremeditated humiliations that they inflict on others. Yet such characters also seem to suffer from profound guilt, following their action. Their insults resemble the hubris of ancient Greek tragedy, the outrageously boastful claims made by mortals in a moment of madness (*ate*), which invariably bring about disproportionate retaliation from the insulted god, only, in the existential hero's case, the retaliation appears to stem from his own conscience. Such insults could be said to derive from a kind of inebriation of living dangerously, of 'getting away' with something outrageous, expressing a deep wish for self-aggrandisement and for the belittlement of an opponent. If insults like the one described in Narrative 7 represent a public challenge within a shame culture, existential insults, in spite of their public dimension, may be said to represent private challenges that individuals in certain psychological states are apt to set for themselves.

This examination of insults in organizations suggests that insults are quite an important social and organizational phenomenon, one that causes powerful emotions and enters people's personal histories. It was suggested that insults involve a perpetrator, a target, and, often, an audience. The intention to insult is not necessary, as some insults are the result of misunderstanding or accident. However, the experience of being gratuitously offended and the corresponding feelings of shame, guilt, and anger are fundamental to insults. Several types of insults were observed. Exclusion, stereotyping, obliteration of significant identity details, ingratitude, scapegoating, rudeness, broken promises, being ignored or kept waiting, were all seen as insulting by different individuals. It was further suggested that even more potent insults may result from the defamation or despoiling of idealized objects, persons, or ideas.

Different insult dynamics were noted; these included an apology, a commensurate retaliation, a disproportionate retaliation and possible escalation, a retaliation against a surrogate and weaker target than the perpetrator of the initial insult, an affected indifference with a possible delayed retaliation, or more commonly a resigned tolerance that may fuel subsequent insults. Retaliation and resistance led to a discussion of the concept of trading of insults as part of an organization's political process, which establishes, first, lines of domination/subordination, secondly, finer gradations of status and power—a pecking order—and, thirdly, opportunities for building coalitions and alliances. It is argued that insults allow for a certain mobility within a pecking order, by offering 'matches' for contestants to pitch their wit, venom, and courage against each other. They also enable audiences to take sides, thus influencing and testing the operation of coalitions and alliances.

This discussion points at several lines of further enquiry. First, it would be interesting to extend and develop the taxonomy of insults tentatively presented here and to establish other forms that insulting behaviour take. Secondly, it is important to elaborate the nature of multiple *interpretations* in insults. It would be interesting to juxtapose the interpretations offered by the victim with those offered by the assailant, especially in what concerns *intentionality*. How do victims seek to establish the intention of their assailant to insult them? And how do the assailants 'construct' their behaviour, which is seen as insulting by the victim? In some cases, an insult may be unambiguous—a common understanding between assailant and victim. In other cases, different or competing interpretations may be proffered. In some cases, it would be possible to argue that *an insult is a multiple interpretation*, as anyone who has tried to adjudicate disputes between children may realize.[12] Thirdly, intensive qualitative research with victims of particular insults may test the hypothesis presented here, that different insults assault different parts of the mental personality and lead to different defence mechanisms. Under what circumstances are insults repressed, rationalized, or defended against and when do they lead to a burning desire for retaliation? A fourth line of enquiry would be an ethnographic account of insults in different institutions (including schools, business organizations, training colleges, and military outfits) to investigate the extent to which they serve as tests establishing political coalitions and pecking orders. It would be especially interesting to explore the nature and magnitude of permissible retaliations, observing closely the group dynamics involved.

In conclusion, we could argue that the study of insults can be of use to three groups of organizational scholars. Students of organizational culture and symbolism may gain considerable insights by focusing on the nature of insults in particular organizations. Equally, researchers exploring organizational emotions, in particular negative emotions, such as anger, shame, and guilt, would do well to explore how narratives associated with such emotions incorporate insults.

---

[12] Dr David M. Sachs has suggested that an insult that hits the mark is equivalent to a successful psychoanalytic interpretation.

Finally, researchers who are exploring the political dimensions of organizations, including labour-process theorists, would find the study of organizational insults valuable, in understanding why so often resistance is bred not simply by long-term exploitation or oppression but by momentary lapses displaying arrogance and contempt.

Happily Ever After . . .

If this narrative were a story, this would be the moment for the denouement, when all is revealed and all loose ends are tied together. We have followed stories from their early mutations in the folkloric universe, through their crises in modernity, to a late flowering in postmodernity. We have encountered them in and out of organizations and have observed their adventures in the lands of computers, nostalgia, leadership, and insults. Now would be the moment when all becomes clear, leaving the reader with a feeling of completeness, closure, and contentment.

But this narrative is not story, nor are stories characters in a larger narrative. As we have argued throughout this book, stories are special, fragile, and valuable webs of narrative. They are capable of sensemaking wonders, but they can easily be broken and then they call into question the very possibility of sensemaking.

If we cannot offer the reader the satisfaction of a happy ending, or even that of a wholesomely satisfying tragic resolution, we can at least offer a definition. *Stories are narratives with plots and characters, generating emotion in narrator and audience, through a poetic elaboration of symbolic material. This material may be a product of fantasy or experience, including an experience of earlier narratives. Story plots entail conflicts, predicaments, trials, coincidences, and crises that call for choices, decisions, actions, and interactions, whose actual outcomes are often at odds with the characters' intentions and purposes.* If human action always achieved the results it intended, there would be no space for stories. Nor would there be a space for stories, if we lived in a perfectly ordered and rational world, like Plato's *Republic.* But the world (both outer and inner) is irrational, disorderly, puzzling, and threatening, our actions often lead to unanticipated results, and, in spite of our best attempts to control our lives, we constantly face situations that we had not anticipated. Under these circumstances, science, with its multi-causal analysis, its statistical and probabilistic links, can at best partially meet our sensemaking needs. So, we turn to narrative forms of explanation, interpretation, and sensemaking. By attributing motive, agency, or purpose to our human predicaments, we may not always make them enjoyable or even tolerable, but at least we make them sensical, capable of being understood. When motive, agency, or purpose cannot be found, we lapse into meaninglessness and despair.

This book has followed stories in one particular milieu, contemporary organizations. Storytelling in organizations has, as we have seen, attracted considerable attention among scholars in recent years, being viewed as one of the principal or even as the chief sensemaking device. Our approach has presented a more cautious view. Unlike the café and the pub, the village square and the family table, organizations do not appear to be a natural habitat of storytelling— after all, most people in organizations are far too busy appearing to be busy to be able to engage in storytelling. Nor is trust, respect, and love among members of organizations such as to encourage free and uninhibited narration. Moreover, stories in organizations compete against other narrativities, especially against information and data, but also against clichés, platitudes, acronyms, artefacts small and large, arguments, opinions, and so forth. In such an environment, amidst the noisy din of facts, numbers, and images, the delicate, time-consuming discourse of storytelling is easily ignored or silenced. Few organizations are spontaneous storytelling cultures. Yet, there *is* storytelling going on in organizations, and some organizational stories are good stories. It is precisely because organizational stories are relatively special phenomena that they are of great value to researchers, as sources of clues about the symbolic and emotional life of organizations. Organizational stories take us directly to those events and experiences that generate strong emotions; these events may be exceptional and unusual and presented as such; alternatively, they may be constructed as typical of a certain state of affairs, though the state of affairs is then constructed as untypical. By highlighting the untypical, the critical, and the extraordinary, stories give us access to what lies behind the normal and mundane.

The exploration of narratives in the human sciences is still in its early stages. Nevertheless, the enthusiasm with which researchers have embraced narratives is making up for lost time. Those of us studying organizations who love stories can at last mix research with pleasure with no fear of marginalization and derision. In concluding this book, however, it is worth reiterating the danger of allowing our current fascination with text and narrative to occlude deeper issues of justice, politics, and human suffering. Between the Scylla of objectivism and the Charybdis of pantextuality, this book has sought to promote the study of organizational stories as poetic elaborations on actual events, as wish-fulfilling fantasies built on everyday experience, and as expressions of deeper organizational and personal realities. Treating a story simply as text, disregarding the extent to which it deviates from or distorts facts and ignoring the effort and ingenuity that it demands, does grave injustice to story and storyteller alike.

Once upon a time, a cat drank a bottle of green ink. At once, the cat turned green . . .

So what happened to the cat?

The cat was distraught, he felt sick. However, he was soon spotted by an advertising executive looking for a mascot for a 'cleaner, greener' campaign; he was snapped up and went on to have a successful media career, promoting cat food and even having a talk show of his own. The cat lived a life of luxury, enjoying the finest fish and milk that money could buy and marrying the pussycat of his dreams.

The cat had been cut from ink blotting paper.

The cat then decided to try some red ink, whereupon he turned red. Next the cat decided to try some black ink. He quickly turned black and disappeared into the pages of a book.

Or at least, this is the story for now . . .

REFERENCES

ADORNO, T. W., FRENKEL-BRUNSWIK, E., LEVINSON, D., and SANFORD, N. (1950), *The Authoritarian Personality*. New York: Harper & Row.

ALLAIRE, Y., and FIRSIROTU, M. E. (1984), 'Theories of Organizational Culture', *Organization Studies*, 5/3: 193–226.

APTE, M. L. (1983), 'Humor Research, Methodology, and Theory in Anthropology', in M. P. E. and J. H. Goldstein (eds.), *Handbook of Humor Research*. New York: Springer Verlag.

ARISTOTLE (1963), *Poetics*. London: Dent.

AUSTER, E. (1993), 'Demystifying the Glass Ceiling: Organizational and Interpersonal Dynamics of Gender Bias', *Business and the Contemporary World*, 5 (Summer), 47–68.

BACHARACH, S. B., and LAWLER, E. J. (1980), *Power and Politics in Organizations*. San Francisco: Jossey-Bass.

BAKHTIN, M. (1929/1973), *Problems of Dostoevsky's Poetics*, trans. R. W. Rotsel. New York: Ardis.

—— (1981), *The Dialogic Imagination*, trans. Caryl Emerson and Michael Holquist. Austin, Tex.: University of Texas Press.

BARKER, J. R. (1993), 'Tightening the Iron Cage: Concertive Control in Self-Managing Teams', *Administrative Science Quarterly*, 38: 408–37.

BARNARD, C. (1938), *The Functions of the Executive*. Cambridge, Mass.: Harvard University Press.

BARTHES, R. (1964/1972), 'The Structuralist Activity', in R. DeGeorge and F. DeGeorge (eds.), *The Structuralists: From Marx to Lévi-Strauss*. Garden City, NY: Anchor Books.

—— (1966/1977), 'Introduction to the Structural Analysis of Narratives', in S. Heath (ed.), *Image — Music — Text*. Glasgow: Collins.

—— (1973), *Mythologies*. London: Paladin Books.

BATE, P. (1990), 'Using the Culture Concept in an Organization Development Setting', *Journal of Applied Behavioral Science*, 26/1: 83–106.

—— (1994), *Strategies for Cultural Change*. Oxford: Butterworth-Heinemann.

—— and MANGHAM, I. (1981), *Exploring Participation*. Chichester: John Wiley.

BAUDRILLARD, J. (1983a), *In the Shadow of the Silent Majorities*. New York: Semiotext(e).

—— (1983b), *Simulations*. New York: Semiotext(e).

BAUM, H. S. (1987), *The Invisible Bureaucracy*. Oxford: Oxford University Press.

REFERENCES

BAUM, H. S. (1989), 'Organizational Politics against Organizational Culture: A Psychoanalytic Perspective', *Human Resource Management*, 28/2: 191–207.

BAUMAN, Z. (1988), *Freedom*. Milton Keynes: Open University Press.

—— (1992), *Intimations of Postmodernity*. London: Routledge.

BAUMEISTER, R. F. (1986), *Identity: Cultural Change and the Struggle for Self*. Oxford: Oxford University Press.

BECKER, E. (1962), *The Birth and Death of Meaning*. Harmondsworth: Penguin.

BENEDICT, R. (1931), 'Folklore', *The Encyclopaedia of the Social Sciences*, vi. New York: Longman.

BENJAMIN, W. (1968*a*), *Illuminations*. London: Jonathan Cape.

—— (1968*b*), 'The Storyteller: Reflections on the Works of Nikolai Leskov', in H. Arendt (ed.), *Walter Benjamin: Illuminations*. London: Jonathan Cape.

BENNIS, W. G. (1989), *Why Leaders can't Lead: The Unconscious Conspiracy Continues*. San Francisco: Jossey-Bass.

—— and NANUS, B. (1985), *Leaders: The Strategies for Taking Charge*. New York: Harper & Row.

BENTON, G. (1988), 'The Origins of the Political Joke', in C. Powell and G. E. C. Paton (eds.), *Humour in Society*. London: Macmillan.

BERG, P. O. (1985), 'Organization Change as a Symbolic Transformation Process', in P. J. Frost, L. F. Moore, M. R. Louis, C. C. Lundberg, and J. Martin (eds.), *Organizational Culture*. London: Sage.

BERGER, P., BERGER, B., and KELLNER, H. (1973), *The Homeless Mind*. Garden City, NY: Anchor.

BERGSON, H. (1980), ' Laughter', in G. Meredith (ed.), *Comedy*. Baltimore: Johns Hopkins University Press.

BETTELHEIM, B. (1976), *The Uses of Enchantment: The Meaning and Importance of Fairy Tales*. London: Thames & Hudson.

—— (1990), *Recollections and Reflections*. London: Thames & Hudson.

BIGGART, N. (1988), *Charismatic Capitalism*. London: University of Chicago Press.

BLOOMFIELD, B. P. (1989), 'On Speaking about Computing', *Sociology*, 23/3: 409–23.

BLY, R. (1990), *Iron John: A Book about Men*. New York: Addison Wesley.

BOJE, D. M. (1991), 'The Storytelling Organization: A Study of Story Performance in an Office-Supply Firm', *Administrative Science Quarterly*, 36: 106–26.

—— and DENNEHY, R. F. (1993), *Managing in the Postmodern World: America's Revolution Against Exploitation*. Dubuque, Io.: Kendall-Hunt.

—— FEDOR, D. B., and ROWLAND, K. M. (1982), 'Myth Making: A Qualitative Step in OD Interventions', *Journal of Applied Behavioral Science*, 18/1: 17–28.

BORN, M. (1979), *L' Île aux Lépreux*. Paris: Grasset.

BOURDIEU, P. (1984), *Distinction: A Social Critique of the Judgement of Taste*. London: Routledge.

BOWLES, M. L. (1989), 'Myth, Meaning and Work Organization', *Organization Studies*, 10/3: 405–21.

BOYCE, M. E. (1995), 'Collective Centring and Collective Sense-Making in the

REFERENCES

Stories and Storytelling of One Organization', *Organization Studies*, 16/1: 107–37.

—— (1996), 'Organizational Story and Storytelling: A Critical Review', *Journal of Organizational Change Management*, 9/5: 5–26.

BRAVO, A., LILIA, D., and JALLA, D. (1990), 'Myth, Impotence, and Survival in the Concentration Camps', in R. Samuel and P. Thompson (eds.), *The Myths We Live By*. London: Routledge.

BROWN, A. D. (1997), 'Narcissism, Identity, and Legitimacy', *Academy of Management Review*, 22/3: 643–86.

BRUNER, J. (1986), *Actual Minds, Possible Worlds*. Cambridge, Mass.: Harvard University Press.

BURAWOY, M. (1979), *Manufacturing Consent*. Chicago: Chicago University Press.

—— (1985), *The Politics of Production*. London: Verso.

BURKE, K. (1945/1969), *A Grammar of Motives*. Berkeley and Los Angeles: University of California Press.

—— (1962), *A Grammar of Motives and a Rhetoric of Motives*. Cleveland, Oh.: Meridian.

—— (1966), *Language as Symbolic Action: Essays on Life, Literature, and Method*. Berkeley and Los Angeles: University of California Press.

BURNS, J. M. (1978), *Leadership*. New York: Harper & Row.

CALASSO, R. (1983), *The Marriage of Cadmus and Harmony*. London: Jonathan Cape.

CAMPBELL, J. (1949/1988), *The Hero with a Thousand Faces*. London: Paladin Books.

—— (1975), 'Folkloristic Commentary', in P. Colum (ed.), *The Complete Grimm's Fairy Tales*. London: Routledge.

—— (1976), *Occidental Mythology*. Harmondsworth: Penguin.

CARR, A. (1998), 'Identity, Compliance and Dissent in Organizations: A Psychoanalytic Perspective', *Organization*, 5/1: 81–99.

—— and ZANETTI, L. A. (1998), 'Metatheorizing the Dialectic of Self and Other: The Psychodynamics in Work Organizations', paper presented at the CSOC Fall Colloquium, University of Missouri–Columbia, 25–7 Sept.

CHASSEGUET-SMIRGEL, J. (1976), 'Some Thoughts on the Ego-Ideal: A Contribution to the Study of the "Illness of Ideality"', *Psychoanalytic Quarterly*, 45: 345–73.

CIBORRA, C. U. (1991), 'The Limits of Strategic Information Systems', *International Journal of Information Research Management*, 2/3: 11–16.

CLARK, T., and SALAMAN, G. (1996), 'Telling Tales: Management Consultancy as the Art of Storytelling', in D. Grant and C. Oswick (eds.), *Metaphor and Organizations*. London: Sage.

CLEGG, S. (1981), 'Organization and Control', *Administrative Science Quarterly*, 26: 545–62.

—— (1990), *Modern Organizations: Organization Studies in the Postmodern World*. London: Sage.

CLEVERLEY, G. (1971), *Managers and Magic*. London: Longman.

COLLINSON, D. (1982), *Managing the Shopfloor: Subjectivity, Masculinity and Workplace Culture*. Berlin: Walter de Gruyter.

COLLINSON, D. (1988), '"Engineering Humour": Masculinity, Joking and Conflict in Shop-Floor Relations', *Organization Studies*, 9/2: 181–99.

—— (1994), 'Strategies of Resistance: Power, Knowledge and Subjectivity in the Workplace', in J. Jermier, W. Nord, and D. Knights (eds.), *Resistance and Power in Organizations*. London: Routledge.

COLUM, P. (1975), 'Introduction', in P. Colum (ed.), *The Complete Grimm's Fairy Tales*. London: Routledge.

COSER, R. L. (1959), 'Some Social Functions of Laughter', *Human Relations*, 12: 171–82.

—— (1960), 'Laughter among Colleagues: A Study of the Functions of Humor among the Staff of a Mental Hospital', *Psychiatry*, 23: 81–95.

CREWS, F. (1995), *The Memory Wars: Freud's Legacy in Dispute*. New York: New York Review of Books.

CZARNIAWSKA, B. (1997), *Narrating the Organization: Dramas of Institutional Identity*. Chicago: University of Chicago Press.

CZARNIAWSKA-JOERGES, B. (1995), 'Narration or Science? Collapsing the Division in Organization Studies', *Organization*, 2/1: 11–33.

—— and JOERGES, B. (1990), 'Linguistic Artifacts at Service of Organizational Control', in P. Gagliardi (ed.), *Symbols and Artifacts: Views of the Corporate Lanscape*. Berlin: Walter de Gruyter.

DANIELS, E. (1985), 'Nostalgia and Hidden Meaning', *American Imago*, 42/3: 371–82.

DAVIDSON, M. P. (1992), *The Consumerist Manifesto: Advertising in Postmodern Times*. London: Routledge.

DAVIES, C. (1984), 'Commentary on Anton C. Zijderveld's Trend Report on "The Sociology of Humour and Laughter"', *Current Sociology*, 32/1: 142–57.

—— (1988), 'Stupidity and Rationality: Jokes from the Iron Cage', in C. Powell and G. E. C. Paton (eds.), *Humour in Society*. London: Macmillan.

DAVIS, F. (1979), *Yearning for Yesterday: A Sociology of Nostalgia*. London: Macmillan.

DE CERTEAU, M. (1984), *The Practice of Everyday Life*. Berkeley and Los Angeles: University of California Press.

—— (1986), *Heterologies: Discourse on the Other*, trans. Brian Massumi, xvii. Minneapolis: University of Minnesota Press.

DEAL, T. E., and KENNEDY, A. A. (1982), *Corporate Cultures: The Rites and Rituals of Corporate Life*. Reading, Mass.: Addison Wesley.

DICKS, H. (1972), *Licensed Mass Murder: A Socio-Psychological Study of Some SS Killers*. London: University of Sussex Press.

DIXON, N. (1976), *On the Psychology of Military Incompetence*. Harmondsworth: Penguin.

DODDS, E. R. (1950/1968), *The Greeks and the Irrational*, Berkeley and Los Angeles: University of California Press.

DORSON, R. M. (1969), 'Theories of Myth and the Folklorist', in H. A. Murray (ed.), *Myth and Mythmaking*. Boston: Beacon Press.

DOUGLAS, M. (1967), 'The Meaning of Myth: With Special Reference to "The Story of Asdiwal"', in E. Leach (ed.), *The Structural Study of Myth and Totemism*. London: Tavistock.

REFERENCES

—— (1975), 'Jokes', in M. Douglas (ed.), *Implicit Meanings: Essays in Anthropology.* London: Routledge.

DU GAY, P. (1996), *Consumption and Identity at Work.* London: Sage.

DUNDES, A. (1965), *The Study of Folklore.* Englewood Cliffs, NJ: Prentice Hall.

—— (1980), *Interpreting Folklore.* Bloomington, Ind.: Indiana University Press.

—— (1989), *Folklore Matters.* Knoxville, Tenn.: University of Tennessee Press.

ECO, U. (1990), *The Limits of Interpretation.* Bloomington, Ind.: Indiana University Press.

EDWARDS, R. (1979), *Contested Terrain: The Transformation of the Workplace in the Twentieth Century.* London: Heinemann.

ERIKSON, E. H. (1968), *Identity: Youth and Crisis.* London: Faber & Faber.

FEATHERSTONE, M. (1991), *Consumer Culture and Postmodernism.* London: Sage.

FEYERABEND, P. (1975), *Against Method.* London: New Left Books.

—— (1978), *Science in a Free Society.* London: New Left Books.

FINE, G. A. (1983), 'Sociological Approaches to the Study of Humor', in P. E. McGhee and J. H. Goldstein (eds.), *Handbook of Humor Research.* New York: Springer Verlag.

FINEMAN, S. (1993), 'Organizations as Emotional Arenas', in S. Fineman (ed.), *Emotion in Organizations.* London: Sage.

—— (1996), 'Emotion and Organizing', in S. Clegg, C. Hardy, and W. R. Nord (eds.), *Handbook of Organization Studies.* London: Sage.

—— and GABRIEL, Y. (1996), *Experiencing Organizations.* London: Sage.

FISKE, J. (1987), *Television Culture.* London: Methuen.

—— (1989), *Understanding Popular Culture.* London: Unwin Hyman.

FLAM, H. (1990*a*), 'Emotional "Man" I: The Emotional "Man" and the Problem of Collective Action', *International Sociology,* 5/1: 39–56.

—— (1990*b*), 'Emotional "Man" II: Corporate Actors as Emotion-Motivated Emotion Managers', *International Sociology,* 5/2: 225–34.

FLESCH, R. (1959), *The Book of Unusual Quotations.* London: Cassell.

FORRESTER, J. (1997), *Dispatches from the Freud Wars.* Cambridge, Mass.: Harvard University Press.

FOUCAULT, M. (1980), *Power/Knowledge: Selected Interviews and Other Writings 1972–1977.* Brighton: Harvester Books.

FREUD, A. (1936), *The Ego and the Mechanisms of Defense.* New York: International Universities Press.

FREUD, S. (1900), *The Interpretation of Dreams.* Harmondsworth: Penguin.

—— (1914), *On Narcissism.* London: Hogarth Press.

—— (1921), *Group Psychology and the Analysis of the Ego.* London: Hogarth Press.

—— (1927), 'Humour', in A. Dickson (ed.), *Sigmund Freud: Art and Literature.* Harmondsworth: Penguin.

FROMM, E. (1941/1966), *Escape from Freedom.* New York: Avon Library.

FRUDE, N. (1983), *The Intimate Machine.* London: Century.

FRYE, N. (1957), *Anatomy of Criticism: Four Essays.* Harmondsworth: Penguin.

—— (1969), 'New Directions from Old', in H. A. Murray (ed.), *Myth and Mythmaking.* Boston: Beacon Press.

GABRIEL, Y. (1982), 'Freud, Rieff and the Critique of American Culture', *Psychoanalytic Review*, 69/3: 341–66.

—— (1983), *Freud and Society*. London: Routledge.

—— (1984), 'A Psychoanalytic Contribution to the Sociology of Suffering', *International Review of Psychoanalysis*, 11: 467–80.

—— (1988), *Working Lives in Catering*. London: Routledge.

—— (1991a), 'On Organizational Stories and Myths: Why it is Easier to Slay a Dragon than to Kill a Myth', *International Sociology*, 6/4: 427–42.

—— (1991b), 'Organizations and their Discontents: A Psychoanalytic Contribution to the Study of Corporate Culture', *Journal of Applied Behavioral Science*, 27: 318–36.

—— (1991c), 'Turning Facts into Stories and Stories into Facts: A Hermeneutic Exploration of Organizational Folklore', *Human Relations*, 44/8: 857–75.

—— (1993), 'Organizational Nostalgia: Reflections on the Golden Age', in S. Fineman (ed.), *Emotion in Organizations*. London: Sage.

—— (1995), 'The Unmanaged Organization: Stories, Fantasies, Subjectivity', *Organization Studies*, 16/3: 477–501.

—— (1999), *Organizations in Depth*. London: Sage.

——and LANG, T. (1995), *The Unmanageable Consumer: Contemporary Consumption and its Fragmentation*. London: Sage.

GEORGES, R. (1969), 'Toward an Understanding of Story-Telling Events', *Journal of American Folklore*, 82: 314–28.

—— (1980), 'A Folklorist's View of Story-Telling', *Humanities in Society*, 3/4: 317–26.

—— (1981), 'Do Narrators Really Digress? A Reconsideration of "Audience Asides" in Narrating', *Western Folklore*, 40: 245–52.

GIDDENS, A. (1991), *Modernity and Self-Identity: Self and Society in the Late Modern Age*. Stanford, Calif.: Stanford University Press.

GINZBURG, C. (1980), 'Morelli, Freud and Sherlock Holmes: Clues and Scientific Method', *History Workshop*, 9: 5–36.

GOFFMAN, E. (1959), *The Presentation of Self in Everyday Life*. Garden City, NY: Anchor.

—— (1961), *Asylums*. Garden City, NY: Doubleday.

—— (1974), *Frame Analysis: An Essay on the Organization of Experience*. New York: Harper & Row.

GOLENBOCK, P. (1989), *Personal Fouls: The Broken Promises and Shattered Dreams of Big Money Basketball*. New York: Carol & Graf Publishers.

GOTT, R. (in press), *Our Empire Story*.

GOULD, S. J. (1996), *Life's Grandeur (Full House)*. London: Jonathan Cape.

GOULDNER, A. W. (1954), *Patterns of Industrial Bureaucracy*. Glencoe, Ill.: Free Press.

GREGORY, K. L. (1983), 'Native-View Paradigms: Multiple Cultures and Cultural Conflicts in Organizations', *Administrative Science Quarterly*, 28: 359–76.

GRÜNBAUM, A. (1984), *The Foundations of Psychoanalysis: A Philosophical Critique*. Berkeley and Los Angeles: University of California Press.

GUTEK, B. A. (1985), *Sex and the Workplace: Impact of Sexual Behaviour and*

REFERENCES

Harassment on Women, Men and Organizations. San Francisco: Jossey-Bass.

—— (1989), 'Sexuality in the Workplace: Key Issues in Social Research and Organizational Practice', in J. Hearn, D. L. Sheppard, P. Tancred-Sheriff, and G. Burrell (eds.), *The Sexuality of Organization*. London: Sage.

HAAS, J. (1977), 'Learning Real Feelings: A Study of High Steel Ironworkers' Reactions to Fear and Danger', *Sociology of Work and Occupations*, 4/2: 147–70.

HABERMAS, J. (1977), 'A Review of Gadamer's "Truth and Method"', in F. R. Dallmayr and T. A. McCarthy (eds.), *Understanding and Social Inquiry*. Notre Dame, Ind.: University of Notre Dame Press.

HANSEN, C. D., and KAHNWEILER, W. M. (1993), 'Storytelling: An Instrument for Understanding the Dynamics of Corporate Relationships', *Human Relations*, 46/12: 1391–409.

HARRIS, R., and TIMMS, N. (1993), *Secure Accommodation in Child Care: Between Hospital and Prison or Thereabouts*. London: Routledge.

HELMERS, S. (1993), 'The Occurrence of Exoticism in Organizational Literature', paper presented at the EGOS Conference, Paris, 6–8 July.

HETHERINGTON, K. (1992), 'Stonehenge and its Festival: Spaces of Consumption', in R. Shields (ed.), *Lifestyle Shopping: The Subject of Consumption*. London: Routledge.

HIRSCHHORN, L. (1988), *The Workplace Within*. Cambridge, Mass.: MIT Press.

—— (1989), 'Professionals, Authority and Group Life: A Case Study of a Law Firm', *Human Resource Management*, 28/2: 235–52.

—— (1997), *Reworking Authority: Leading and Following in the Post-Modern Organization*. Cambridge, Mass.: MIT Press.

—— and GILMORE, T. N. (1989), 'The Psychodynamics of a Cultural Change: Learning from a Factory', *Human Resource Management*, 28/2: 211–33.

HOBBES, T. (1651/1962), *Leviathan: Or the Matter, Forme and Power of a Commonwealth Ecclesiastical and Civil*. London: Collier-Macmillan.

HOCHSCHILD, A. (1983), *The Managed Heart: Commercialization of Human Feeling*. Berkeley and Los Angeles: University of California Press.

HOLDAWAY, S. (1988), 'Humour in Police Work', in C. Powell and G. E. C. Paton (eds.), *Humour in Society*. London: Macmillan.

HÖPFL, H. (1995), 'Organizational Rhetoric and the Threat of Ambivalence', *Studies in Culture, Organizations and Society*, 1/2: 175–88.

INGERSOLL, V. H., and ADAMS, G. B. (1986), 'Beyond the Organizational Boundaries: Exploring the Managerial Myth', *Administration and Society*, 18/3: 105–36.

JACKALL, R. (1988), *Moral Mazes: The World of Corporate Managers*. Oxford: Oxford University Press.

JANIS, I. (1972), *Victims of Groupthink*. Boston: Houghton Mifflin.

JAQUES, E. (1955), 'Social Systems as a Defence against Persecutory and Depressive Anxiety', in M. Klein, P. Heimann, and R. E. Money-Kyrle (eds.), *New Directions in Psychoanalysis*. London: Tavistock.

JERMIER, J. M. (1998), 'Introduction: Critical Perspectives on Organizational Control', *Administrative Science Quarterly*, 43: 235-56.

JERMIER, J. M., KNIGHTS, D., and NORD, W. R. (1994), *Resistance and Power in Organizations*. London: Routledge.

JONES, B. (1982), *Sleepers, Wake: Technology and the Future of Work*. London: Wheatsheaf.

JONES, E. (1938), 'The Theory of Symbolism', in E. Jones (ed.), *Papers on Psychoanalysis*. London: Baillière, Tindall & Cox.

JONES, M. O. (1984), 'Works of Art, Art as Work, and the Arts of Working: Implications for the Study of Organizational Life', *Western Folklore*, 43: 172–9.

—— (1985), 'On Folklorists Studying Organizations: A Reply to Robert S. McCarl', *American Folklore Society Newsletter*, 14/5: 8.

—— (1990), 'A Folklore Approach to Emotions at Work', *American Behavioral Scientist*, 33: 278–86.

—— (1991), 'On Fieldwork, Symbols, and Folklore in the Writings of William Foote Whyte', in P. J. Frost, L. F. Moore, C. C. Lundberg, and J. Martin (eds.), *Reframing Organizational Culture*. London: Sage.

JUNG, C. G. (1969), *On the Psychology of the Trickster-Figure*, ix. Princeton: Princeton University Press.

KANTER, R. M. (1977), *Men and Women of the Corporation*. New York: Basic Books.

—— (1983), *The Change Masters*. New York: Simon & Schuster.

KAPLAN, H. A. (1987), 'The Psychopathology of Nostalgia', *Psychoanalytic Review*, 74/4: 463–86.

KAPUSCINSKI, R. (1983), *The Emperor*. London: Picador.

KEMPER, S. (1984), 'The Development of Narrative Skills: Explanations and Entertainment', in S. A. Kuczaj II (ed.), *Discourse Development: Progress in Cognitive Development Research*. New York: Springer-Verlag.

KERNBERG, O. (1980), *Internal World and External Reality*. New York: Jason Aronson.

KETS DE VRIES, M. F. R. (1988), 'Prisoners of Leadership', *Human Relations*, 41: 261–80.

—— (1990), 'The Organizational Fool: Balancing a Leader's Hubris', *Human Relations*, 43/8: 751–70.

—— and MILLER, D. (1984), *The Neurotic Organization*. San Francisco: Jossey-Bass.

KIDDER, T. (1982), *The Soul of a New Machine*. Harmondsworth: Penguin.

KLEIN, M., and RIVIERE, J. (1974), *Love, Hate and Reparation*. New York: Norton.

KLEINER, J. (1970), 'On Nostalgia', *Bulletin of Philadelphia Association of Psychoanalysis*, 21: 11–30.

KNIGHTS, D. (1990), 'Subjectivity, Power and the Labour Process', in D. Knights and H. Willmott (eds.), *Labour Process Theory*. Basingstoke: Macmillan.

—— and MORGAN, G. (1991), 'Selling Oneself: Subjectivity and the Labour Process in Selling Life Assurance', in C. Smith, D. Knights, and H. Willmott (eds.), *White-Collar Work*. London: Macmillan.

—— and VURDUBAKIS, T. (1994), 'Foucault, Power, Resistance and All That', in J. Jermier, W. Nord, and D. Knights (eds.), *Resistance and Power in Organizations*. London: Routledge.

KOHUT, H. (1985), *Self Psychology and the Humanities*. New York: Norton.

REFERENCES

KRANTZ, J. (1989), 'The Managerial Couple: Superior–Subordinate Relationships as a Unit of Analysis', *Human Resource Management*, 28/2: 161–76.

—— (1990), 'Lessons from the Field: An Essay on the Crisis of Leadership in Contemporary Organizations', *Journal of Applied Behavioral Science*, 26/1: 49–64.

KUHN, T. S. (1962), *The Structure of Scientific Revolutions*. Chicago: University of Chicago Press.

KUNDA, G. (1992), *Engineering Culture: Control and Commitment in a High-Tech Corporation*. Philadelphia: Temple University Press.

LA BARRE, W. (1979), 'Species-Specific Biology, Magic and Religion', in R. H. Hook (ed.), *Fantasy and Symbol*. London: Academic Press.

LABIER, D. (1986), *Modern Madness*. Reading, Mass.: Addison-Wesley.

LABOV, W., and WALETZKY, J. (1967), 'Narrative Analysis: Oral Versions of Personal Experience', in J. Helm (ed.), *Essays on the Visual and Verbal Arts*. Seattle: University of Washington Press.

LASCH, C. (1980), *The Culture of Narcissism*. London: Abacus.

—— (1984), *The Minimal Self: Psychic Survival in Troubled Times*. London: Pan Books.

LEIDNER, R. (1991), 'Serving Hamburgers and Selling Insurance: Gender, Work and Identity in Interactive Service Jobs', *Gender and Society*, 5/2: 154–77.

LÉVI-STRAUSS, C. (1958/1976), 'The Story of Asdiwal', in C. Lévi-Strauss (ed.), *Structural Anthropology*, ii. Harmondsworth: Penguin.

—— (1963a), 'The Structural Study of Myth', in C. Lévi-Strauss (ed.), *Structural Anthropology*, i. Harmondsworth: Penguin.

—— (1963b), 'Structure and Dialectics', in C. Lévi-Strauss (ed.), *Structural Anthropology*, i. Harmondsworth: Penguin.

—— (1966), *The Savage Mind*. Chicago: Chicago University Press.

—— (1978), *Myth and Meaning: The 1977 Massey Lectures*. London: Routledge.

LIEBOW, E. (1981), *Tally's Corner: A Study of Negro Streetcorner Men*. Boston: Little, Brown & Company.

LINDHOLM, C. (1988),'Lovers and Leaders: A Comparison of Social and Psychological Models of Romance and Charisma', *Social Science Information*, 27/1: 3–45.

LINN, P. (1985),'Micro-Computers in Education: Dead and Living Labour', in T. Solomonides and L. Levidow (eds.), *Compulsive Technology: Computers as Culture*. London: Free Association Books.

LINSTEAD, S. (1985), 'Breaking the "Purity" Rule: Industrial Sabotage and the Symbolic Process', *Personnel Review*, 14/3: 12–19.

—— (1988), 'Jokers Wild: Humour in Organizational Culture', in C. Powell and G. E. C. Paton (eds.), *Humour in Society*. London: Macmillan.

MACCOBY, M. (1976), *The Gamesman: New Corporate Leaders*. New York: Simon & Schuster.

McDOUGALL, W. (1908/1932), *An Introduction to Social Psychology* (22nd edn.). London: Methuen.

MACINTYRE, A. (1981), *After Virtue*. London: Duckworth.

MAHLER, J. (1988), 'The Quest for Organizational Meaning: Identifying and Interpreting the Symbolism in Organizational Stories', *Administration and Society*, 20: 344–68.

REFERENCES

MANGHAM, I. L. (1986), *Power and Performance in Organizations: An Exploration of Executive Process*. Oxford: Blackwell.

—— (1995), 'Scripts, Talk and Double Talk', *Management Learning*, 2/4: 493–512.

—— and OVERINGTON, M. A. (1987), *Organizations as Theatre: A Social Psychology of Dramatic Appearances*. Chichester: John Wiley.

MANNING, P. K. (1979), 'Metaphors of the Field: Varieties of Organizational Discourse', *Administrative Science Quarterly*, 24: 660–71.

MARSDEN, R. (1993), 'The Politics of Organizational Analysis', *Organization Studies*, 14: 93–124.

MARTIN, J. (1982), 'Stories and Scripts in Organizational Settings', in A. Hastorf and A. Isen (eds.), *Cognitive and Social Psychology*. New York: Elsevier-North Holland.

—— (1990), 'Deconstructing Organizational Taboos: The Suppression of Gender Conflict in Organizations', *Organization Science*, 1: 1–22.

—— FELDMAN, M. S., HATCH, M. J., and SITKIN, S. B. (1983), 'The Uniqueness Paradox in Organizational Stories', *Administrative Science Quarterly*, 28: 438–53.

—— and POWERS, M. E. (1983), 'Truth or Corporate Propaganda: The Value of a Good War Story', in L. R. Pondy, P. J. Frost, G. Morgan, and T. C. Dandridge (eds.), *Organizational Symbolism*. Greenwich, Conn.: JAI Press.

MARTINKO, M. J. (1995), 'Stereotyping', in N. Nicholson (ed.), *Encyclopedic Dictionary of Organizational Behaviour*. Oxford: Blackwell.

MAYER, J. P. (1956), *Max Weber and German Politics*. London: Faber.

MEEK, V. L. (1988), 'Organizational Culture: Origins and Weaknesses', *Organizational Studies*, 9/4: 453–73.

MENZIES, I. (1960), 'A Case Study in Functioning of Social Systems as a Defence against Anxiety', *Human Relations*, 13: 95–121.

MITROFF, I. I. (1984), *Stakeholders of the Corporate Mind*. San Francisco: Jossey-Bass.

—— and KILMAN, R. H. (1976), 'On Organization Stories: An Approach to the Design and Analysis of Organizations through Myths and Stories', in R. H. Kilman, L. R. Pondy, and D. Slevin (eds.), *The Management of Organization Design*. New York: New Holland.

MORIARTY, S. E., and McGANN, A. F. (1983), 'Nostalgia and Consumer Sentiment', *Journalism Quarterly*, 60/1: 81–6.

MORSON, G. S., and EMERSON, C. (1990), *Mikhail Bakhtin: Creation of a Prosaics*. Stanford, Calif.: Stanford University Press.

NEWALL, V. (1980), 'Tell Us a Story', in J. Cherfas and R. Lewin (eds.), *Not Work Alone*. London: Temple Mead.

NOVAK, M. (1975), ' "Story" and "Experience" ', in J. B. Wiggins (ed.), *Religion as Story*. New York: Harper & Row.

OGLENSKY, B. D. (1995), 'Socio-Psychoanalytic Perspectives on the Subordinate', *Human Relations*, 48/9: 1029–54.

PARKER, M. (1992), 'Post-Modern Organizations or Postmodern Theory?', *Organization Studies*, 13/1: 1–17.

—— (1995), 'Critique in the Name of What? Postmodernism and Critical Approaches to Organization', *Organization Studies*, 16/4: 553–64.

REFERENCES

PERRY, S. E. (1978), *San Francisco Scavengers: Dirty Work and the Pride of Ownership*. Berkeley and Los Angeles: University of California Press.

PETERS, T. S., and WATERMAN, R. H. (1982), *In Search of Excellence*. New York: Harper & Row.

PETTIGREW, A. M. (1979), 'On Studying Organizational Cultures', *Administrative Science Quarterly*, 24: 570–81.

PFEFFER, J. (1981), *Power in Organizations*. Marshfield, Mass.: Pitman.

—— (1992), *Managing with Power*. Boston, Mass.: Harvard Business School Press.

PLATO (1993), *Republic*, trans. Robin Waterfield. Oxford: Oxford University Press.

POLANYI, L. (1979), 'So What's the Point?', *Semiotica*, 25: 207–41.

POLKINGHORNE, D. E. (1988), *Narrative Knowing and the Human Sciences*. Albany, NY: State University of New York Press.

POLLIO, H. R. (1980), 'What's So Funny?', in J. Cherfas and R. Lewin (eds.), *Not Work Alone*. London: Temple Mead.

—— (1983), 'Notes toward a Field Theory of Humor', in P. E. McGhee and J. H. Goldstein (eds.), *Handbook of Humor Research*. New York: Springer Verlag.

PORTELLI, A. (1990), 'Uchronic Dreams: Working Class Memory and Possible Worlds', in R. Samuel and P. Thompson (eds.), *The Myths We Live By*. London: Routledge.

POWELL, C. (1988), 'A Phenomenological Analysis of Humour in Society', in C. Powell and G. E. C. Paton (eds.), *Humour in Society: Resistance and Control*. London: Macmillan.

PROPP, V. (1968), *Morphology of the Folktale*. Austin, Tex.: University of Texas Press.

—— (1984), *Theory and History of Folklore*. Manchester: Manchester University Press.

REASON, P., and HAWKINS, P. (1988), 'Storytelling as Inquiry', in P. Reason (ed.), *Human Inquiry in Action: Developments in New Paradigm Research*. London: Sage.

REICH, W. (1970), *The Mass Psychology of Fascism*. New York: Farrar, Straus & Giroux.

RICŒUR, P. (1970), *Freud and Philosophy: An Essay on Interpretation*. New Haven: Yale University Press.

ROBINS, D. (1984), *We Hate Humans*. Harmondsworth: Penguin.

ROBINSON, J. A. (1981), 'Personal Narratives Reconsidered', *Journal of American Folklore*, 94: 58–85.

ROBINSON, J. A., and HAWKE, L. (1986), 'Narrative as a Heuristic Process', in S. R. Sarbin (ed.), *Narrative Psychology*. New York: Praeger.

ROSEN, M. (1985a), 'Breakfast at Spiro's: Dramaturgy and Dominance', *Journal of Management*, 11/2: 31–48.

—— (1985b), 'The Reproduction of Hegemony: An Analysis of Bureaucratic Control', *Research in Political Economy*, 8: 257–89.

—— and ASTLEY, W. G. (1988), 'Christmas Time and Control: An Exploration in the Social Structure of Formal Organizations', *Research in the Sociology of Organizations*, 6: 159–82.

REFERENCES

ROTHSCHILD, J., and MIETHE, T. D. (1994), 'Whistleblowing as Resistance in Modern Work Organizations: The Politics of Revealing Organizational Deception and Abuse', in J. Jermier, W. Nord, and D. Knights (eds.), *Resistance and Power in Organizations*. London: Routledge.

SCHEIN, E. H. (1985), *Organizational Culture and Leadership*. San Francisco: Jossey-Bass.

—— (1988), 'Organizational Socialization and the Profession of Management', *Sloan Management Review* (Fall), 53–65.

SCHWARTZ, H. S. (1985), 'The Usefulness of Myth and the Myth of Usefulness: A Dilemma for the Applied Organizational Scientist', *Journal of Management*, 11/1: 31–42.

—— (1987a), 'Anti-Social Actions of Committed Organizational Participants: An Existential Psychoanalytic Perspective', *Organization Studies*, 8/4: 327–40.

—— (1987b), 'On the Psychodynamics of Organizational Totalitarianism', *Journal of Management*, 13/1: 45–54.

—— (1988), 'The Symbol of the Space Shuttle and the Degeneration of the American Dream', *Journal of Organizational Change Management*, 1/2: 5–20.

—— (1990), *Narcissistic Process and Corporate Decay*. New York: New York University Press.

—— (1993), 'Narcissistic Emotion and University Administration: An Analysis of Political Correctness', in S. Fineman (ed.), *Emotion in Organizations*. London: Sage.

SCOTT, P. (1973), *The Day of the Scorpion*. London: Granada.

SELZNICK, P. (1943), 'An Approach to a Theory of Bureaucracy', *American Sociological Review*, 8/1: 47–54.

SENNETT, R. (1980), *Authority*. New York: Alfred A. Knopf.

—— and COBB, J. (1973), *The Hidden Injuries of Class*. New York: Random House.

SHEPPARD, D., L. (1989), 'Organizations, Power and Sexuality: The Image and Self-Image of Women Managers', in J. Hearn, P. Sheppard, P. Tancred-Sheriff, and G. Burrell (eds.), *The Sexuality of Organization*. London: Sage.

SIEVERS, B. (1986), 'Beyond the Surrogate of Motivation', *Organization Studies*, 7/4: 335–51.

—— (1990), 'Thoughts on the Relatedness of Work, Death and Life Itself', *European Journal of Management*, 8/3: 321–4.

—— (1994), *Work, Death and Life Itself*. Berlin: Walter de Gruyter.

—— (1998), 'Psychotic Organization as a Metaphoric Frame for the Study of Organizational and Interorganizational Dynamics', paper presented at the International Society for the Psychoanalytic Study of Organizations, Jerusalem, 1–3 July.

SIMS, D., FINEMAN, S., and GABRIEL, Y. (1993), *Organizing and Organizations*. London: Sage.

SMIRCICH, L. (1983a), 'Concepts of Culture and Organizational Analysis', *Administrative Science Quarterly*, 28: 339–58.

—— (1983b), 'Organizations as Shared Meanings', in L. R. Pondy, P. J. Frost, G. Morgan, and T. C. Dandridge (eds.), *Organizational Symbolism*. Greenwich, Conn.: JAI Press.

REFERENCES

SOHN, L. (1983), 'Nostalgia', *International Journal of Psychoanalysis*, 64: 203–11.

STEFFENSMEIER, D. (1986), *The Fence: In the Shadow of Two Worlds*. Boston, Mass.: Rowman & Littlefield.

STEIN, H. F. (1994), 'Workplace Organizations and Culture Theory: A Psychoanalytic Approach', paper presented at the International Society for the Psychoanalytic Study of Organizations, Chicago, 2–4 June.

STURDY, A. (1992), 'Clerical Consent: Shifting Work in the Insurance Office', in A. J. Sturdy, D. Knights, and H. Willmott (eds.), *Skill and Consent: Contemporary Studies in the Labour Process*. London: Routledge.

—— (1998), 'Customer Care in a Consumer Society: Smiling and Sometimes Meaning it?', *Organization*, 5/1: 27–53.

TALLMAN, R. S. (1974), 'A Generic Approach to the Practical Joke', *Southern Folklore Quarterly*, 38: 259–315.

TERKEL, S. (1985), *Working*. Harmondsworth: Penguin.

THOMPSON, P. (1990), 'Crawling from the Wreckage: The Labour Process and the Politics of Production', in D. Knights and H. Willmott (eds.), *Labour Process Theory*. London: Macmillan.

—— (1993), 'Postmodernism: Fatal Distraction', in J. Hassard and M. Parker (eds.), *Postmodernism and Organizations*. London: Sage.

TODOROV, T. (1981), *Introduction to Poetics*, trans. Richard Howard. Brighton: Harvester.

TOLSTOY, L. (1869/1982), *War and Peace*, trans. Rosemary Edmonds. Harmondsworth: Penguin.

TOWNLEY, B. (1993), 'Foucault, Power/Knowledge and its Relevance for Human Resource Management', *Academy of Management Review*, 18/3: 518–45.

TURKLE, S. (1984), *The Second Self*. London: Granada.

TURNER, B. A. (1983), 'The Use of Grounded Theory for the Qualitative Analysis of Organizational Behaviour', *Journal of Management Studies*, 20/3: 333–48.

—— (1986), 'Sociological Aspects of Organizational Symbolism', *Organization Studies*, 7/2: 101–15.

TURNER, V. (1974), *Dramas, Fields and Metaphors*. Ithaca, NY: Cornell University Press.

—— (1980), 'Social Dramas and Stories Told about Them', *Critical Inquiry*, 7: 141–68.

UNGER, L. S., McCONOCHA, D. M., and FAIER, J. A. (1991), 'The Use of Nostalgia in Television Advertising: A Content Analysis', *Journalism Quarterly*, 68/3: 345–53.

VAN DIJK, T. A. (1975), 'Action, Action Description, and Narrative', *New Literary History*, 6: 275–94.

WALLEMACQ, A., and SIMS, D. (1998), 'The Struggle with Sense', in D. Grant, T. Keenoy, and Oswick (eds.), *Discourse and Organization*. London: Sage.

WALLRAFF, G. (1985), *Lowest of the Low*. London: Methuen.

WARDE, A. (1994), 'Consumers, Identity and Belonging: Reflections on Some Theses of Zygmunt Bauman', in R. Keat, N. Whiteley, and N. Abercrombie (eds.), *The Authority of the Consumer*. London: Routledge.

REFERENCES

WATSON, T. J. (1994), *In Search of Management: Culture, Chaos and Control in Managerial Work*. London: Routledge.

WEICK, K. E. (1985), 'Cosmos vs Chaos: Sense and Nonsense in Electronic Contexts', *Organizational Dynamics*, 14/2: 51–64.

—— (1995), *Sensemaking in Organizations*. London: Sage.

WERMAN, D. (1977), 'Normal and Pathological Nostalgia', *Journal of American Psychoanalytic Association*, 25: 313–20.

WHITE, H. (1978), *Topics of Discourse*. Baltimore: Johns Hopkins University Press.

WHYTE, W. F. (1943), *Street Corner Society*. Chicago: University of Chicago Press.

WILKINS, A. L. (1978), 'Organizational Stories as Expressions of Management Philosophy: Implications for Social Control in Organizations', unpublished Ph.D., Stanford University, Palo Alto, Calif.

—— (1983), 'Organizational Stories as Symbols which Control the Organization', in L. R. Pondy, P. J. Frost, G. Morgan, and T. C. Dandridge (eds.), *Organizational Symbolism*. Greenwich, Conn.: JAI Press.

—— (1984), 'The Creation of Company Cultures: The Role of Stories in Human Resource Systems', *Human Resource Management*, 23: 41–60.

—— and MARTIN, J. (1979), 'Organizational Legends' (Research Paper No. 521), Stanford University Research Paper Series. Palo Alto, Calif.: Stanford University.

—— and OUCHI, W. G. (1983), 'Efficient Cultures: Exploring the Relationship between Culture and Organizational Performance', *Administrative Science Quarterly*, 28/468–81.

WILLIAMS, R. (1974), *The Country and the City*. Oxford: Oxford University Press.

WILLIS, P. (1979), *Learning to Labour*. London: Saxon House.

WILLMOTT, H. (1990), 'Subjectivity and the Dialectics of Praxis: Opening up the Core of Labour Process Analysis', in D. Knights and H. Willmott (eds.), *Labour Process Theory*. Basingstoke: Macmillan.

—— (1993), 'Strength is Ignorance; Slavery is Freedom: Managing Culture in Modern Organizations', *Journal of Management Studies*, 30: 515–52.

WINNICOTT, D. W. (1964), *The Child, the Family and the Outside World*. Harmondsworth: Penguin.

—— (1980), *Playing and Reality*. Harmondsworth: Penguin.

WRIGHT, P. (1985), *On Living in an Old Country: The National Past in Contemporary Britain*. London: Verso.

ZALEZNIK, A. (1989), 'The Mythological Structure of Organizations and its Impact', *Human Resource Management*, 28/2: 267–77.

ZIJDERVELD, A. C. (1983), 'The Sociology of Humour and Laughter', *Current Sociology*, 31/1: 1–100.

ZILLMANN, D. (1983), 'Disparagement Humor', in P. E. McGhee and J. H. Goldstein (eds.), *Handbook of Humor Research*. New York: Springer Verlag.

—— and CANTOR, J. R. (1976), 'A Disposition Theory of Humour and Mirth', in A. J. Chapman and H. C. Foot (eds.), *Humour and Laughter: Theory, Research and Applications*. London: Wiley.

ZUBOFF, S. (1985), 'Automate/Informate: The Two Faces of Intelligent Technology', *Organizational Dynamics*, 14/2: 5–18.

—— (1988), *In the Age of the Smart Machine*. Oxford: Heinemann.

INDEX OF STORIES

INDEX OF WORDS

INDEX OF WORDS

INDEX OF WORDS

INDEX OF WORDS

INDEX OF WORDS

s of

ntal

Nursing

SEVENTH EDITION

Louise Rebraca Shives,
MSN, ARNP, CNS

*Psychiatric–Mental Health Nurse Practitioner
and Clinical Nurse Specialist*

Consultant in Long-Term Care

Legal Nurse Consultant

Orlando, Florida

Health Ministry Cabinet, St. Stephen Lutheran Church

Co-Director C.A.R.E. Team Ministry, St. Stephen Lutheran Church

Longwood, Florida

 Wolters Kluwer | Lippincott Williams & Wilkins
Health

Philadelphia · Baltimore · New York · London
Buenos Aires · Hong Kong · Sydney · Tokyo

Senior Acquisitions Editor: Peter Darcy
Managing Editor: Michelle Clarke
Senior Production Editor: Debra Schiff
Director of Nursing Production: Helen Ewan
Senior Managing Editor/Production: Erika Kors
Design Coordinator: Holly Reid McLaughlin
Interior/Cover Designer: Candice Carta-Myers
Manufacturing Coordinator: Karin Duffield
Indexer: Kathy Pitcoff
Compositor: Spearhead
Printer: RR Donnelley-Crawfordville

Seventh Edition

9 8 7 6 5 4 3 2 1

LCCN 98643499
ISBN 978-0-7817-9707-8

Care has been taken to confirm the accuracy of the information presented and to describe generally accepted practices. However, the author, editors, and publisher are not responsible for errors or omissions or for any consequences from application of the information in this book and make no warranty, expressed or implied, with respect to the currency, completeness, or accuracy of the contents of the publication. Application of this information in a particular situation remains the professional responsibility of the practitioner; the clinical treatments described and recommended may not be considered absolute and universal recommendations.

The author, editors, and publisher have exerted every effort to ensure that drug selection and dosage set forth in this text are in accordance with the current recommendations and practice at the time of publication. However, in view of ongoing research, changes in government regulations, and the constant flow of information relating to drug therapy and drug reactions, the reader is urged to check the package insert for each drug for any change in indications and dosage and for added warnings and precautions. This is particularly important when the recommended agent is a new or infrequently employed drug.

Some drugs and medical devices presented in this publication have Food and Drug Administration (FDA) clearance for limited use in restricted research settings. It is the responsibility of the health care provider to ascertain the FDA status of each drug or device planned for use in his or her clinical practice.